MW00635718

MANAGING COMPLEX PROJECTS AND PROGRAMS

MANAGING COMPLEX PROJECTS AND PROGRAMS

How to Improve Leadership of Complex Initiatives Using a Third-Generation Approach

RICHARD J. HEASLIP, PHD

WILEY

Cover Design: Wiley
Cover Photograph: White Abstract Construction © iStock.com/chernetskiy

This book is printed on acid-free paper.

Copyright © 2014 Richard J. Heaslip. All rights reserved

Published by John Wiley & Sons, Inc., Hoboken, New Jersey
Published simultaneously in Canada

No part of this publication may be reproduced, stored in a retrieval system, or transmitted in any
form or by any means, electronic, mechanical, photocopying, recording, scanning, or otherwise,
except as permitted under Section 107 or 108 of the 1976 United States Copyright Act, without
either the prior written permission of the Publisher, or authorization through payment of the
appropriate per-copy fee to the Copyright Clearance Center, 222 Rosewood Drive, Danvers, MA
01923, (978) 750–8400, fax (978) 646–8600, or on the web at www.copyright.com. Requests to the
Publisher for permission should be addressed to the Permissions Department, John Wiley & Sons,
Inc., 111 River Street, Hoboken, NJ 07030, (201) 748–6011, fax (201) 748–6008, or online at
www.wiley.com/go/permissions.

Limit of Liability/Disclaimer of Warranty: While the publisher and author have used their best
efforts in preparing this book, they make no representations or warranties with the respect to
the accuracy or completeness of the contents of this book and specifically disclaim any implied
warranties of merchantability or fitness for a particular purpose. No warranty may be created or
extended by sales representatives or written sales materials. The advice and strategies contained
herein may not be suitable for your situation. You should consult with a professional where
appropriate. Neither the publisher nor the author shall be liable for damages arising herefrom.

For general information about our other products and services, please contact our Customer
Care Department within the United States at (800) 762–2974, outside the United States at
(317) 572–3993, or fax (317) 572–4002.

Wiley publishes in a variety of print and electronic formats and by print-on-demand. Some
material included with standard print versions of this book may not be included in e-books or in
print-on-demand. If this book refers to media such as a CD or DVD that is not included in the
version you purchased, you may download this material at http://booksupport.wiley.com. For
more information about Wiley products, visit www.wiley.com.

Library of Congress Cataloging-in-Publication Data:

Heaslip, Richard J., 1955–
    Managing complex projects and programs : how to improve leadership of
complex initiatives using a third-generation approach / Richard J. Heaslip.
        pages   cm
    Includes index.
    Summary: "Focuses on aligning projects and programs within the complex
environments of today's business models"—Provided by publisher.
    ISBN 978-1-118-38301-8 (hardback); 978-1-118-41741-6 (ebk);
978-1-118-42076-8 (ebk); 978-1-118-91994-1 (o-book)
    1. Project management.   I. Title.
    HD69.P75H434   2014
    658.4'04—dc23

                                                              2014018964

Printed in the United States of America

10 9 8 7 6 5 4 3 2 1

To family:

To my parents, Dick and Marie Heaslip,
Who taught me to treat life as a program—
Always embracing the richness to be found in its uncertainty and complexity

and

To Julie, Rick, Cody, and Kelley
My life's incredible program team

CONTENTS

Preface   xiii
Acknowledgments   xxi

Part 1   **Professional Project and Program**
               Management—Yesterday and Today   **1**

Chapter 1 The Exhilaration and Exasperation of Project
               and Program Leadership   3
               Leading Projects and Programs   4

Chapter 2 The Emergence of Project Management:
               First-Generation Programmatics   13
               Project Management's Beginnings   13
               Project Management Processes   17
               A Growing and Challenging Profession   19
               Organizational Responses   21

Chapter 3 The Evolution of Project Management:
               Second-Generation Programmatics   25
               Phase-Gate Approaches   25
               Circumstance-Specific Approaches   26
               Current Perspectives and Needs   29
               An Identity Crisis   31
               A Time for Action   32

Chapter 4 Rethinking the Roles and Responsibilities
               of Project Management Professionals   35
               The Exasperados   35
               Programmaticists and the Management
                 of Complexity   38
               A New Credo   40
               Understanding Project and Program Complexity   41
               Operational Uncertainty and Complexity   43
               Outcome Uncertainty and Complexity   45

	Stakeholder Uncertainty and Complexity	47
	Environmental Uncertainty and Complexity	49
	Organizational Uncertainty and Complexity	51
	Reactions to the Complexity Framework	53
	Use of the Complexity Framework	55
Chapter 5	Stakeholder Views about the Roles and Responsibilities of Programmaticists	61
	Diversity of Views	61
	Three Conceptions of a Programmaticist's Role	63
	The Traditionalist Perspective	63
	The Operationalist Perspective	66
	The Inclusivist Perspective	68
	Adoption and Value	70
	The Need for Different Kinds of Programmaticists	72
Chapter 6	Modern Problems with Traditional Management Models	77
	The Two-Party Fully Governed Project Oversight Model	77
	Limitations of the Model	81
	Problems with Background Documents	83
	Problems with Operational Decision Making	86
	Problems with Strategic Decision Making	89
	Unsatisfied Needs for Expertise	92
	A Search for Solutions	94
Chapter 7	Adaptations of the Traditional Two-Party Fully Governed Project Oversight Model	97
	Stakeholder Stories	97
	Organizational Growth	99
	The Benefits of Growth	99
	Responding to Growth-Related Challenges	100
	Operational, Technical, and Strategic Review Committees	102
	The Unintended Consequences of Review Committees	105
	Impact on Decision Making and Programmatic Complexity	107
	Portfolio Expansion	110

The Benefits of Pursuing Larger
    Numbers of Projects   110
Responding to Portfolio-Related Challenges   111
Mixed-Function Review and Governance
    Committees   115
Business Governance Committees   117
More Unintended Consequences   120
Increased Project Size, Uncertainty,
    and Complexity   122
The Benefits of Large and Uncertain Projects   122
Establishment of Within-Project Infrastructure 123
The Unintended Consequences of
    Within-Project Infrastructure   126
The Establishment of Specialty Review and
    Governance Committees   130
The Unintended Consequences of Specialty
    Review and Governance Committees   133
Challenges Ahead   134

Chapter 8   Moving Forward   137

Other Approaches   137
Downsizing the Organization   137
Transferring Governance   139
Redefining the Role of a Programmaticist   140
Operationalist Approaches Re-Examined   140
Inclusivist Approaches Re-Examined   145
Building a Centaur   148
Elements of an Improved Project
    Oversight Model   153

Part 2   **The Promise and Practice of Third-Generation**
             Programmatics   **155**

Chapter 9   Leading Complex Endeavors   157

The Journey So Far   157
Leadership That Resolves Complex Problems   159
Critical Leadership Roles   163
Adaptive Leadership and the Outcome
    Sage–Programmaticist   168

Chapter 10   A New Perspective on Programs and
Program Management   171

From Adaptive Leadership to Program
Management   171
What Is a Program, Really?   174
Redefining Program Management   180
Redefining Projects and Project Management 183
Is It a Program or Is It a Project?   185
Barriers to Acceptance   192

Chapter 11   Introducing Third-Generation Programmatics   195

The Complexity-Management Roles of Project and
Program Management   195
Defining Third-Generation Programmatics   197
Roles and Responsibilities in the
Three-Party System   200
Projects Sponsored by Governing Committees 203
*Programs Sponsored by the Governing
Committee*   204
Subprograms Sponsored by Programs   209
Other Activities Sponsored by Programs   212
Benefits Expected from the Third-Generation
Programmatics Approach   213
*Benefits of Distinguishing Projects from
Programs*   214
*Benefits of Distinguishing Project
Management from Program Management*   217
*Benefits of Implementing the
Three-Party System*   223

Chapter 12   The Decision to Implement Third-Generation
Programmatics   225

Choosing Between Two-Party and
Three-Party Systems   226
Challenges Faced When Implementing
Third-Generation Programmatics   229
*Organizational Maturity in the
Programmatic Sciences*   229
*Defining Programmaticist Authority
and Autonomy*   230

(Re-)Assigning Current Project and
   Program Managers   235
Identifying and Assigning New Project
   and Program Managers   238
Defining Reporting Relationships for
   Program and Project Managers   240
Establishing Departments of Program
   Management and of Programmatic Science   244

Chapter 13 Developing Programmatic Leadership
              Competencies   247

              The Needs of a Leader   247
              Defining "Appropriate" Leadership Behaviors 253
              Insights from Research on Program Management
                 Competency   260
              Leadership Challenges   264
              Defining "Ideal" Leadership Systems
                 and Behaviors   268

Chapter 14 Becoming a Third-Generation
              Programmatics Organization   271

              Applying the Principles of Third-Generation
                 Programmatics   271
              Twelve Questions to Answer   275
              Deciding to Use a Third-Generation
                 Programmatic Oversight System   279
              Life, Viewed Programmatically   282
              Final Thoughts   283

Afterword   285
Glossary of Newly Introduced Terms   287
Suggested Readings   295
              Standards and Guides in Program and Project
                 Management   295
              First- and Second-Generation Programmatics 295
              Distinctions between Projects and Programs, Project
                 Management and Program Management   296
              Complexity Management   296
              Program Leadership Competency Development 297
Index   299

PREFACE

I have learned over the years that exasperation can be a very valuable thing. Not every exasperation, mind you—not the exasperation of discovering that your wallet is at home when you are halfway through a supermarket checkout line—but chronic exasperation, certainly. Chronically exasperating things fester and foment in unusual and sometimes priceless ways. They roil about in the semiconscious and unfettered part of the brain, coalescing into ideas that can burst forth in response to an unexpected trigger. I pay attention to that kind of exasperation because once in a while when it congeals and erupts, it reveals insights that are unexpectedly sensible, enlightening, and clear. Exasperation can beget inspiration, and if we are lucky it can stimulate innovation.

This book, in many ways, is about exasperation. It is about a journey that I started while trying to understand the exasperation experienced by my colleagues and I as we tried to fix a broken pharmaceutical industry. It is about how that journey led to a broader examination of exasperation shared by leaders across many other of today's knowledge-based industries. And it is about how the collective exasperation of many leaders, boiled to its essence, can lead to new and seemingly sensible perspectives about the unique leadership needs of modern knowledge-based industries.

I started my career in a place that was very different from where I am now. I was a biochemical pharmacologist with every intention of spending my life as one. I cherished my profession for the challenges that it presented me—the opportunity to explore a problem through cycles of hypothesis, testing, and fact-finding. It was exasperating at times, but always in a good way. Every failed experiment brought frustrations, but those frustrations were always based on a truth that needed to be uncovered and understood. Examined appropriately, those frustrations often turned into discoveries. They had creative value because they enabled me to see things differently, and they led to some of my favorite "Aha!" moments. I might have enjoyed that role for the entirety of my career.

Over time, however, I came to recognize that being a good scientist was only the first part of a successful scientific career. Big and impactful science was advanced through research programs, and being a good program (or project) leader was equally critical to success. But program leadership was not something I had been formally schooled in, and the exasperation associated with it was quite different. Big programs were complex—technically, strategically, and operationally. Pursuing them required the support of large organizations, and large organizations had specific expectations as to how complexity should be managed. Those expectations were rarely articulated well. Program leaders in large organizations needed to precisely balance their exercise of individual leadership with the constraints imposed by their organizational hierarchies. It could be a precarious balance that was inconsistently defined and difficult to maintain. Sustaining that balance could be exasperating for a leader.

As my career progressed and I assumed an executive role (as a Vice President of Program, Project and Portfolio Management), I came to be responsible for the actions of many others who led or managed programs and projects. The time I spent developing those leaders (and trying to ensure that they exhibited appropriately balanced leadership) grew— and with it grew my personal exasperation about poorly defined organizational conceptions of leadership. Organizations within my industry lacked a cohesive framework for defining their leadership expectations. Then, in 2006, after I had spent more than twenty years as a program or project leader, I had three experiences that brought my exasperation forever to the surface. Each of them led to a moment of clarity—a specific realization that would trigger my journey seeking to define a better approach to leadership of complex projects and programs—and eventually, to this book.

My first experience occurred while interviewing a candidate who had applied to fill a program leader job within my department. Early in the interview, he asked me to define the specific roles and responsibilities of a program leader within my organization. On that day the question made me uneasy. Program leaders in my department were assigned widely different roles and responsibilities based on their personal skills and capabilities. It was too early in the interview to know what expectations I might set for this candidate.

I began my answer by noting that a single widely accepted "best practice" for leading programs and projects had not been established within the pharmaceutical industry. Because each program was unique, I needed to match candidate skills with program needs as part of building an effective program team. And then I said this: "You will be given responsibilities according to your skills. Your responsibilities as a program leader will be whatever the president of the company agrees them to be." I quickly praised our president for his empowerment of program leaders and talked about the responsibilities that the candidate might expect to have. It was an honest answer that I might have given on any other day, and the candidate seemed satisfied by it. But on that day, it did not satisfy me. There was something troubling about it.

Over the previous fifteen or so years, my organization had been led by five different presidents (each, I am sure, with a five-year plan). Each president had a somewhat different approach to his interactions with program and project leadership. Given my answer, how could I be sure that my organization would continue to pursue a clear long-term vision for leadership by my department? How could I promise to a job applicant that I knew what his role would be in the years to come? In the absence of an industry standard, could I feel secure about the vision of program and project leadership that I had been working to build? And why, after decades of pursuing team-based development programs, had my industry not succeeded in defining more generally accepted program and project leadership "best practices"? The questions nagged at me.

In fact, the pharmaceutical industry had struggled mightily in its attempts to develop appropriate models for managing complex research and development programs. In its attempts to strike the right balance between agile autonomous teams and rigorous executive oversight it had flitted between models that alternately emphasized strategically focused versus operationally focused roles for program and project leaders. It seemed that the industry was never comfortable that it had achieved the right balance. And as I thought more about it, I came to an unsettling conclusion:

My industry's inability to agree on best practices in the leadership and management of programs (or projects) represented a failure of my profession.

Complexity of our projects notwithstanding, something was wrong if the most experienced and professional of program and project leaders could not uniformly and unambiguously define their leadership roles within the industry and within their own host organizations. I wondered how common this was in industries other than my own.

The second event occurred just a few weeks later. It began with a phone call from Joel Adler, a faculty member in Organizational Dynamics at the University of Pennsylvania. He wanted to discuss Penn's master's degree program in the Organizational Dynamics of Project, Program and Portfolio Management. Joel was interested in establishing a partnership with my organization, and he wondered whether I would find value in sending program and project leaders to an academic program such as Penn's. I feigned a moment of thought and then quickly said "No" with a simple explanation: My program management staff was already experienced. A number of them had earned certifications as project or program management professionals. I did not believe that academic studies were the best way to further advance my staff's capabilities. I explained that program management in complex knowledge-based industries was far different from the process-focused forms of program management that were described in textbooks and training manuals. They were much more pragmatic. "The dynamics of program leadership need to be learned and developed within the context of an organization."

My response was clear, and at the surface, quite certain. But deep inside, on that day, I found myself almost immediately questioning my own beliefs. Again, I felt troubled.

If leading programs in my organization did not require formal education, then why would program leaders be more qualified than anyone else (for example, my organization's president) to define their "ideal" roles? Is it just because of their prior experience, or their unique understanding of the program's needs, or their professional focus? Somehow, those things did not seem like compelling enough differentiators. (Too many of my experienced, knowledgeable, and previously successful program leaders had struggled and failed in their next program leadership assignments.) What makes program leadership a profession, and not just an assignment? And perhaps most importantly, what education would leaders need if we were to design (from scratch if necessary) a better system for leading organizational programs?

The pharmaceutical industry had struggled for years to achieve greater success via its programs and projects—and to a large extent, it had failed. What reason did I have to believe that we had the knowledge necessary to fix our problems? As I asked myself these questions, I came to my second unsettling conclusion:

We did not understand everything that we needed to know in order to dramatically improve our leadership of programs and projects; something important was missing.

Program leaders should be clearly recognized as having knowledge, capabilities, and skills that are unique and specific to their own professional "science"—the science of managing an organization's complex and innovative endeavors. I became dissatisfied with my response to Joel because it asserted that the science of managing programs could not be taught. And the admonition of British theorist Stafford Beer began to haunt me:

"Our institutions are failing because they are disobeying laws of effective organization which their administrators do not know about, to which indeed their cultural mind is closed, because they contend that there exists and can exist no science competent to discover those laws."

Stafford Beer
Designing Freedom, **1974**

Was I contending that a competent "science" of program leadership did not exist? This second observation was as unsettling as the first.

My third experience came shortly thereafter, in the form of a comment from a colleague and friend. It felt like a kick in the groin—my first reaction was surprise, and then there was pain, followed by a lingering discomfort that was very hard to forget. I was in a program team meeting where we were debating the significance of a technical outcome from one of our projects. After voicing my opinion, I was asked half-jokingly to let the others decide, because I was now a program leader and "no longer a scientist." The suggestion that I was no longer viewed as a scientist was surprising and painful. (Did they forget that my research had resulted in more scientific publications than the rest of the team's combined?) And then it made me uncomfortable for a very long time—because my friend and colleague, without realizing why, was so very right.

As a scientist, I had been trained to begin every endeavor with an investigation of the current knowledge in the field. I knew that uncovering new knowledge required a thorough understanding of what was already known: what was hypothesized versus proven, what should be accepted and what should be questioned. How could I expect to discover the "missing piece" without a thorough knowledge of all that was already known? I had ceased to be a scientist, but not because my capabilities as a biochemical pharmacologist had diminished. I had ceased to be a scientist because I had failed to approach my program leadership role with the diligence of a scientist. In my professional transition from scientist to leader and then to executive, I had not taken enough time to study the theory, the research, and the knowledge that had preceded me in my new fields. I had allowed myself somehow to accept that the appropriate understanding could be learned on the job. I would never have accepted that premise in my previous role as a biochemical pharmacologist, and now I was all the more embarrassed by my earlier response to Joel.

My exasperation with myself grew, and I reached a third conclusion:

Leaders of programs and projects should hold themselves accountable for becoming experts in the "science" of leadership if they are to advance their capabilities and their profession.

I was guilty of the very transgressions that Stafford Beer had attributed to institutional "administrators." As a consequence of my promotions, I had become one of them.

Together, these three events exposed elements of my profession that were at first troubling, and eventually exasperating. They raised fundamental questions about my profession in program leadership:

Why and when does it become exasperatingly difficult to lead complex programs and projects within an organization?

Why had we, as professional leaders, been unsuccessful in anticipating and addressing that?

What new knowledge or insight would be necessary to correct it?

And was it already available, or could we attain it?

And so I set out on a journey to find answers to my questions.

It started with an investigation of what was known about the "science" of leading programs and projects—published standards that described the principles, practices, and processes considered to best capture cross-industry knowledge of my profession. It progressed to the examination of published research on the leadership attributes critical to a program or project leader's success. It led to the academic study of theories relevant to the leadership of cross-functional programs and projects in dynamic organizations (for example, systems thinking, and complexity and adaptive leadership theories). And it revealed a rich body of literature that together suggested (at least to me) that improving the leadership of complex programs and projects in knowledge-based organizations of today required a new approach.

It is not my intention to conduct an academic review of all that material here (lest this book begin to read like a thesis). I have chosen instead to pursue a more practice-based narrative in the hope that the book will appeal not only to program and project leaders, but also the executives who control the organizational environments in which program and project leaders work. However, that research led to two important conclusions. The first was that studying the more academic material is a very worthwhile endeavor for anyone who is responsible for (or dependent upon) the effective leadership and management of programs or projects. That conclusion clearly validated my friend Joel.

The second was more surprising, and seemingly much more signifi-cant. Examined thoughtfully, the material does seem to provide new and valuable insight about the unique leadership needs of modern organiza-tions. It convinced me that my personal exasperation was an understand-able consequence of having applied unsuitable (bureaucratic) thinking to the management of complex modern-day programs. And it seemed to provide at least one of the critical "missing pieces" that my exasperation had left me looking for—a new framework for examining, understand-ing, and developing program and project management leadership. But one question remained: Was this framework uniquely germane to the needs of my organization or my industry, or did it have much broader applications?

I returned to my discussions with Joel at the University of Pennsylvania, this time to discuss the curriculum being used at Penn for teaching the dynamics of program and project leadership. Our conversation was stimulating. And before it was over (and much to my surprise) I had agreed to join Penn's faculty, teaching coursework in Program Management Skills and Systems as part of a master's degree executive education program. I had not accepted this position because I was looking for another job; it was because I was looking for another laboratory.

Teaching at Penn has provided a perfect opportunity to further the journey described in this book. Each semester has presented an oppor-tunity to study the challenges of program leadership with a different group of diverse, intelligent, experienced, and thoughtful professionals who were eager to examine the application of leadership theory and pro-fessional standards to his or her own organizational context. My students came from diverse industries—aerospace and defense, healthcare, infor-mation technology, telecommunications, consumer products, finance, and energy, to name a few. They had widely different training and expe-rience. They each brought new insights gleaned from their diverse prac-tices. Some were exhilarated by their professional leadership experience; others were exasperated. And together over a seven-year period, we have conducted hundreds of case studies examining the potential re-invention of program leadership principles, and the potential significance of those principles to their own organizations.

The body of work gathered from my colleagues, my students, and the many professional contacts that we have made, reveals surprising consistencies in the issues that are being faced by organizations that otherwise seem to be very, very different. It reveals common threads that tie together the experiences of many program and project leaders.

And it provides a framework by which those threads can be woven into a fabric that is different and better than any we have seen before. The result is a perspective about where program and project leaders (and the organizations that employ them) have been, and a proposal about where we should go if we are to enhance the leadership of complex and innovative endeavors.

I invite you to experience that journey and its interesting conclusions in the chapters that follow.

Richard Heaslip
March 2014

ACKNOWLEDGMENTS

Readers of *Managing Complex Projects and Programs* will quickly recognize that it could not have been written without the significant contributions of my colleagues, students, and friends. Part 1 of the book bears witness to the generosity that each of them has shown in sharing their experiences, their knowledge, and their professional and personal insights with me. Part 2 applies their experience, their advice, and their wisdom in the design of new approaches for managing such endeavors. The entire book is a testimony to the contributions that they have made. Unfortunately, I am unable to cite the many contributors to that effort; for the most part, they participated under the promise or presumption of anonymity. But I am humbled and grateful for the enthusiasm each of them showed. So to my colleagues, my students, and my friends who have participated in this journey: Let me say thank you so very much. This book would not exist without you. I only hope that it somehow fulfills the promises that I made to you along the way.

Readers will also note that throughout *Managing Complex Projects and Programs*, I have made reference to my belief that we need to advance the "science" of managing programs and projects. It is my hope that professionals will continue to explore and develop that concept. It is a subject that I had at first found myself ill-prepared to study; I began this journey accidentally, as a practitioner-turned-student of the profession, not as its academician or philosopher. I have been lucky, however, to have had the opportunity to research the foundations of "programmatic science" while being supported by a particularly well-prepared group of colleagues—the Organizational Dynamics faculty at the University of Pennsylvania. They pointed me in directions that I might not otherwise have discovered. For their encouragement and help, I offer my heartfelt thanks to: Joel Adler PhD, Jean-Marc Choukroun PhD, Richard Bayney PhD, Keith Hornbacher MBA, Larry Starr PhD, John Pourdehnad PhD, Alan Barstow PhD, and Martin F. Stankard PhD.

I am also appreciative of the wisdom, the knowledge, and the support bestowed upon me by another remarkable group of colleagues and friends—a group that I came to know and admire by working on the third edition of the *Project Management Institute's Standard for Program Management*. Their rich contributions and learned advice were invaluable to me as I worked to make sense of my research in the field. They challenged me to consider a variety of perspectives, and never failed to remind me that (despite the despair voiced by many individual program and project managers) there were organizations and professionals out there who had already "gotten it right." Thank you so much: James Carilli PMP PgMP, Michael Collins PMP, Andrea Demaria PMP, Brian Grafsgaard PMP PgMP, Richard Krulis MSE PMP, Penny Pickles MA PMP, Chris Richards PMP, Sandra Smalley ME, Matthew Tomlinson PMP PgMP, Bobbye Underwood PMI-ACP PMP, Kristin Vitello CAPM, and Lynn Wendt PMP PgMP. Most especially from this group, I would like to thank and acknowledge Eric Norman PMP PgMP, for the many hours we spent immersed in thoughtful discussion and debate about our visions of Program and Project Management.

I would also like to offer special thanks for the patience, guidance, and support provided by the team at John Wiley & Sons: Amanda Shettleton, Margaret Cummins, Doug Salvemini, and Bob Argentieri, as well as copyeditor Suzanne Rapcavage. They have been most gracious in ignoring my publishing naiveté, in improving my content, and in making my first trip through the publishing process as painless as possible.

And lastly, but most importantly, I would like to acknowledge the incredible support that I have received from my friends and my family as I have written this book. Each, in various ways, has contributed to my efforts. They encouraged me to continue when I was most tired, they offered me support when I was most in need of it, and they listened with the most empathetic of expressions as I droned on about my struggles. I know none of that was easy. Thank you for pretending it was.

To my wife Julie, and my children Rick, Cody, and Kelley—thank you for being there to support me in this and every journey, and at the same time for holding the rest of the world at bay. Your love, your understanding, and your support energize and expand my life.

And to Mom and Dad—yes, it is done; you can stop asking. Thank you for worrying that I've been working too hard; the apple doesn't fall far from the tree. I love you.

PART 1

Professional Project and Program Management—Yesterday and Today

CHAPTER 1

The Exhilaration and Exasperation of Project and Program Leadership

Irecall to this day the first time I acted as a project leader. It happened quite by accident. I was a fifteen-year-old volunteer who, for reasons I didn't understand, had just been asked to co-manage the opening of a coffee house for teens in the basement of a local church. It was an unlikely request; I was a very quiet kid who didn't really like coffee, and it wasn't my church. But Martin, the adult in charge of the project, had for some reason picked me from among a group of interested friends to fill the role "for a while." (I learned later that such deception is common in the recruitment of first-time project leaders!) I hesitantly agreed after recognizing that it would enable me to assign my closest friends to the choice roles. (I thought that was a good thing.) The goal, I believed, was simple: To organize coffee house events that gave teens someplace fun to go on cold Saturday nights. For Martin, though, it was something different. The project was part of a bigger program intended to teach teens about accepting responsibility, working in teams, and developing leadership skills—perhaps as a diversion from the riskier distractions of the early 1970s.

The coffee house openings became popular events in our town, but preparing for them was a lot more work than I had anticipated. I wasn't really sure of what was expected of me in my "leader" role. I filled the role as best I could, mostly by cataloging the work activities that we needed to complete and soliciting volunteers from our team to help in getting them done. At first it was a reasonably easy task. Over time, however, our committees grew weary and I found that I needed to pressure team members into fulfilling their commitments. In one of our meetings, an argument broke out. Steve (a close friend of mine) was accused of not doing his share of the work. He didn't understand that his commitment was necessary, and other team members resented him for not doing his part. As the argument got uglier, I shrank into my chair and made a silent vow to stay out of it. And then Martin called for a timeout and asked for my opinion. I was cornered.

After a silence filled with inner conflict and panic, I said to my friend, "The coffee house is like a galley ship where we all have to row. If someone stops rowing on his side, we will go in a circle. People are upset because last week you stopped rowing . . . and this week it sounds like you want to water-ski. Your friends are saying, 'You can't.'"

It was a silly metaphor. (Let me apologize at the outset. I may use too many of those.) But it broke the tension. The people at the meeting burst out laughing. Some applauded, and others who I hardly knew got out of their chairs to give me a high five. Steve gave me a thumbs up to indicate he understood, and we were back on track. Martin smiled and nodded at me. He asked me to run the rest of the meeting and then he left.

It seemed like forever before my heart stopped racing. It might have been out of fear that I could have lost a good friend. Maybe it was fright about running the rest of the meeting, or alarm about what other surprises were up Martin's sleeves. But I now suspect that in some unexpected way, that moment changed my life. I realized later that I was able (in a manner befitting my then-quiet personality) to help a group of friends re-align in their commitment to each other and to their shared goals.

My friends thanked me afterwards for exerting influence that I didn't know I had, and the coffee houses that followed went smoothly and successfully. I had achieved my goal, and (though I didn't realize it at the time) so had Martin. I had experienced for the first time what it was like to be a project *leader*. I was quietly exhilarated, and I suspect Martin was too.

I have since come to believe that the best reason to become a project or program leader is to personally experience that exhilaration.

LEADING PROJECTS AND PROGRAMS

It should be easy to understand why those who are responsible for leading or managing projects or programs would find the role to be exhilarating. To be associated with projects or programs is to be "where the action is." Projects and programs provide the means for pursuing new and important things. To be asked to lead or manage one is to be entrusted with delivering a promise for the future, and being successful in that should certainly be exciting. Whether the intent is to open a coffee house or to pursue much more important project or program goals—the personal exhilaration that comes with success is always gratifying.

Project or program leadership can also be challenging and scary, however. It is common that success does not come easily. Leaders can expect to be held personally accountable for ensuring that they pursue success in the best possible way. They must ensure that their goals are clearly defined and communicated, and that they are accepted by stakeholders who may have quite different perspectives, desires, and motivations. Project or program leaders are responsible for designing effective and supportable plans and for managing the long periods of the often intense and difficult work required to complete them. Within an organizational environment, each of these tasks can be daunting. And yet, for some—for uniquely skilled and passionate leaders who are good at overcoming challenges to achieve important goals—it seems only to increase the exhilaration that they experience.

Over the years, I have had the privilege of working with some extremely talented project and program leaders. The best of them possess a unique blend of leadership competencies that they skillfully call upon in just the right moments. They exude passion and dedication for the goals they are pursuing and for the teams with whom they work. And each of them is invigorated by the success that their teams achieve. They are, in my view, *organizational athletes*. As they lead, they are exhilarated by the thrill of moving their teams forward with deftly executed plays, managing the clock, analyzing their options, and defining and re-defining strategy in the moment. They find that working on their program and project teams is exciting in the same ways that competing on the athletic field might be. They understand that they won't always win. In fact, some of them work in environments where their goals can rarely be achieved— where factors that cannot be anticipated or controlled will stymie even the best of their endeavors. Still, they love what they do. They take pride in their work as they pursue elusive goals, and they are enlivened by the prospect of making a real difference.

To work with such people can be inspiring; I would wish it on anyone. For those who have (or could develop) the appropriate personal and technical skills, I would advise that being a leader of a project or program team is a wonderful, even ideal profession. And I believe it bears repeating—the best reason to become a project or program leader is to personally experience that exhilaration.

My enthusiasm for the profession of project and program management has served me well in my professional life. It has carried me forward. However, over time I have found that my perspective does not resonate as well with some of my peers. Increasingly often, when I discuss this "ideal" career, I have found that successful members of my profession question whether my views are, well, too "idyllic." They agree that their careers have been exhilarating, but many of them lament that there is something about their careers that has been changing over time. They confide that they are tiring, and with increasing frequency, they admit to periods where they are more *exasperated* than exhilarated. And they suggest that it is somehow related to changes in their organizations' expectations, or in their organizations' cultures.

It would be easy to dismiss such perspectives as isolated events were they to be made infrequently, or by those who are seemingly less successful in or knowledgeable about their leadership roles, or if (deep down) I didn't recognize some of those same feelings within myself. But after two decades in a variety of organizational roles, I cannot help but observe that these views have been expressed with increasing frequency by many of my most successful colleagues—those whom I would consider to be any organization's "franchise" athletes. And as I have listened to them, and examined my own feelings more deeply, I cannot help but conclude that there is a growing, even urgent, need to understand why.

This book is about the journey I have taken to answer that question, and to explore changes that would enable these athletes and the organizations in which they work to more successfully deliver the exhilarating outcomes that they both desire. It is based on observations made by some of the best leaders and managers whom I have come to know through my professional lives—as a project and then program leader, as an executive responsible for developing such leaders, as an academic who studies the "science" of program leadership, and an advisor to organizations striving to improve their leadership capabilities. It seeks to take the perspectives of these very smart and successful people and, after combining them with insights from a rich literature on leadership, to propose a new framework for managing complex projects and programs being pursued by modern organizations.

My journey began with a search for the answer to a seemingly simple question: *What circumstances have led experienced, successful project and program leaders to become exasperated with their professions?*

As might be expected, individual professionals gave different answers to that question. To my surprise, however, I found that when answering the question, experienced project and program leaders did not usually point to professional challenges commonly discussed in so many other good books. They did not cite difficulties of learning the "body of knowledge" of a project manager, or of building a winning team, or of leading without authority, or of listening and communicating effectively. In fact,

I have found that they focused very little on the challenges of developing personal skills and competencies, despite the critical importance of each of them. As their organizations' franchise athletes, experienced leaders seemed to believe that the need to develop those skills was a given, akin to basic conditioning. It was a prerequisite of their positions.

Instead, project and program management professionals most often pointed to challenges that were related to the organizational environments in which they worked—the constraints that were imposed upon them by their organizations' governing processes, bureaucracy, or politics. Their greatest expressions of exasperation related to organizational behaviors that (they felt) limited their abilities to be effective and to succeed. They related to their organization's culture and its approach in managing change. And they related to an increasing need to manage project and program change, based on their organizations' pursuit of initiatives that were uncertain and complex.

In our discussions, experienced leaders observed that their projects and programs progressed reasonably smoothly when they were able to deliver the outcomes that were expected. Issues that emerged during those times were generally manageable. However, they noted that projects and programs did not always deliver their expected outcomes. Outcomes achieved from their truly complex projects and programs (those that pursued unprecedented solutions, or that relied on assumptions about human perception and behavior, for example) were often difficult to predict. And because unexpected outcomes led to learning, and learning led to new ideas about the best ways to pursue goals, it was common that uncertain outcomes resulted in the need to significantly change the plans or to alter the priorities of an ongoing project or program.

Project and program leaders confided that much of their growing frustration was related to the difficulty of obtaining organizational agreement to re-examine strategies or priorities in response to uncertain outcomes, or to obtain agreement on the precise changes that were most appropriate. They observed that when pursuing uncertain outcomes, project and program leaders spent far too much of their time navigating increasingly complex organizational processes—processes that required formal subcommittee reviews and the approval of various executives. They reported that their energies were being shifted from managing programs or projects that intended to deliver change, to managing organizational processes that seek to control or monitor change.

As organizational athletes trying to manage activities on "the field," program and project leaders had grown exasperated with the amount of time they spent managing those in "the seats and the suites." Seasoned but exasperated project and program leaders seemed to share a common longing to work in organizations that had better, faster, and smarter approaches for managing their programs and projects.

These project and program leaders—even the most exasperated of them—recognized there were good reasons for their organizations' behaviors: Their organizations were struggling to identify the best approach for managing the uncertainty that was associated with the very complex projects and programs that they were now sponsoring. The truth be told, there had been many times when their organization's executive leaders were also becoming exasperated—with the seemingly unscripted behaviors of their project and program leaders!

Project and program leaders observed that their organizations were struggling with important questions: Should they grant team leaders more autonomy in an effort to improve project and program agility, or should they exert more influence and control over them so as to monitor strategy and manage their use of resources? How much authority should they place in the hands of program or project team leaders versus the executive leaders who had responsibilities for managing line-function operations and strategies? Are the organization's project and program leaders competent enough to be entrusted with greater autonomy, authority, and individual responsibility? At the core of each of these questions was the same inquiry:

What are the roles and responsibilities of an ideal project or program leader in our organization?

To reduce the exasperation of project and program leaders, organizations would need to answer that question more clearly. But is there a framework that organizations can apply to every program or project to clarify how its leadership needs are intended to be filled? Could we identify a framework that promotes the athleticism of project and program leaders?

I believe that the answer is yes.

Organizations have already spent many years trying to improve their management of projects and programs. They have conducted what amounts to a series of experiments to define how they could better manage their complex endeavors. We can begin by learning from them. Their responses should reveal the specific competencies that must be developed.

Next, we should look for the pieces that are missing. We need a framework that enables us to make sense of what we have learned—a framework for examining the unique roles, responsibilities, and relationships that need to exist if organizations are to improve their management and leadership of complex projects and programs. One goal of this book is to propose such a framework.

The core of the book's proposal is based on recognition that to effectively manage complex projects and programs, organizations must develop three distinct managerial competencies, and then clearly define how they will be brought together within an organization's "leadership system." Poorly developing one or more of these competencies, or poorly defining how they should come together in a leadership system, leads to issues—and to exasperation. The proposed framework describes how these three leadership specialties should work together synchronously and dynamically in a symbiotic relationship within an organization, to enable its leaders to better define and fill the role(s) most exhilarating to them.

The book is about developing an advanced knowledge and understanding of what I will refer to as ***programmatic science***.[1] Programmatic science is defined as the study of managerial systems, principles, practices, and processes used by organizations to pursue their goals via programs and/or projects. The purpose of programmatic science is to develop a more advanced understanding of how organizations can more effectively lead and manage their projects and programs. Programmatic science should be viewed as a social science that seeks to study and understand the dynamics of managing programs and projects within an organization, much the same as political science is a social science that seeks to study and understand the dynamics of managing governments and governmental institutions.

Programmatic science examines the key factors that should be considered when designing an organization's approach to the management of programs and projects. For ease of reference, a specific combination of applied systems, principles, practices, and processes, used by an

---

[1] I will, throughout the course of this book, introduce a number of terms that are new. To make it easier to recognize such terms, they will be bolded and italicized the first time they are used. The formal definitions for these terms will be included in the text, and also at the end of the book in a section (predictably) entitled Glossary of Newly Introduced Terms.

organization for the purpose of managing its programs and projects will be referred to as the organization's ***programmatics*** or its ***programmatic approach***.

Why is the study of programmatics and programmatic science critical? Because the many hours spent exploring the exhilaration and exasperation of students, colleagues, and organizational leaders reveals that *organizations that have not carefully and knowledgeably defined their systems for managing the pursuit of their goals through programs and projects have too often sought to improve their capabilities reactively, through successive rounds of well-intentioned but poorly understood organizational restructuring in which old problems are often exchanged for new ones.* Such organizations are conducting costly experiments in search of solutions, and they are often surprised by the unintended consequences of their actions.

Too often, they have entered a world in which program or project management is treated much the same as a vending machine. Shiny and new when it is first installed, the organization will be pleased when it reliably delivers what is expected (products and change). It will be trusted and recognized for its value. Over time, however, as its customers' needs change, it will be asked to deliver many different things. The customers will be happy when it does. But if it does so less effectively or less consistently, its customers will notice. They may begin to mumble, then to complain, and finally to curse. Some may be willing to put a bit more money into it, remembering that it has previously worked well. But others will stop trusting it until they are assured that it has received some "adjustments." Adjustments may help. But if the machine still doesn't deliver properly, someone will eventually kick it. Sometimes vending machines respond to that. Unfortunately, kicking can become commonplace (first in one spot, then in another). It may help the customer, but it is clearly not good for the machine. It leaves marks. When the kicking no longer produces results, someone else (usually someone powerful) will demonstrate that when vending machines are "stuck" it can help to shake them. Sometimes that also works; when shaken vigorously enough some machines will even give you more than what you paid for. However, a shaken machine is usually less capable of responding to its next customer. It may no longer be able to deliver even those things that it had previously delivered reliably. Eventually, its reputation will be so damaged that no one will place their trust in it. Few will want to use it, and everyone will agree with a proposal to replace it.

So it often is with organizations that have historically viewed their project and program management infrastructure as a machine, and expected it to deliver new and very different things—things it was not originally built to deliver; things that were uncertain. Without an understanding of how the machine works (or should work), they could not know if their expectations were reasonable.

To optimize our organizational environments for the pursuit of complex projects and programs, I propose that we examine and better understand when that machine works and when it doesn't. Only then can we explore how it can be made to operate flexibly enough to deliver "products and change" of every shape and size in environments that are complex, diverse, and highly uncertain.

Does the solution lie in adjustment of the current machine, in the acquisition of a replacement, or in the design of something completely new? It depends. (The best answer to most complex questions is "it depends." This one is no different.)

For some projects or programs and their organizations, adjustment or replacement might work. But it would seem that for highly uncertain and complex endeavors the introduction of something new might be the best answer. For those projects and programs, we would do better to think of project and program management and the infrastructure that supports them not as parts of a machine, but as distinct vital organs, each of which has a unique, specialized function that is critical to survival of the entire organization. We might expect that any examination of their expected function and required fitness would need to begin with an understanding of how they could optimally contribute to the system that they are part of. Only then could we most clearly define the expectations we should have for them, and enable them to more fully demonstrate the prowess that is required to produce exhilarating results.

We will begin that process in the next chapter with an examination of the managerial dynamics that led to the introduction, acceptance, and evolution of "project management" in many modern organizations. My intent is not to provide excruciating detail about the history of project management or the evolution of industrial business models, or to review the extensive literature on these subjects. Instead, I seek to provide a contextual description of circumstances that commonly led to the adoption of project management in the late twentieth century, and to the assumptions we still make about it today. My purpose is to provide background that helps us to understand how the strengths and weaknesses of project management have contributed to its evolving role in organizations, and to the exhilaration and exasperation felt by those working in the profession.

CHAPTER 2

The Emergence of Project Management: First-Generation Programmatics

PROJECT MANAGEMENT'S BEGINNINGS

Project management became widely recognized as a managing discipline in the mid-1900s, when its principles, practices, processes, and value to project-based engineering endeavors became more generally understood and accepted. The conditions that enabled its birth and shaped its purpose had been established long before that time, however—perhaps a century earlier, with the birth of the Industrial Age.

During the Industrial Age, organizations dramatically advanced their capabilities for industrial manufacturing and production by introducing specific organizational philosophies and approaches. It was an age in which they discovered (among many other things) that by organizing themselves into individual "line function" groups and enabling their staff to develop the technical skills of each, they could rapidly advance their capabilities. They could quickly develop new knowledge and competencies, perform job functions with greater efficiency, and achieve higher quality in areas critical to their success. If an organization focused on manufacturing consumer products, for example, it could develop research and engineering functions explicitly focused on designing and developing the specific products that it targeted. It could hire specialists who were uniquely skilled at the processes required to efficiently manufacture and package those products. And it could develop specialized sales teams and a distribution system catered to the products and to the customers of greatest importance. To achieve this, organizations hired leaders—usually highly skilled technical leaders—whose primary responsibility was to optimize performance related to each area of expertise. These leaders were, in turn,

---

13

responsible for employing and organizing staff with the required training and knowledge. In each area the effect was the same—advancement of the organization's ability to efficiently and effectively get the desired work done in its key competency areas.

Functional specialization also led to the establishment of specific organizational structures and management practices. Often, managing committees were formed and management practices were established to coordinate organizational operations that required support from more than one functional group (see, for example, Figure 2.1). These committees were usually staffed by the leaders of each functional group to ensure that each line-function's knowledge and insight was effectively communicated to the other line functions. Under this system, leaders would work together to define the organization's cross-functional goals and then make commitments as to how each of their groups would contribute to achieving them. Jointly, they were responsible for assuring that the operational activities of the functional groups remained appropriately coordinated and synchronized. Individually, they were accountable for dedicating the resources that were necessary to satisfy their group's commitments, and for monitoring their group's progress in completing assignments according to the committee's plan.

Establishing cross-functional committees provided organizations with an important mechanism for supervising cross-functional activities. It enabled line function managers to maintain control over their departmental resources while ensuring that they could support and influence organization-wide strategic initiatives. However, it also had its drawbacks. Functionally-centered organizational models were not ideally

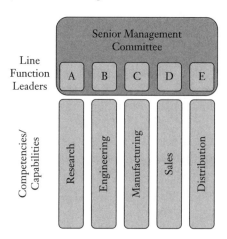

Figure 2.1   An organizational model based on functional groups.

suited for managing cross-functional activities on a day-to-day basis. It was inherently inefficient to depend upon high-level management committees (whose members had complete responsibility for their own functional groups) to coordinate cross-functional work (for which they were only partially responsible).

To maximize cross-functional efficiency (particularly in larger organizations), managing committees needed to establish collaborative relationships at multiple organizational levels. Middle-level managers from a given line function generally needed to manage their cross-functional work in collaboration with the middle-level managers from the other functional groups. Lower-level employees often needed to coordinate their activities with other lower-level employees. Relying on senior managing committees for such communication could not by itself stimulate the establishment of important collaborative relationships that often needed to exist between lower levels of the functional groups. Organizations sought to improve the everyday middle-level and lower-level management of cross-functional initiatives via organizational constructs designed specifically for that purpose—via "projects."

In various organizations projects of diverse types were initiated. They shared a general definition—temporary initiatives organized with the purpose of doing something new. Employees from the required functional groups were assigned to work collaboratively on projects with the appropriate level of employees from the other functional groups. The concept was simple: Organize people who needed to work on these temporary initiatives into temporary "organizations" that would focus on the specific goals and needs of that initiative.

Projects provided an excellent vehicle for managing cross-functional activities that sought to achieve a specific organizational goal. They were recognized to be critical to an organization's success; they were the means by which organizations sought to develop new products and capabilities, to pursue new initiatives, and to enable internal change. They were different from line-function "operations" in that they were explicitly recognized to be temporary. And as such, they were managed differently than the operational activities of typical functional groups, which seemed to need a more permanent model of leadership.

To support the pursuit of projects, employees from line function organizations would be commissioned to work together as a "project team" under the direction of a "project manager" (or "project leader") responsible for oversight of the cross-functional work (see Figure 2.2). Project managers assumed responsibility for creating a collaborative

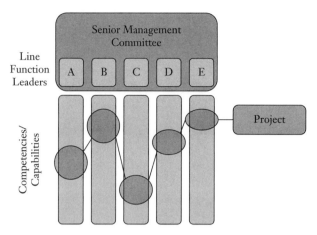

Figure 2.2   Participation of specific elements of functional groups in a cross-functional project.

environment that enabled team members to work closely together. For example, within a project environment, researchers and engineers could work closely with manufacturers to ensure that the new product could be produced efficiently; together they could work directly with sales and distribution professionals to ensure that the products would reach the right customers in an efficient way. The commissioning of a project was quickly recognized as an excellent means of improving communication, coordination, and collaboration between employees who were jointly responsible for pursuing goals that spanned more than one functional group. The impact of project-based management structures was significant, because projects could be introduced at any level of an organization to coordinate the work of otherwise-independent people, making them responsible for developing new and important organizational capabilities.

To facilitate their organizations' management of cross-functional projects (and ensure that properly trained professionals would be available to do so) many organizations established a formal "project management" line function, which focused on managing projects as its core competency. It should not be a surprise that they did. It had been demonstrated in the Industrial Age that remarkable advances could be made by forming functional groups with specific core competencies; it stood to reason that developing a core competency in project management would enable the development of even more advanced and efficient project management capabilities. The development of advanced competencies in project management dramatically improved the effectiveness of many organizations in managing cross-functional initiatives.

PROJECT MANAGEMENT PROCESSES

The work products of project management proved invaluable in helping organizations to understand and plan for the needs of cross-functional projects: Project managers introduced processes for precisely defining the activities that needed to be completed to achieve the project's goals. They ensured that the assumptions about those activities were understood and accepted by the line function managers who sponsored their projects. They provided "PERT" (Project Evaluation and Review Technique) analyses, which depicted the relationships between important activities within a project. They provided project plans, in the form of "Gantt Charts," that summarized the appropriate time for starting and completing key project activities, and the functional group responsible for it. Together, Gantt and PERT analyses provided a foundation for improving cross-functional communication, coordination, and resource planning. They formed the basis for many implied "contracts" between line functions and project managers for the exchange of line function resources in return for specific project results.

As organizations' competencies in managing projects matured, project management became more widely accepted as a profession that was critical to organizational success. New "best practices," standard processes, tools and techniques, and a formal "body of knowledge" related to them emerged. A common framework for managing project lifecycles was defined, with each project progressing through five distinct phases (Initiation, Planning, Executing, Controlling, and Closing). Over 40 processes were identified as being important to the effective management of these phases, and each was grouped into "knowledge areas" for study and teaching purposes. Professionals were trained and eventually certified for their understanding of (and presumably, competency in) the profession's practices and processes. And from all of this emerged a mission that defined a standard of success for a project management professional—to complete projects within the organization's imposed constraints: on time, on budget, and to specifications. It became a project management credo. I would not be surprised to learn that there are project managers out there who have "on time, on budget, and to specifications" tattoos. (Send me a picture!)

Perhaps most significantly, there also emerged a powerful mindset—that important organizational initiatives could be carefully planned and then efficiently managed through the rigorous application of highly controlled processes. It was a mindset entirely consistent with the Industrial Age that led to its conception, because it was grounded in the belief that improved efficiency could be achieved by breaking down work responsibilities into subcomponents, improving the understanding, management, and execution of each as a specialty, and then sequentially reassembling them to produce the desired output.

Project management principles and processes proved extremely valuable to organizations that sought to produce specific work outputs (products). They were usually embraced with enthusiasm by line function leaders, who appreciated that the establishment of a project management function enabled them to delegate their oversight responsibilities for important cross-functional projects without relinquishing their leadership authority over them. They appreciated that they could enter into specific, somewhat "contractual" agreements for projects to deliver their organization's desired operational results. And, as acceptance of these principles spread within organizations, each organization developed an internal culture that defined the relationship that was expected to exist between those who led or managed projects and those who led or managed line functions.

The "first generation" of programmatic approaches adopted by most organizations to manage their projects were usually similar and built on a few simple assumptions: Managing committees authorized projects and approved their strategies and plans, while project teams (usually under the direction of project management professionals) assumed accountability for pursuing those plans precisely as defined to assure efficient delivery of their intended outputs. Significant changes to project strategies and plans (and in particular, changes that affected timelines, budgets, or specifications) needed to be approved by the managing committees.

We will refer to this as a *first-generation programmatic approach* (or as *first-generation programmatics*). Under first-generation programmatics, projects are managed under an organizational system in which the managing committee retains strict authority and control over its project's strategies, plans, timelines, budgets, and specifications.

Under first-generation programmatics, project managers assumed primary responsibility for assuring that their project plans were completed precisely as approved. Successful project managers became well-recognized for their abilities to anticipate, avoid, and address issues related to the completion of cross-functional activities, and thus for their critical role in managing operational risk. It came to be expected that under the appropriate direction of a good project manager, and with rigorous adherence to an organization's established programmatic processes, projects would be completed successfully—on time, on budget, and to expectations.

A GROWING AND CHALLENGING PROFESSION

The attractiveness of project management as a profession and a career path grew under first-generation programmatic managing systems. Most project managers enjoyed the leadership responsibilities that came with their roles. The establishment of a project was, in essence, the creation of a new organization (within their existing organization), and to be named as the project's leader or manager was to be put in charge of it. Project leaders and managers embraced the authority that came with their roles and the importance of their work to the larger organization. Many enjoyed that their roles gave them access to (and visibility with) higher-level executives via their interactions with the senior management who sat on their projects' governing committees. And, as a group, project management professionals cherished the autonomy that came with their authorization to manage cross-functional initiatives. They treasured the satisfaction, and exhilaration, that came with being successful in that role.

Working on clearly defined goals using clearly understood principles and processes to deliver clearly recognizable success was clearly fulfilling. As the profession of project management matured, its capabilities and organizational impact also grew, and its contribution to the success of organizations became more widely recognized. Over time, experienced project managers were often given greater latitude for implementing operational changes within their projects, as necessary to ensure that their projects were able to deliver on their intended outputs on time, on budget and to specifications.

Over time, organizations' use of projects and project teams also expanded. They commissioned teams to pursue goals that were progressively more strategic and increasingly more complex, such as organizational change initiatives and research and development efforts. Here too, the use of projects and common first-generation programmatic management systems seemed to have a positive effect. However, it was observed (and attested to in the growing project management literature) that improving the pursuit of complex strategic projects through the application of traditional project management practices was much more difficult. It was much more complex.

Most observers would come to agree that project management principles and processes did improve their abilities to manage the activities of complex strategic projects. However, they would also observe that complex or strategic projects differed from other (more operationally focused) projects, in an important way: They relied more often and more critically on assumptions about the outcomes that would be achieved as a consequence of a project's activities. It was commonly observed that reliance on *outcomes* was very different than reliance on *outputs*. In an organizational change program, for example, the activities conducted as part of a project plan might be expected to lead to changes in the behaviors, satisfaction, or productivity of employees. However, the appropriate behavioral changes could not be guaranteed because perceptions, feelings, and responses of people to a specific action, no matter how carefully planned or controlled, were often quite uncertain. Similarly, the activities conducted in a research and development project plan might be predicted to lead to a technical breakthrough; however, they could not be promised to lead to a breakthrough because research results were uncertain. (That's why they put the "re" in research!) Delivering the strategic value of a project "to specifications" was less assured when there was uncertainty about outcomes. Outcomes resulted in learning, and learning often resulted in the need to change a project's strategy and/or plan. Project managers were painfully aware that learning disrupts projects.

The significant differences between success that is defined in terms of outputs, and success that is defined in terms of outcomes can easily be appreciated when considering the example of a project leader I know who was responsible for a drug research and development program. One of her "projects" was to conduct a clinical study to demonstrate a drug's effectiveness and safety in a new patient population and to deliver a study report to support a regulatory filing. Her project team was highly efficient in doing so. It produced their desired *output*—a high-quality regulatory report—on time, on budget, and to specifications. Unfortunately, however, it did not produce the desired *outcome*. It was learned from the project that the drug was not as effective as was expected or desired; the project plan (which presumed a regulatory filing based on effectiveness) needed to be changed. A second (different) study was required to support the filing. The value of the project was directly linked to the outcome of the first study, but only indirectly linked to its output.

Project leaders and managers who were held solely responsible for producing predictable outputs might reasonably be expected to deliver according to their credo (and perhaps their tattoos). But how should one define the responsibilities of leaders and managers whose plans depended upon the sequential achievement of several uncertain outcomes? Is it sufficient to define project management success based on the efficient delivery of outputs, or is it better (or necessary) for project management professionals to be responsible for ensuring that their projects eventually achieve their desired outcomes? How much responsibility should a project leader or manager have for redefining the strategy of his or her project in response to (or in developing anticipation of) unpredicted or unexpected outcomes? Should an experienced project leader or manager be allowed similar autonomy and independence when managing changes to improve the delivery of project outcomes, as when managing changes to improve the delivery of project outputs?

Such questions were critical to project managers (and to their organizations) whenever their projects were pursuing uncertain outcomes. But they were also critical to the profession of project management and to organizations that believed in managing projects according to the output-focused assumptions of first-generation programmatics. They had a profound influence on how one should define a project manager's roles and responsibilities, and how one might measure his or her success. Organizations that left these questions unanswered (or unclearly answered) unwittingly left their project managers guessing about their intended roles and responsibilities, and about the knowledge and leadership behaviors expected of project leaders and managers.

ORGANIZATIONAL RESPONSES

Organizations that expected project leaders and managers to focus on the pursuit of project *outputs* had historically preferred to recruit individuals with a full-speed-ahead, command-and-control mindset that sought first to deliver outputs as promised. They had recruited project managers with traditional project management training, who focused on precisely predicting their operational capabilities and who then dedicated themselves completely to demonstrating (even proving) that their predictions were correct (by delivering their promised outputs on time, on budget, and to specifications). This was, after all, the mindset that led to the acceptance and advancement of project management as an Industrial Age profession, and to its delivery of value under traditional first-generation programmatic systems.

However, organizations that expected project leaders and managers to assume responsibility for delivering *outcomes* found that they needed leaders and managers with a different mindset—a mindset that more readily recognized a need to pause and reconsider their project's or program's direction. They needed leaders and managers who more consciously and continuously monitored outcomes in anticipation of the possible need to change project plans, sometimes radically. Such leaders might be less likely to hold time, budget, or specifications as absolutely sacrosanct. They would need to balance their "command-and-control" mindset with a "learn-and-adapt" mindset; it is not easy to proceed with full-speed-ahead and pause-and-consider mandates at the same time.

Consider the case of a project manager who is faced with evidence that his project plan might need to be changed because of emerging outcomes. Under project management "best practices," changing that plan might require the re-activation of several of the 20 or so processes that are important to the planning stage of projects. At what point should re-planning be pursued? An output-focused leadership style might lead the project manager to focus on the seeming inefficiency of re-planning his project until there was incontrovertible proof of the need. An outcome-focused leadership style might instead lead the project manager to be preoccupied with the seeming inefficiency of continuing the project as planned.

Entrusting project managers with responsibility for balancing these two mindsets requires that organizations allow a project manager to use his or her personal and professional judgment, or else define a more formal (and teachable) basis for their prioritization. It may require that organizations rethink or redefine their organizations' assumptions about the strategic role of a project management professional. It may require a somewhat revised model of project management—one that enables project managers to manage their initiatives more flexibly. Recognizing this, project leaders and managers proposed a number of "new" approaches to project management for use in what we might label as **second-generation programmatic approaches,** or **second generation programmatics**.

Second-generation programmatic approaches may be defined as management approaches that provide project or program management professionals with greater responsibility for managing the adaptation of project strategies or plans in response to outcomes that are realized or knowledge that is attained. Second generation programmatic approaches are used to support the management of projects whose timelines, budget, and/or specifications need to be managed more adaptively because pursuing the project is expected to result in the generation of outcomes or knowledge that will influence subsequent elements of the project. Under second generation programmatic approaches, project management professionals may be given greater authority for managing the adaptation of timelines, budget, and specifications (usually within previously established constraints), so as to enable the more effective pursuit of desired benefits. In the next chapter we will review some of the more common second-generation programmatic approaches.

CHAPTER 3

The Evolution of Project Management: Second-Generation Programmatics

PHASE-GATE APPROACHES

The first and best-accepted approach for striking a balance between the "command-and-control" and "learn-and-adapt" mindsets required for outcome-based projects involved the fragmentation of projects into distinct stages, which could be managed, in effect, as projects within projects. The concept was reasonably straightforward: Define the project work expected to produce the desired outputs and outcomes; break the plan into work periods ("stages" or "phases") punctuated at their beginning and end by periods of review; manage the work periods according to traditional project management practices; and, at each review period, examine the appropriateness of continuing with the next work period as planned, versus adapting it based on outcome-related learning. This method has been labeled generically as a "phase-gate" approach, in reference to its management of projects in phases and its treatment of each review period as a "gate" through which the project would (or would not) pass.

The phase-gate approach was well accepted by a wide variety of organizations for its value in enabling the management of diverse outcome-focused projects. It enabled project teams to pursue large, complicated, and complex projects somewhat autonomously during their work phases using traditional project management processes, while ensuring that managing organizations could participate actively in the review and adaptation of each project in response to its newly attained outcome. The phase-gate approach provided sponsoring organizations with the option of significantly modifying or discontinuing projects at the key gate periods in their lifecycles. And it generally did not require that organizations deviate drastically from their use of traditional principles and practices for managing work (as defined in traditional standards of project management practice). One might suggest, in fact, that the approach was so amenable to the use of traditional project management practices that it hardly qualified as a second-generation programmatic approach at all. Its use, however, did represent a first step toward defining project management principles and practices that were more flexible and adaptive. The division of projects into distinct phases enabled project teams to apply a great deal of rigor in the planning of near-term phases while being more qualitative in the planning of phases that would not be pursued for some time.

CIRCUMSTANCE-SPECIFIC APPROACHES

Other second-generation approaches deviated more significantly. Some proposed that the approaches to leading or managing projects needed to be modified on a project-by-project basis, according to specific attributes of the project, such as its novelty, its complexity, its dependence on new technology, or its time constraints. Others proposed that the approaches to leading or managing projects could be adapted according to project types; that information technology projects, new product development projects, or research projects, for example, were best managed using project management approaches tailored specifically to them, and to their sponsoring organizations' unique needs. Each proposed approach was thought to provide specific advantages not available when using traditional project management principles and practices. And each might be recognized to also have specific disadvantages. Consider, for example, some of the more popular proposals for the modification or "advancement" of project management to achieve second-generation programmatic goals:

Adaptive or agile project management approaches have been described and widely implemented. Under agile project management approaches, "just in time" planning is used to manage short, successive phases of a project, in an attempt to reduce the time wasted in continuous re-planning of projects whose uncertain outcomes were realized frequently. By this approach, it was generally proposed that projects should be managed carefully to their intended time and budget, while adaptations to project scope or specifications were made based on the learning from the project's emerging outcomes and the remaining uncertainty for the project. Agile project management approaches have been well-received by the project management community because of the value they bring when managing certain kinds of projects. They were found to be especially valuable for software development projects, for example, because they enabled the dynamic management of project plans that needed frequent adjustment based on progress that was realized in short and yet meaningful bursts. Agile approaches to project management were lauded for their responsiveness. However, their use of very short planning horizons did not enable the same degree of oversight by organizational managing committees. Agile approaches required that the project leader or manager be given a more autonomous role in authorizing changes to specifications. And because their short planning periods were managed in rapid succession, agile approaches generally required that those who were assigned to the project have personal competency in (or rapid access to) all the expertise required to complete each successive series of work activities.

There also emerged a proposal for the establishment of a discipline of complex project management. Complex project management approaches recognized that traditional project management tools, techniques, practices, and processes are particularly inadequate for managing projects that are highly complex. Complex project management approaches sought to provide improved capabilities for managing projects that involved the parallel pursuit of component activities whose outcomes may have substantial influence on each other and/or the project's environment. They recognized that complex projects must be managed in a way that allows for significant amounts of unpredictable change. Complex project management is similar to agile project management in that it embraces periodic reassessment of projects to enable one to reconsider their scope. However, complex project management principles and processes focused on reassessments that were made necessary as a consequence of the asynchronous realization of outcomes from major project components that were being pursued concurrently. They emphasized management of the cross-component impact of outcomes as they became available. In complex project management it was also explicitly recognized that outcomes could result in the need for significant changes to budgets and timelines. Thus, the adoption of complex project management approaches necessitated an organization-wide acceptance of a nontraditional role for project management—where scope, time, and budget are all subject to change, and where the project manager may need to develop advanced skills in managing highly complex change. Use of complex project management approaches also required that oversight committees give project leaders and managers increased responsibility for recognizing the need for change, managing its impact, and (ultimately) implementing it.

For projects that were considered highly complex, highly variable, and very difficult to define (such as exploratory projects), the concept of extreme project management was introduced. By this approach, the project plan was intentionally left vague. The plan was seen as a series of as-yet undefined steps which would be taken in an appropriate direction, with the intention of defining and achieving the project's goal over time. Under extreme project management, a project's goals, timeline, budget, and specifications were all treated as unknowns. It was proposed that adoption of extreme project management would enable organizations to pursue more abstract projects, seeking change that may yet be undefined or unimagined. Extreme project management's adoption would require that managing committees accept a radically different view of the roles and responsibilities of a project manager or leader. In fact, some might argue that traditional project management can hardly be recognized within it. "Extreme" project management has defined project management as "the art and science of facilitating and managing the flow of thoughts, emotions, and interactions, in a way that produces valued outcomes."[1] Executives in most organizations would have difficulty recognizing this at all as a definition of project management.

There have been many additional proposals (and permutations of proposals) for the further adaptation of project management—too many to summarize in this book. The faithful proponents of each proposal have touted the value of their adaptations, and many have been well received for the insights and understanding that they have provided. Each of them, at its core, has sought to achieve the same purpose: To redefine the principles and practices of project management so as to improve its ability to dynamically manage the knowledge-sensitive, outcome-driven projects being pursued by modern organizations. Each of these "second-generation" approaches proposed that project management step back to some extent from its historical mission of completing projects as originally conceived—"on time, on budget, and to (exacting) specifications." They defined project management principles and practices that could be used when one or more of these constraints are uncertain because a project depends upon unsure outcomes. And they sought to broaden the definition of a professional project manager's roles and responsibilities beyond those of project management's first-generation credo. Each of these proposals served to further advance thinking about how the project manager role could be re-interpreted to contribute optimally to the unique needs of very diverse organizations pursuing very different projects.

---

[1] See DeCarlo, 2004.

CURRENT PERSPECTIVES AND NEEDS

By most accounts, second-generation approaches to project management have been successfully adopted by the organizations most in need of them. Development projects that face technical uncertainty now commonly use phase-gate methodologies; "best practice" software development projects frequently use agile project management approaches; organizational change and technological development initiatives leverage the practices of complex project management; exploratory innovation-driven projects often adopt extreme project management principles.

Many would suggest that such advancements in the practice of project management should make this an exciting time for those in the profession. They might note that the introduction of second-generation principles and practices has provided a means for project management practitioners to contribute more dynamically and significantly to the delivery of their projects' outcomes. They would be right. And yet (if we are to acknowledge the angst that we discussed in Chapter 1) it still seems that something is wrong. Experienced managers and leaders of projects or programs appear increasingly to be exasperated with their professions. Why?

It is helpful to again consider the input from leaders and managers of organizational projects and programs (from Chapter 1). Those experienced leaders and managers had noted that:

- Their projects and programs progressed reasonably smoothly when they were able to proceed according to plan and deliver the outcomes that were expected.

- They were not as exasperated by issues commonly known to be important to project management (team-building, managing without authority, or communication, for example).

- They were increasingly exasperated by difficulties related to their organizations' governing processes, bureaucracy, or politics.

- They worked in organizations that were struggling with important questions about the roles, responsibilities, and degree of autonomy that project management professionals should be given.

The exasperation that they expressed, while derived from diverse experiences managing very different projects in dissimilar organizations and industries, seemed to be rooted in a common question: What are (or should be) the roles and responsibilities of an "ideal" project (or program) management professional in modern-day organizations?

The significance of this question to the professional is obvious. Having a clear understanding of its answer is critical to his or her ability to be successful (and to be recognized as such). However, the significance of the question to the *profession* is perhaps greater. It is not a question that was difficult to answer in "Industrial Age" organizations, or in modern organizations that were using traditional, first-generation conceptions of project management when pursuing their projects. The role of project management seemed clearer for those organizations; it could be summarized in a seven-word credo (on time, on budget, and to specifications). It was also not a question that burned strongly in the minds of inexperienced project managers whose responsibilities were constrained to traditional practices and processes.

This was a question that seemed to have grown in importance with professionals as they assumed broader responsibilities for managing the need for change within their projects using second-generation programmatic approaches. It grew in importance as those professionals sought to interpret (each within their own unique project management environment) their personal responsibilities for delivering their projects' intended outcomes. And it grew in importance as they sought to balance their responsibilities for leading and managing projects that needed to strike a balance between their "full speed ahead" and "pause and consider" mandates.

Project leaders and managers who assumed responsibility for continuously assessing project outcomes as part of managing the uncertainty associated with delivering "to specifications" found that they were assuming responsibilities for managing the changes to project strategy. This was a role that had been reserved for governing committees under traditional first-generation programmatic systems. Under second-generation programmatic systems, however, project leaders and managers were assuming more independent responsibility for the day-to-day management of program strategy. Often their organizational mandate and authority for assuming independent responsibility were not clearly defined. Were project managers now responsible for adapting their timelines, budgets, and specifications as they supervised the day-to-day activities of their projects? Strategic options were constrained by budgets and allowable timelines. How much autonomy should project managers have in adapting strategy, timelines, budget, or specifications? It was not always clear, and it was not always easy to define an organization's expectations. The leadership and management of more uncertain and complex projects and programs, it turned out, was itself an uncertain and complex endeavor.

AN IDENTITY CRISIS

It seems—based on interviews with scores of experienced (and often exasperated) project leaders and managers—that the introduction of second-generation programmatic systems may have led project management professionals to an unappreciated identity crisis.

In hindsight, it is perhaps understandable that it would.

It is common for organizations to simultaneously pursue many different kinds of projects and programs, and to leverage the best practices of the principles and practices of first- or second-generation project management approaches as appropriate. Organizations might, for example, pursue product launch initiatives using strict first-generation practices that require project activities to be completed on time, on budget, and to specifications. However, the products they are launching may have been derived from development projects that were better managed using agile, adaptive, or complex project management approaches. Alternatively, organizations may find that it is in their interests to use different project management approaches simultaneously to manage the different workstreams of a single project or program. Or they might leverage the benefits of several project management approaches to form "hybrid" approaches best suited to the needs of a given project within their organizations. They might find that it is best if different approaches are used as that project advances through various phases within its lifecycle. As a consequence, it is understandable that *the adaptation of project management principles and practices to fit the specific needs of a given project or organization often results in the adoption of versions of project management that defy neat and standard descriptions.*

In the absence of a clear understanding of the tenets of each second-generation approach, and the organization's intent for applying them selectively to a given project within its portfolio, it is also understandable that individuals within an organization might have inconsistent expectations about the roles, responsibilities, and behaviors of that project's leader or manager. Individuals might have *vastly* different expectations about how time, budget, and scope should be managed. And those different expectations might result in organizational dynamics that are exasperatingly unpredictable.

A TIME FOR ACTION

The evolution and adoption of second-generation programmatic approaches seems to have caused enough confusion about the roles and responsibilities of a professional project manager to warrant some attention. As a member of the profession, I would suggest that it is time to raise a provocative new question: *When would changes intended to advance the profession of project management (by making it more responsible for managing the delivery of outcomes) actually result in the decline of project management (by creating confusion over the project manager's role)?*

There are signs they may already have.

I have observed that when one asks project managers and leaders in modern knowledge-based organizations about their roles and responsibilities, many no longer find it sufficient to identify themselves as project managers or leaders. They feel obliged to annotate their title with a description of how project management is practiced in their organizations, or to explain their personal roles and responsibilities within their specific project assignment. They find it necessary to define which "denomination" of project management they subscribe to. Why? Because they recognize that those details are essential if a person is to understand their role, their skills, and the value that they bring. And despite their desire to accurately describe their roles, they do not seem to have a vocabulary capable of precisely communicating the denominational nuances important to them and to their organizations.

Some take delight in detailing their abilities to deliver outputs on time, on budget, and to specifications. However, others highlight the strategic contributions that they make by ensuring that their projects remain focused on their intended outcomes, benefits, and value. Still others, in emphasizing their strategic roles, go so far as to distance themselves from the traditional first-generation notion of project management, as if it somehow cheapened their job descriptions. When one asks modern-day project managers and leaders about their roles and responsibilities, their answers can sound something like a riddle: I am a project manager, but I may not be what you think. I work in an industry, in an organization, and on a project with a unique culture and specific needs. I manage and lead in ways that might be different or surprising. I do what is required to deliver optimal benefits and value. (Who am I?)

Similar conclusions might be reached when observing the questions asked of experienced project management professionals who are interviewing for a management or leadership position. It is common that a large amount of interview time is spent assessing the "types" of project management experience that a given professional has, or is best suited for—the degree to which they have been responsible for managing outputs versus outcomes, or for controlling versus initiating change, or for demonstrating operational versus strategic leadership skills.

In some organizations, identifying candidates with the "right" blend of project management experience is not hard. Organizations pursuing software development projects, for example, may know to seek managers and leaders who are adept at agile project management. They may advertise specifically for leaders or managers with "agile" experience, and find that their inboxes are filled with applicants identifying themselves as agile project management specialists. However, not all organizations can be so specific in defining their needs, or so informed as to know how those needs would best be served by a specific denomination of the recognized second-generation project management approaches. And many project management professionals (because they have been trained principally in a single approach to project management) do not adequately appreciate that their experience is limited to a specific type of project management—that there is great diversity in the practice of their chosen profession, and that they might be required to practice differently when leading or managing projects with different needs or challenges.

One is left to question whether in seeking to *redefine* project management, members of the profession have inadvertently taken a step toward *de-defining* it in the eyes of practitioners and the critical stakeholders in their organizations. We might ask whether in seeking to address traditional project management's perceived weaknesses (its potential insensitivity to outcome-based reasons to change direction), we might have unwittingly eroded confidence in its strength (its unwavering promise to deliver outputs on time, on budget, and to specifications).

Perhaps when solving the riddle of project management's identity, we should heed the advice of author Marilyn vos Savant, who observed that, "Success is achieved by development of our strengths, not by elimination of our weakness."[2] She might suggest that project management has done itself a disservice; that it should instead seek to grow stronger by focusing on its traditional strengths in assuring effective delivery of outputs from approved project plans. Humorist Jack Handey might

---

[2]Marilyn vos Savant. BrainyQuote.com, Xplore Inc, 2014. http://www.brainyquote.com/quotes/quotes/m/marilynvos385323.html, accessed March 20, 2014.

agree. He warned that, "If you think a weakness can be turned into a strength, I hate to tell you this, but that's another weakness."[3]

We will explore these perspectives much more in the second half of this book. Before doing so, however, it would be beneficial to further examine what experienced project and program management professionals and their organizational executives believe about the roles and responsibilities of project management in modern knowledge-based industries. Their insights are quite interesting.

---

[3] Jack Handey, http://deepthoughtsbyjackhandey.com/index.html

CHAPTER 4

Rethinking the Roles and Responsibilities of Project Management Professionals

THE EXASPERADOS

None are more conscious of project management's "identity crisis" than the project management professionals we discussed earlier—those "franchise athletes" who have grown exasperated in their long careers as project management professionals. We might call them project management's *Exasperados*. It is important that we understand their perspectives.

As a group, Exasperados yearn to deliver more than just project *outputs*. They believe that their knowledge, skills, and experience make them uniquely capable of leading and managing the most complex of projects in pursuit of value. They seek to deliver their project's desired *outcomes*. To be more effective in delivering outcomes, they have embraced many second-generation programmatic approaches. They have tried to assume more personal responsibility for balancing their projects' sometimes-conflicting mandates to efficiently complete projects as planned, while also being prepared to quickly suspend and adapt those project plans in response to emerging outcomes. And to achieve an appropriate balance they have found it necessary to expand the scope of their roles and responsibilities.

Exasperados believe that they can, through their personal actions, make their projects more capable of adapting to emerging outcomes. Many have begun to manage their projects in ways that are more subjectively determined. And as they have, their courses of action have become perceptively less predictable to their senior management sponsors. As a consequence, Exasperados acknowledge, their direction has more often been subject to question or criticism by organizational leaders who would themselves prefer to maintain control of project planning and strategy.

Exasperados report that their roles as change agents, and their responsibilities for managing change, are not always clearly defined or consistently accepted. They recognize that there is confusion and debate about the degree of autonomy that project management professionals should have. And they recognize that project management's identity crisis—the ambiguity surrounding the profession's roles and responsibilities—lies at the root of their exasperation. They long for its resolution.

It is interesting to ask the Exasperados their views about second-generation programmatic systems. *How would they prefer to define the roles and responsibilities of project and program management professionals?* As a group, they are some of project management's most experienced and successful professionals; their perspectives can be enlightening.

Most Exasperados are quite happy with the expansion of their roles under second-generation programmatic systems. Any longing that they might have for the simplicity of the "good old days" (when they were expected to deliver outputs—on time, on budget, and to specifications) is usually fleeting. For the most part, Exasperados are exhilarated to contribute to the refinement of project and program strategies in the fast-paced environments of their teams. They are "organizational athletes" who like to improvise and adapt when faced with challenges. They appreciate that second-generation programmatic systems give them a more strategically balanced mandate by making them responsible for delivering benefits and value via *both* outputs and outcomes. And they believe that second-generation programmatic approaches are critical for the effective day-to-day management of their projects. Most Exasperados are convinced that the demand for adaptive approaches to project management will continue to grow as their organizations pursue initiatives that are increasingly uncertain, unpredictable, and complex.

As a group, the Exasperados I have interviewed believe that the adoption of second-generation programmatics was a natural consequence of the evolution of their organizations from the Industrial Age of the past to the "knowledge era" of today. They believe that project success in the Industrial Age was more likely to have been based on generation of outputs, whereas project success in the knowledge era is more likely to be based on outcomes—and so the adoption of second-generation approaches was necessary in most knowledge-based industries. Exasperados tend to view their frustration with second-generation approaches as an understandable (and in hindsight, maybe even predictable) consequence of organizational evolution. They believe that a project manager's challenge is to adapt successfully, so that he or she can survive and thrive in evolving organizational environments. (Their views, I suppose, are very Darwinian.)

Exasperados believe that the most important question is "How?" How can project management professionals more clearly define, for themselves and their organizations, their optimal roles and responsibilities under second-generation programmatic systems? As organizational and professional leaders, most Exasperados acknowledge that it is their responsibility to figure that out. And that so far they haven't.

In the views and experience of the Exasperados, project managers and their organizations desperately need to develop a clearer, more commonly understood framework for defining the roles and responsibilities of project management professionals. In the absence of such a framework, Exasperados will continue to find that they are not consistently empowered to do what they believe is required for the most effective pursuit of success. For them, specific second-generation approaches to project management have not provided an adequate solution. The diversity of projects that are being pursued within most organizations seems to preclude the specific use of agile or complex or extreme project management as singular approaches for managing and leading the many different kinds of projects and programs that those organizations pursue. And none of these second-generation approaches provides universal guidance on how to effectively balance the need for traditional (execution-oriented) first-generation project management practices with those of adaptive second-generation approaches. Exasperados note that they are constantly questioning (and being questioned about) whether they are using appropriate judgment in defining the balance. It seems, at least based on the perspectives of these practitioners, that second-generation programmatic systems are a necessary but not sufficient step in the evolutionary development of programmatic systems.

But what is the next step? How can professional project managers more clearly define the roles and responsibilities of those who are placed in charge of an organization's complex outcome-based endeavors? How can an improved definition of their roles enable them to contribute better to their organizations, now and in the future?

PROGRAMMATICISTS AND THE MANAGEMENT OF COMPLEXITY

These are not easy questions to resolve; organizations have been struggling to address them for many years. Professionals who function as the leaders or managers of an organization's projects and programs—we might generically refer to them as *programmaticists*—are not a homogeneous professional group.[1] They have diverse knowledge, experience, and skills, and different strengths and weaknesses. They may have quite different leadership roles and responsibilities. And they may have been given titles (made by combining the words "project" or "program" with titles like "manager" or "leader" or "director," and modifiers like "assistant" or "associate" or "global" or "executive") that, while commonly used, are ambiguous designators of professional roles and responsibilities. See Figure 4.1. When trying to answer the questions that programmaticists face, it is easy to get entangled in misunderstood meanings and misplaced assumptions.

When asked how professional project managers could more clearly define the roles and responsibilities of those responsible for managing an organization's uncertain, complex, outcome-based endeavors, I have found that Exasperados respond in quite different ways. Each has a portfolio of stories that provide examples of the confusion and frustration that can result from the introduction of second-generation programmatic approaches. Each has specific suggestions for what could have been done to address the particular issues that they have faced. One

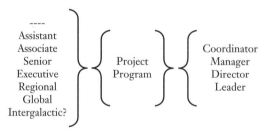

Figure 4.1   The creation of common programmaticist titles.

---

[1] I have introduced the term "programmaticist" because it provides a simple means of generically referring to all those who lead or manage an organization's projects or programs, without invoking titles (such as project manager or program leader) that often have organization-specific meanings.

could fill books with them. Every circumstance is different, and at first each solution seems unique. And yet, when one considers the stories and solutions together, I have found that a consistent theme emerges: Much of the confusion over project and program management's roles and responsibilities, and much of the exasperation expressed by project management's Exasperados, results from inadequate definitions or inconsistent agreements about how much personal responsibility programmaticists should take for managing the various kinds of uncertainty and complexity associated with their projects and programs. The issues that these professionals face and the solutions that they offer seem to reflect a need to better understand how uncertainty and complexity is meant to be managed within the programmatic systems being used by a given organization.

After thoughtful (and usually long) conversations, most Exasperados conclude that confusion over the roles and responsibilities of programmaticists (and their own resultant exasperation) could be resolved if organizations would more clearly define and more consistently recognize the roles and responsibilities of those who will take primary responsibility for managing each kind of uncertainty and complexity that is associated with their projects and programs. In fact, the stories of Exasperados are so consistent in their messages about the importance of defining these responsibilities, that most agree that the management of uncertainty and complexity could (and should) be used as the foundation for a new approach for defining their roles and responsibilities. Most Exasperados, I have found through my interviews, would enthusiastically embrace an uncertainty- and complexity-based definition of their programmatic roles:

> The primary role of a programmaticist is to manage the uncertainty and complexity associated with pursuing the goals of projects or programs, so that a project's or program's intended benefits and value might be most effectively delivered.

To them, this is what project and program management has always been about. They observe that under first-generation programmatic systems, project managers are asked to focus specifically on managing uncertainty that is related to the delivery of outputs according to their credo—on time, on budget, and to specifications. They observe that *under first-generation programmatic systems the value of projects is often associated with the delivery of project outputs. The role of a project management professional is to manage the complexity and uncertainty associated with the pursuit of projects that may have very large, detailed, and complicated operational plans*, and to thereby ensure delivery of the value that is inherent in their outputs.

Exasperados observe and agree that under second-generation programmatic systems, a greater focus is placed on managing uncertainty associated with the pursuit of outcomes that are difficult to predict or control. *Under second-generation systems, the role of a programmaticist is to manage the complexity and uncertainty associated with delivering outcome-based benefits that are being pursued by their projects or programs.* The role of a programmaticist under these systems is to manage the complexity and uncertainty associated with both outputs and outcomes, and to optimize the delivery of their project's or program's intended value.

A NEW CREDO

This newly proposed high-level definition of a programmaticist's roles and responsibilities is a holistic one that resonates well with most of the project management professionals and executive management teams I have worked with. It is consistent with a practical and conventional wisdom that is commonly accepted in many organizations. Its logic goes something like this:

> The role of a project management professional is to ensure that projects or programs efficiently deliver their intended benefits and value.
>
>> To be effective in delivering them, project management professionals must assume responsibility for preventing or managing any issues that would impede their delivery.
>>
>>> To prevent or manage issues, project management professionals must be effective in managing project and program uncertainty, and
>>>
>>>> Managing project and program uncertainty in today's organizations is often a very complex endeavor.

It is a logic that leads one to accept that the role of a programmaticist should indeed be: To manage the uncertainty and complexity that is associated with the pursuit of projects and programs, so that a project's or program's intended value might be most effectively delivered. Moreover, it leads one to consider whether a new credo should also be adopted—a credo that reflects the central importance of managing uncertainty, complexity, and value:

> To manage the uncertain, solve the complex, and deliver the value.

It is a credo that captures the resolve and promise of first-generation programmatic approaches while fully embracing the mandate of second-generation approaches. Moreover, we will find (in later chapters) that it applies equally well to our proposal of a new, third-generation approach.

But how well would it be received by the majority of project and program management professionals? I have found that the initial reaction of many professionals to this credo is caution—understandable caution. They have questions. What exactly do we mean by "complexity"? How does this perspective align with my previous understanding of project and program management (and a vision for its future)? How can it improve my organizations' understanding of the profession? Is it tattoo-worthy?

UNDERSTANDING PROJECT AND PROGRAM COMPLEXITY

I suspect that it will take some time to fully answer these questions; the answers that I propose will certainly need to withstand a test of time. As a first step, however, we should recognize that uncertainty and complexity in projects and programs are intimately connected; as the uncertainty associated with a project increases, so does the universe of possible outcomes from that project, and the complexity of preparing to manage each of them. Uncertainty and complexity must therefore be managed together.

Programmatic complexity may be viewed as a characteristic of projects and programs that reflects the difficulty of understanding and defining the most appropriate approach for pursuing their goals. Programmatic complexity gets greater when the uncertainty associated with a project or program's strategy or plan increases, and when the number of possible responses to that uncertainty increases. Managing programmatic complexity can be difficult because it must be done dynamically—as elements of a project's or program's plan are completed, the impact of its uncertainty is realized, issues emerge, and viable options for responding to that uncertainty under current organizational (or environmental) conditions are clarified.

To examine how we might create a new framework for redefining the programmaticist's role in managing uncertainty and complexity we will need to examine the kinds of uncertainty and complexity that the programmaticist typically faces. In doing so, we will begin to reveal how many of the standard practices, processes, tools, and techniques of project and program management already provide a powerful basis for managing uncertainty and complexity'.[2]

What does the new framework reveal? Two critical observations can be made:

1. The sources of uncertainty and complexity that need to be managed in the project or program environment, as cited by experienced programmaticists and the organizational executives with whom they work, can be examined within a framework that identifies five distinct types of uncertainty and complexity (we will call this the *five-complexities framework*); and

2. The roles and responsibilities of programmaticists can be defined by describing programmaticists' accountability for managing each type of uncertainty and complexity within the five-complexities framework.

The five principle types of uncertainty and complexity are: operational, outcome, stakeholder, environmental, and organizational uncertainty and complexity; see Figure 4.2.

---

[2]When examining complexity I have chosen (as I have throughout this book) to draw heavily from perspectives harvested from hundreds of interviews, discussions, and case study analyses that I have conducted with experienced programmaticists and organizational executives. It should be noted, however, that the observations from these discussions are quite consistent with observations made in other academic, theoretical, and practice-based publications on the management of project and program complexity (see the Additional Reading section at the end of this book). For this review, I have chosen to discuss project complexity using the terms and framework that have resonated best with the professionals I interviewed. (The terms may differ slightly from terms used by those who have published previously on the science of complexity and its management. For that I apologize.)

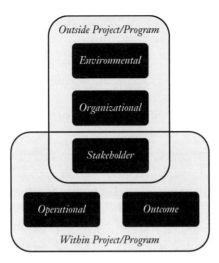

Figure 4.2   The five types of uncertainty and complexity in programmatic endeavors.

Operational Uncertainty and Complexity

Perhaps the best-recognized sources of uncertainty and complexity in the project and program environment are *operational uncertainty and complexity*.

Operational uncertainty may be described as the uncertainty that is associated with defining, scheduling, and completing those activities required to generate the outputs and outcomes of a project or program—the project or program plan. Operational uncertainty is a lack of certainty that a project plan adequately captures the activities that need to be performed as part of a project or program, or the lack of certainty that the plan can be completed precisely as intended. Endeavors with high operational uncertainty are more likely to have project plans whose timing, budget, or specifications change.

The amount of operational uncertainty faced within a project or program usually depends upon the number of activities that must be conducted as part of its plan, the number and significance of assumptions that are made when defining those activities or when constructing that plan, and the number and significance of interdependencies that exist between the various activities within the plan. In general, as each of these increases, the certainty that a plan will be completed exactly as expected decreases. The reasons should be apparent: An increase in the number of activities increases the number of things that can go wrong within a plan; an increase in the number of assumptions increases the likelihood that things will go wrong; and an increase in the number of dependencies between activities usually increases the consequences (to other activities in the plan) when things do go wrong.

Operational uncertainty is present within all projects and programs; when seeking to deliver outputs and outcomes according to a strictly defined plan, unforeseen needs arise and foreseen activities progress in unforeseen ways.

The impact of operational uncertainty and the challenges of managing it may be quite variable, however. In projects that are small or highly predictable, managing operational uncertainty may not be difficult. Operational variances might be easily accommodated by making adjustments to the timing, the resources, or the scope of activities. However, the management of operational uncertainty often becomes much more complicated when projects are bigger, or their activities are less predictable, or they rely heavily on the carefully choreographed completion of their activities, or they must be completed quickly (i.e., with little time allowed for variances). Extremely large projects or programs (such as very large construction projects, for example) often have correspondingly extreme amounts of operational uncertainty associated with them.

Operational uncertainty can also be observed to increase when projects or programs must share organizational resources. The need to share resources between projects and programs increases the probability that unforeseeable external events will disrupt a given project's or program's operational plan (see environmental uncertainty, below).

Operational complexity is encountered when the management of operational uncertainty becomes a complex endeavor—when operational uncertainty results in issues that need to be managed dynamically and holistically as they emerge. Operational complexity is first managed during the construction of a project or program plan, when the activities that will be conducted are identified and the intended plan for conduct of those activities is defined and optimized relative to the known constraints of the project or program and its sponsoring organization. Its management becomes most urgent, however, during pursuit of a project or program, as operational variances (or other types of uncertainty and complexity) produce a need for project plans to be changed significantly while they are ongoing.

Anticipating and managing operational complexity can be difficult. It requires that a programmaticist understand operational variance that may originate simultaneously from several of a project's interconnected activities, recognize the issues that may be caused by such variance, and then identify solutions to those issues that can be implemented under an organization's constraints. When project plans are tightly scheduled, the impact of variation or constraints may be exaggerated, leaving few options for complexity-solving strategies. To manage operational complexity, a programmaticist usually seeks to limit its emergence while simultaneously adjusting project plans to mitigate its future impact. Doing so requires an intimate knowledge of the operational capabilities of the project or program and its sponsoring organization—and advanced knowledge, skills, and experience in competency areas important to operational project planning and resourcing.

It should not be a surprise that project and program management professionals and executive managers in their sponsoring organizations are acutely aware of operational uncertainty and complexity, and the role of a programmaticist in managing and solving them. Leaders and managers of projects or programs recognize that managing operational complexity has been a principle focus of programmaticists since the introduction of first-generation programmatic systems; project management's standards for managing a project's lifecycle, its PERT analyses and Gantt charts, and many of the standard principles and practices, tools and techniques of project management (as described, for example, in the Project Management Body of Knowledge®) were developed and widely adopted because of the significant value they provide for the management of operational uncertainty and complexity. In my many hundreds of discussions and interviews with programmaticists; executive sponsors and stakeholders; and students, colleagues, and clients from diverse organizational environments, I cannot recall a single person who would argue with the assertion that *a principal role of project and program management professionals is to manage operational uncertainty and complexity*.

Outcome Uncertainty and Complexity

A second source of uncertainty and complexity that must be managed by programmaticists is *outcome-based uncertainty and complexity*.

Outcome uncertainty may be defined as the uncertainty that is associated with a plan's dependence on activities that do not have known or predictable results. Outcome uncertainty is a lack of certainty that a project plan will produce the results that are intended or desired. Projects or programs with high outcome uncertainty are more likely to need to adapt their strategies and plans in response to what they learn as they pursue their goals.

Outcome uncertainty becomes significant when projects or programs depend upon plans whose results may vary in unpredictable ways, or when their plans pursue goals that are unprecedented. For example, project or program plans that seek to improve morale or to influence public opinion would be expected to have high outcome uncertainty, because plans that depend upon human perceptions or behavior (no matter how well conceived and executed) cannot be guaranteed to produce the desired effects. Plans that seek to make new discoveries, develop new technologies, or establish new applications for known technologies might also be expected to have high outcome uncertainty because of their novelty.

Within a project or program, outcome uncertainty may be expected to increase with the novelty of the actions to be taken to produce the desired results, the variability (irreproducibility) of results that might be obtained from a planned set of actions, the degree of dependence of other project or program activities on achieving a specific result, the potential impact of the results that might be realized and the variety of actions that one might consider taking in response to those results.

Outcome complexity is the complexity associated with managing outcome uncertainty within a project or program. It is the complexity that is associated with the need to dynamically adapt a project's or program's strategy or plan in response to outcomes that are realized as the endeavor is pursued.

Programmaticists may seek to limit outcome complexity during the planning stages of a project or program—for example when decisions are being made to pursue multiple (sometimes redundant) approaches for achieving desired outcomes, in an effort to increase the likelihood that those outcomes will be achieved using a project's or program's initial plan. However, the most dynamic management of outcome complexity occurs after outcomes are realized from an activity plan that contained significant outcome uncertainty. Whenever outcomes result in the acquisition of new knowledge about how best to pursue a project's intended goals and value (or about the inadequacy of a previous plan for pursuing it), it may become necessary to modify the strategy or plans of projects or programs that are in progress—and to manage the complexity associated with doing so. Programmaticists are quick to agree that within the context of an organization, defining, defending, approving, and implementing outcome-driven change is often a highly complex endeavor.

In my interviews with programmaticists responsible for leading projects and programs in very diverse modern organizations (and especially in my interviews with those who would identify themselves as programmaticist Exasperados), there was a consistent theme relating to outcome uncertainty and complexity. Programmaticists believed: *Organizational competencies in managing outcome-based uncertainty and in solving outcome-based complexity are essential to the success of the knowledge-based organizations that are common today.* The projects and programs sponsored by such organizations are subject to large amounts of outcome uncertainty—many of them are, by their very design, knowledge-generating endeavors that must adapt regularly to the results that they produce. But managing the impact of outcome uncertainty can be a very complex endeavor, especially when an organization's projects or programs are large or when that organization must juggle the simultaneous pursuit of many of them. As a group, programmaticists felt that both they and the organizations in which they worked needed to improve their effectiveness in managing outcome uncertainty and complexity.

Programmaticists have already adapted their approaches to project management to improve their abilities to manage outcome uncertainty and complexity. As we discussed in Chapter 3, this was the primary reason for introducing many of the principles, practices, tools, and techniques common to second-generation programmatic systems. These new approaches have been successfully used for managing projects and programs with specific needs. However, none seems to provide a universally applicable framework for managing outcome-based uncertainty and complexity in the various diverse endeavors being pursued by many modern organizations. The simultaneous management of operational- and outcome-based complexity represents a challenge that many programmaticists struggle with to this day. (It is a challenge that we will discuss in far more detail in the second half of this book.)

Stakeholder Uncertainty and Complexity

A third source of uncertainty and complexity that must be managed in the project and program environment is *stakeholder-based uncertainty and complexity*.

Stakeholder uncertainty may be described as the uncertainty that is associated with a reliance on stakeholders to support the strategy or plan being used to achieve project or program goals. Stakeholder uncertainty might also be thought of as *directional uncertainty* because it relates to a reliance on stakeholders to support a project's or program's direction. Stakeholder uncertainty is a lack of certainty that stakeholders will support the strategy and plan of a programmatic endeavor as desired, or that they will agree to support changes in the strategy or plan that become necessary in the future. Projects and programs at risk of losing the support of key stakeholders as they pursue their goals or those that only receive conditional stakeholder support should be viewed as having high stakeholder uncertainty.

Stakeholder uncertainty often becomes significant when programmaticists rely on support from stakeholders who interpret their project's or program's key elements (objectives, strategies, assumptions, or needs) subjectively, or from stakeholders whose support for a project or program is based substantially on the stakeholders' personal motivations. Stakeholder uncertainty is also more likely to become significant when support is required from different groups of stakeholders who have competing views, interests, or responsibilities, or who have professional reward systems that are not aligned with those of the project or program. Stakeholder uncertainty may be increased, for example, when a project or program relies on stakeholders whose performance is measured more by their achievement of line function goals than by their achievement of project or program goals. It should be noted that stakeholder uncertainty may originate from either within a project or program team (from team-member stakeholders) or outside the team (from influential external stakeholders).

As stakeholder uncertainty increases, so too does the complexity associated with defining a project's or program's direction.

Stakeholder complexity (or *directional complexity*) may be defined as the complexity associated with managing stakeholder uncertainty.

Stakeholder complexity is first managed by programmaticists in the early stages of a project or program, when stakeholder support is required for the endorsement of an endeavor's initial objectives, strategies, and plans. Stakeholder understanding and agreements secured at this time are intended to establish a clearly defined direction for a project or program, and to thereby reduce stakeholder uncertainty. However, managing stakeholder uncertainty remains critically important throughout the life of any programmatic endeavor, inasmuch as stakeholder motivations, needs, assumptions, and goals are all subject to change, and the subjectivity of a stakeholder's initial agreement or understanding becomes more apparent as it is tested over time.

Programmaticists are aware (some, painfully aware) of the importance of their roles in understanding and managing stakeholder complexity. Stakeholder Management and Stakeholder Engagement are well documented as critical knowledge areas in published "standards" of project and program management. The principles, practices, tools, and techniques described in those standards should be recognized as critically important because of their value in helping to reduce stakeholder uncertainty and in facilitating the management of stakeholder complexity. In fact, I have found that it is common for project and program management professionals to note that the primary value of several well-recognized project management tools (for example, project management information systems and enterprise project management systems) and numerous project management competencies (for example, effective communication, listening, and negotiation skills) relates principally to their importance in reducing stakeholder uncertainty and (therefore) in preventing and managing issues related to stakeholder complexity. These tools and competencies are well recognized for their importance and value to both the first- and the second-generation programmatic systems discussed in previous chapters.

In discussions and interviews, programmaticists consistently stressed that the management of stakeholder uncertainty and complexity is especially critical when the strategies and plans of complex projects or programs need to be adapted in response to operational or outcome uncertainty. Thus, the successful management of stakeholder complexity is critically important to the successful management of operational and outcome complexity.

Environmental Uncertainty and Complexity

A fourth source of uncertainty and complexity that must be managed in the project and program environment is *environmental uncertainty and complexity*.

Environmental uncertainty may be described as the uncertainty that is external to a project or program, but that may influence its direction. Environmental uncertainty is a lack of surety that environmental conditions will remain stable and thereby continue to support pursuit of the project or program as planned. Projects or programs exposed to environmental uncertainty may need to adapt their strategies and plans significantly (or even discontinue their efforts completely) as a consequence of changes that occur in the environment in which they operate. Usually, projects and programs have little control over such changes.

In discussions with programmaticists from various organizations, I was observed that the sources of environmental uncertainty are quite diverse. Environmental uncertainty sometimes results from changes in the programmatic environment that are introduced by the host organization. Such changes include, for example, changes to the organization's goals or its strategy for pursuing those goals, or to a project's or program's priority, or to the funding or resources allocated to a project or program. They might also include changes related to the organization's continuation or termination of alliances, partnerships, or contracts.

Environmental uncertainty may also result from changes external to the organization, such as change in a project's or program's competitive environment. The launch of a competitor's product, or the emergence of a disruptive technology may both result in the need for change to a project or program in order to preserve its expected value, for example. In fields that are highly regulated by external agencies (such as in the aerospace, defense, pharmaceutical, or environmental industries), the imposition of new standards, requirements, or constraints often results in the need to adapt projects or programs. In governmental settings, political agendas and budget approvals were identified as common sources of environmental uncertainty.

In general, environmental uncertainty was observed to be of greatest significance when a project's or program's timeframe was long enough to make environmental change likely to occur. Environmental uncertainty could be important to projects or programs conducted in environments that are characterized by rapid change, or to projects or programs conducted over very long periods of time in environments that change more slowly. Programmaticists in either of these environments were quick to agree that environmental uncertainty could be profoundly disruptive to their projects and programs as they pursued their goals and objectives.

Environmental complexity may be defined as the complexity associated with managing environmental uncertainty.

Programmaticists face the need to manage environmental complexity when events external to their projects or programs force them to alter their strategies or plans in disruptive ways. Managing such disruption can be a highly complex endeavor, inasmuch as the changes that are triggered by environmental events are often sudden, surprising, and substantial. They may have dramatic effects on the strategy or plan required or desired for a project or program.

The skills that may be required of a programmaticist for managing environmental complexity depend on the nature of the uncertainty that has impacted his or her endeavor. Clearly, change management skills are required (as they are for the management of all other types of project complexity). However, specific competencies in other areas (for example, technical, behavioral, operational, or regulatory) may also be beneficial, depending on the issues that must be resolved.

Organizational Uncertainty and Complexity

A fifth source of uncertainty and complexity that must be managed in the project and program environment is *organizational uncertainty and complexity*.

Organizational uncertainty may be defined as the uncertainty that is associated with a programmaticist's need to secure the endorsement or approval of organizational committees in order to implement or change the strategy or the plan of a project or program. Organizational uncertainty is a lack of certainty that a proposed strategy or plan will be supported by a governing body, or that the recommendations of any given governing body will be accepted by another governing body whose support is also required.

Organizational uncertainty might at first be viewed as a form of stakeholder uncertainty, where one views an entire governing body as a project or program "stakeholder." However, organizational uncertainty is fundamentally different from stakeholder uncertainty because the decisions made by groups of individuals depend upon the results of spontaneous interactions of individuals who may disagree with each other; these decisions are subject to high variance based the dynamics of stakeholder participation. Moreover, organizational uncertainty can be more difficult to manage than stakeholder uncertainty because the opportunities to interact with governing bodies *as a whole* (and thereby assess or influence their behavior, or preemptively obtain their endorsements) are generally limited to the specific times when those governing bodies have been formally assembled.

Programmaticists observe that managing operational, outcome, stakeholder, and environmental uncertainty usually requires the effective management of organizational uncertainty. Projects or programs with high organizational uncertainty often need to navigate complex organizational processes, sometimes iteratively, before identifying and implementing changes that have become necessary as a result of these other forms of uncertainty and complexity.

Programmaticists observe that organizational uncertainty increases with the number of committees that must be consulted before defining or changing the strategy or the plan of a project or program. An increase in the number of committees increases the likelihood that one will make recommendations that need to be considered (or reconsidered) by the others. High organizational uncertainty is often encountered when a project or program needs to attain endorsements and approvals from governing bodies that represent different parts of an organization or as part of cross-organizational partnerships, alliances, and ventures.

Organizational uncertainty also increases with the diversity of responsibilities of organizational committees, and with the diversity of interests of the members of any given committee. An increase in diversity of responsibilities increases the likelihood that committees will establish "conditions of approval" that conflict with those of other committees. It also decreases the surety that a clear consensus will be achieved during any particular meeting of a committee.

Finally, organizational uncertainty may be influenced in profound ways by an organization's management system or culture. Organizational uncertainty increases in organizations whose committees do not work well with each other or with their project or program teams. It also increases when the decision-making authority of individual committees is not clearly defined, understood, and respected. We will further explore the influence of organizational management systems and culture on a programmaticist's roles and responsibilities later in this book, beginning in Chapter 6.

Organizational complexity may be defined as the complexity associated with managing organizational uncertainty.

Organizational complexity is managed by programmaticists throughout the life of a project or program, whenever a project's or program's strategies and plans need to be reviewed, endorsed, or approved by groups of organizational stakeholders. Most often, it results from the need to manage another source of uncertainty and complexity; managing operational, outcome, stakeholder, or environmental uncertainty often results in the recommendation of changes to strategy or plans that need to be reviewed and approved. Line function or operations committees may need to review new resourcing plans; portfolio committees may need to review budgets, risk, and value assessments; executive committees may need to review strategic implications; and customer-facing committees may need to assess the consequences of changes on external stakeholders.

Programmaticists note that managing organizational complexity can be made easier or harder as a consequence of organizational agreements. Granting a project or program "high priority" status, for example, may reduce the organizational uncertainty and complexity associated with approval of its resourcing plan. Appointing a high-level executive sponsor or a well-respected leader may reduce the uncertainty and complexity related to accessing, influencing, and aligning high-level organizational committees. Programmaticists also report that managing organizational uncertainty and complexity can be made easier by the establishment of organizational "standards" that clearly define committee responsibilities, organization-wide decision criteria, or hierarchies of decision-making authority.

In interviews with experienced programmaticists—and especially with the Exasperados among them—it is common for them to identify organizational uncertainty and complexity as the most underappreciated source of programmatic uncertainty and complexity. They often identify it as being difficult to manage because of its emergent nature and its dependence on group dynamics, and because of the limited opportunities that they have for influencing it. One Exasperado I interviewed was very clear when expressing her opinion: "Organizational complexity is the biggest reason for my exasperation." We will discuss the organizational confusion that leads her to be exasperated in more detail in Chapter 5. However, before we do, we should further explore programmaticists' reactions to the five-complexities framework.

REACTIONS TO THE COMPLEXITY FRAMEWORK

Those who lead or manage projects and programs have been accepting of the five-complexities framework. They often observe that it "explains why my job is so hard." I have found that programmaticists are, in a strange way, comfortable with the notion that examining and understanding the complexity of their jobs will itself be a complex challenge. It seems somehow to encourage them to accept that there is a "science" behind the management of programmatic complexity—and to accept that they must evolve and learn to be better *programmatic scientists*.

Programmaticists also seem to appreciate a central message that emerges from our many discussions of programmatic complexity: Successfully managing any one form of complexity in an organization's programmatic environment usually requires the simultaneous management of other forms of complexity.

Managing outcome uncertainty and complexity, for example, often requires that an endeavor's plans or strategy be adapted—which, in turn, may require the modification of operational agreements, the concurrence of stakeholders, a reassessment of environmental factors, or the navigation of organizational review processes. Managing outcome uncertainty and complexity (in this example) may require the simultaneous management of all four other types of complexity (operational, stakeholder, environmental, and organizational). The implications of this are significant. They lead to the conclusions that:

- For organizations to be successful in managing complex projects or programs, they need to be prepared to manage all five types of uncertainty and complexity.

- For programmaticists to be successful they need to clearly understand their responsibilities for managing each type of uncertainty and complexity.

- For projects and programs to be successful in delivering their intended value they should be designed not only to minimize complexity wherever possible, but also to ensure that they are ready to solve complexity (of every type) when it arises.

These conclusions align with our proposed programmaticist credo "to manage the uncertain, solve the complex, and deliver the value." They also inevitably lead to the conclusion that programmatic systems used by organizations to oversee their complex projects and programs need to be designed with a focus on the efficient management of complexity.

Some of those who lead or manage projects and programs have had other reactions to the proposed complexity framework. For some, the first response is "Oh no!" In most cases, I have found that this response comes from those who, having recognized the personal implications of such a framework, begin to fear them. Often it comes from programmaticists who are most comfortable in a traditional project management role—those who are trained and inclined to focus their energy on managing operational uncertainty and complexity, and (to varying degrees) the stakeholder and organizational complexities that must be managed when solving operational issues. I have found that these programmaticists sometimes grow uneasy with the thought of being personally responsible for managing the complex issues that can result from outcome uncertainty (which can be highly technical) or environmental uncertainty (which can require deep insights of subjects external to their project or program endeavors). They may not be prepared for that.

Programmaticists who do not want to be personally responsible for managing outcome or environmental uncertainty begin to question whether they would be recognized as being the best candidates to lead or manage their organizations' endeavors. They may recognize that these endeavors have evolved to become increasingly outcome-based and environmentally sensitive. For these programmaticists, the five-complexities framework signals the growing need for a different kind of programmaticist (one who has skills beyond those commonly expected of a "traditional" first-generation project management professional) or for new programmatic management systems that embrace the sharing of programmatic leadership responsibilities among programmaticists with different skill sets.

Or is it both?

We will discuss both of these needs (and the opportunities that they reveal) in the second half of this book, as we explore the development of a new "third-generation" programmatic system.

Use of the Complexity Framework

After the passage of time and long discussions of their "Ah yes" and "Oh no" reactions, there is one question that consistently emerges from both groups of programmaticists—and it is an important question for those seeking to better define a programmaticist's roles and responsibilities.

"What next?" How can an understanding of the five-complexities framework be used to improve our definitions of a programmaticist's roles and responsibilities? The answer, I believe, is that the framework enables four important activities: *assessment, assignment, alignment,* and *advancement*; see Table 4.1.

The first of the activities is *assessment—of the significance of each source of complexity.* Understanding the likely significance of each source of complexity in a given project or program enhances an organization's understanding of the challenges that it will face and the skills that will be most important to the programmaticist who is responsible for leading or managing it.

The second of the activities supported by the complexity framework is *assignment—of personnel with appropriate knowledge, skills, and experience.* Assessment of the likely significance of each form of complexity enhances an organization's ability to ensure that programmaticists with the appropriate competencies are assigned to lead or manage a given organizational

Table 4.1   Use of the Five-Complexity Framework

Assessment	How significant are the uncertainties and complexities that will be faced within a given project or program?
Assignment	What knowledge, skills, and experience will the programmaticist who is assigned to the project or program need?
Alignment	How will we ensure that the organization's oversight of the project or program is aligned with its need to effectively manage uncertainty and complexity?
Advancement	How can we advance the capabilities of our programmaticists and our organization for managing these uncertainties and complexities?

endeavor. A program likely to face significant outcome-based complexity, for example, might be assigned to a programmaticist with technical knowledge, skills, or experience related to the program's outcomes.

The third activity supported by the complexity framework is *alignment—of a project or program with the most appropriate programmatic management (oversight) system*. Understanding the likely significance of each source of complexity and the programmaticist's capabilities for managing them enables a sponsor organization to design its programmatic oversight model according to a project's or program's oversight needs. It enables organizations to ensure that teams are governed within a management system that provides appropriate access to the knowledge and insight that lie outside of the team but within the organization. It may also enable organizations to reduce organizational complexity by avoiding the routine establishment of governing relationships that are of lesser importance.

Finally, the fourth activity supported by the complexity framework is *advancement—of individual and organizational competencies for complexity management*. Understanding the complexities that will be faced by their projects and programs enables organizations and programmaticists to prepare themselves to face those complexities. It enables them to seek education and training opportunities that will advance the complexity management and leadership capabilities of their organization, their programmaticists, and their teams.

How does the "five-complexities framework" improve our definition of a programmaticist's roles and responsibilities? For a programmaticist, the *assessment* of uncertainty and establishment of clear *assignments* of responsibilities for uncertainty and complexity management are important first steps. And *alignment* of those responsibilities with roles that are clearly defined within an organization's programmatic management system is an essential next step. Ultimately, however, for the sake of both the programmaticist and his or her organization, the *advancement* of complexity management competencies might be most critical. The five-complexities framework provides a structure that can be used to map the knowledge and skills that are known to be important when managing complexity within projects or programs, and that can be used to facilitate the development of even more effective competencies; see Table 4.2.

Complexity is a peculiar thing. It is not perceived and understood in the same way by all who encounter it. To those who are unaware of the complexity that they face, the world may seem delightfully simple; blissful ignorance has its benefits. Unfortunately, however, such ignorance does not make programmaticists or their organizations successful. To those who become aware of the complexity that they face, the world may suddenly seem to have become overwhelmingly intricate; knowledge about the complexity of issues can be paralyzing. Fortunately, however, that knowledge also enables one to appreciate what is required from a solution. To those who are aware of the complexity and who have the knowledge and skills to solve it, the world becomes simpler again.

Learning to solve complexity often requires that one progress from a state of mystery to one of misery before attaining a state of mastery. Those who are successful in developing the right knowledge and skills can become uniquely capable of solving the most complex of issues. See Figure 4.3.

I am reminded of my son's attempts to solve a Rubik's Cube. I handed him a cube and a "vision" of its solution (give me back the cube with only one color on each of the cube's six sides). The desired outcomes were clear. With a few casual twists of his wrists, he set out to show that he could quickly produce the results that I wanted. He wasn't aware of the complexity of the task. With each twist to align a color, however, there were unexpected consequences, and as the hours passed he became exasperated with them. For a good while, the more he tried, the more chaotic his results became. After a while, though, he developed approaches for working within the cube's "system"—series of moves that produced changes that were appropriate to one side of the cube without totally disrupting the views of another side. He got closer to a solution. One day, after he returned from school I told him a secret: Start with

Table 4.2   Knowledge and Skills Important in the Management of Complexity

Type of Complexity	Examples of Important Knowledge, Skills, and Capabilities
Operational	Traditional first-generation project management principles, practices, tools, and techniques (as described, for example, in the Project Management Institute's Body of Knowledge); operational risk management; use of project management software or enterprise planning and resource management tools; critical chain planning methodologies; contracting and procurement; change control
Outcome	Technical/subject matter knowledge; second-generation project management methodologies, goal-based planning methods; lean six sigma methods; decision analysis; earned value management; use of information sharing systems
Stakeholder	Stakeholder engagement skills; teambuilding skills; communication and negotiation skills; cultural awareness; active listening skills; impact and influence training
Environmental	Portfolio management skills; budgeting and finance; competitive intelligence and analysis; strategic planning; market research and analysis; related regulatory, legal, and compliance knowledge; environmental benchmarking
Organizational	Organizational governance processes and standard operating procedures; matrix management skills; writing and presentation skills; use of organizational reporting systems; awareness of organizational metrics and performance management targets; budget management

the corners. (I had never solved the cube, but I had heard that corners were important.) He refused my advice, saying that it wouldn't work for him. He needed to solve it his own way, and he offered to make a bet that he could. I laughed (like fathers who think they know better sometimes do). And even though I didn't take the bet, he began his work to solve the cube. Less than three minutes later he had. I was shocked. I thoroughly remixed the cube and gave it back to him; he solved it again, this time in less than two minutes. He had (unbeknownst to me) learned new approaches and developed new insights, and solving the cube was

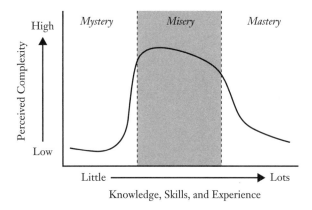

Figure 4.3 The influence of knowledge, skills, and experience on the perceived complexity of a task.

no longer complex to him. I had also learned a few things—to trust him when I had "cubes" that needed to be solved, to enable him to develop complexity-solving perspectives and skills that matched his own mindset and strengths, and to be very careful when he offered to place a bet with me in the future.

I have found that experienced programmaticists are quick to adopt the "five-complexities framework" for examining their roles and responsibilities. They report that it enables them to focus less fixatedly on what they are supposed to *do* (following standard processes, using recognized tools), and more clearly and specifically on what they are supposed to *achieve* (solving complex issues, delivering benefits). It helps them to focus more on the *why* than on the *what*, more on the *outcomes* of their work than on its *outputs*. And, over time, they find themselves more enthusiastically embracing the notion that their primary role is indeed "to manage the uncertainty and complexity that is faced when pursuing the goals of projects or programs, so that their intended benefits and value are effectively delivered."

Unfortunately, programmaticists often lament that their organizations have not (yet) reached the same understanding. They frequently report getting stuck on the third step of implementing the framework—the *alignment* of roles and responsibilities within their organizations' programmatic management systems. Why should that be?

To explore this question, we should examine the views that organizational stakeholders have about the roles and responsibilities of programmaticists within their organizations.

CHAPTER 5

Stakeholder Views about the Roles and Responsibilities of Programmaticists

DIVERSITY OF VIEWS

In my positions as an executive, an academic, and a consultant, I have now had the privilege of interviewing hundreds of organizational stakeholders about the current roles and responsibilities of their project management professionals, and about how those roles and responsibilities could be more "ideally" defined in the future. Many of these stakeholders have been actively seeking to improve the programmatic systems used by their organizations. They each recognize that their organization's success is linked to the success of its programs and projects, and they are anxious to identify any means for improving project and program management.

It should be no surprise (given our prior discussions of Exasperados, first- and second-generation programmatic systems, and project management's potential identity crisis) that the interviews have revealed significant differences in the perspectives of individuals whose organizations were pursuing complex knowledge-based endeavors. Stakeholders often begin their discussions with an acknowledgment that the specific roles and responsibilities of their organizations' programmaticists may be quite different from the roles and responsibilities of programmaticists in other organizations. They observe that their organizations have, over time, adapted the definitions of a programmaticist's roles and responsibilities to suit their organization's specific needs, challenges, and culture. They acknowledge that they would again adapt those definitions if they thought that it would improve their organizations' ability to pursue projects. When prompted appropriately, many stakeholders have "at their fingertips" a list of changes (based on their personal perspectives and experiences) that could (or should) be introduced.

What I found surprising in my interviews was the diversity of opinion that can be found among stakeholders who work *within* the same organizations. In my interviews, it was common to observe that stakeholders from any single organization often disagreed about the "ideal" roles of project and program management professionals. They frequently contradicted one another in their descriptions of what was "right" or "wrong" with the programmatic systems that their organizations were currently using. To one stakeholder, a program's need to manage uncertain technical outcomes may signal the need for a technically trained programmaticist who would be able to quickly and independently manage the challenges associated with outcome-based uncertainty. To another it may signal the need for a governance-focused programmaticist who would schedule reviews of the program before further actions were initiated. The former approach would require a programmaticist who focused primarily on the management of outcome uncertainty and complexity, whereas the latter approach would require a programmaticist who focused first on the management of organizational uncertainty and complexity.

Within an organization, it could be observed that the diversity of stakeholder opinion had resulted in programmaticists receiving different guidance regarding the roles and responsibilities that they were currently filling or ideally assuming in the future.

Moreover, stakeholders commonly reported that their opinions had changed over time. When they were questioned as to why their organizations had adopted their respective views on programmaticist roles and responsibilities, they commonly explained that their organizations had previously tried "other" approaches and had concluded that "they didn't work." They had changed their programmatic approaches and adapted their perspectives of the "ideal" roles and responsibilities of a programmaticist in response to the issues that they had most recently faced within their programmatic systems.

I found it perplexing, however, that stakeholder and organizational opinions about programmaticist roles and responsibilities did not seem to be changing with directional consistency. At any moment in time, two organizations facing the need to manage outcome complexity might have concluded that the best approach for improving their management of that complexity was to move in very different directions. While one organization might conclude that it needed programmaticist leaders who were more technically insightful, another might simultaneously conclude that it needed programmaticists with less technical and greater organizational or operational focus. Within either organization, their conclusions seemed logical; they seemed like necessary responses to current business conditions. However, the lack of directional consistency across many such organizations (and also within individual organizations, when viewed over time)—the inconsistent implementation of "fixes" to problems that seemed similar—might alternatively be taken to suggest something very different. It might suggest that *none* of the approaches commonly being taken was working predictably well for these organizations. Or, alternatively, that they were not predictably adept at executing the approaches they were choosing.

Based on the results of many interviews, this seems clear: A significant number of organizations are struggling to develop a better understanding of how to define the "ideal" roles and responsibilities of the programmaticists who are responsible for managing their complex projects and programs. They are in search of a more consistent means of defining, communicating, and aligning the expectations that they have of their programmaticists and their programmatic systems.

But can that be achieved in an environment where organizational stakeholders express diverse views about the ideal roles and responsibilities of their programmaticists? How? An important first step in answering these questions is to understand the assumptions that stakeholders make when defining their individual views. In fact, when one listens carefully to the perspectives of organizational stakeholders, a surprising observation can be made. When stakeholders are asked what roles and responsibilities should "ideally" be assumed by a programmaticist who is charged with leading or managing a complex project, they generally make recommendations that are based on one of three principle conceptions of a programmaticist's role in managing project or program complexity. It is valuable to understand these conceptions and the reasons that stakeholders choose between them.

THREE CONCEPTIONS OF A PROGRAMMATICIST'S ROLE

The Traditionalist Perspective

The first of these programmatic conceptions, which we will call the *Traditionalist perspective*, is grounded in the belief that programmaticist roles and responsibilities should be defined according to role definitions originally espoused under first-generation programmatic systems. Stakeholders who assume the Traditionalist perspective seek first for a programmaticist to deliver value to the organization by efficiently and effectively managing the completion of work *according to approved project or program plans*—on time, on budget, and to specifications. They believe that the programmaticist's primary role should be defined so as to maximize control over operational uncertainty—to improve the likelihood that projects or programs will deliver their expected results precisely as predicted.

Those who hold the Traditionalist perspective advocate that governing committees should retain responsibility for authorizing any significant changes to the plan or strategy of a project or program. They seek to limit the programmaticist's authority for independently changing project plans or strategy, except perhaps when noncontroversial changes can be implemented to restore a project to its originally approved course of action. They expect that programmaticists will manage organizational uncertainty as necessary to assure that appropriate organizational processes are pursued for the resolution of operational uncertainty. However, Traditionalists believe that a programmaticist should depend on governance systems to endorse the adaptation of a programmatic endeavor's strategy or plans, as may be required to solve any complex issues that arise as a consequence of operational, outcome, environmental, or stakeholder uncertainty.

During interviews, those espousing the Traditionalist perspective cited a number of reasons for their beliefs. The views of many were based on their comfort with the first-generation programmatic management systems that had been prevalent in many of their organizations since the Industrial Age—systems which authorized programmaticists to work under the specific authority of an organization's executive governing bodies, on endeavors that were explicitly defined and approved by those bodies. During interviews, Traditionalist stakeholders often asserted that it was critically important for line function leaders to retain responsibility for approving or disapproving any changes that affected the use of their line function resources (since line function leaders were ultimately held responsible for that), and also for governance committees to review and approve project or program changes that could affect the broader organization (since governance members had the best perspective on organizational needs and strategy). They believed that it should be a governing body's responsibility to make sure that any changes proposed for a project or program are consistent with the strategies, plans, and prior commitments of the larger organization.

It was common for stakeholders who held the Traditionalist perspective to point out that they had a good understanding of programmaticists' roles and responsibilities under Traditionalist assumptions, and that the knowledge, skills, and competencies required of programmaticists who worked under Traditionalist management approaches were clearly defined and highly valued. They often referenced the "standards" of project management as providing sound guidance about the principles, practices, tools, and techniques of traditional project and program management. They noted that this guidance itself provided clear definitions of the roles and responsibilities of project and program management professionals.

Stakeholders who were espousing the Traditionalist perspective tended to assert that the programmaticist's roles should be (1) to limit the uncertainty and complexity associated with projects or programs (by planning for it and controlling it whenever possible) and (2) to facilitate the resolution of complexity by the organization's governance bodies (when it could not be or had not been adequately controlled). Thus, they often suggested that a programmaticist's primary roles and responsibilities for complexity management were: to define and manage their endeavor so as to minimize any potential requirement for change; to monitor information that might signal a need for change; to inform governance bodies of the need for change whenever it arose; to provide governance bodies with information and analyses related to the need for change; and (as appropriate) to recommend the specific change(s) favored or proposed by members of the program or project team.

Those with a Traditionalist perspective clearly recognized the importance of the programmaticist in limiting and managing operational complexity. They often acknowledged that a programmaticist's skills in filling the Traditionalist role were critically important to their organizations' ability to manage complex projects and programs. In their views, a programmaticist who was capable of "mastering" operational complexity might be expected to present highly complex operational information in a manner that would enable stakeholders who sit on organizational governing bodies to more clearly understand the issues at hand so that they might quickly and easily agree on the best approach for solving them.

The Traditionalist perspective of a programmaticist's "ideal" roles and responsibilities was the most common perspective held by stakeholders. During interviews, stakeholders from many different industries and very diverse organizations commonly noted that *the programmatic management systems used by their organizations for overseeing most of their projects and programs were based on Traditionalist conceptions*. It could also be observed, however, that satisfaction with the Traditionalist perspective was expressed less consistently. During interviews, *the Traditionalist approach to defining a programmaticist's roles and the organization's respon-sibilities was also the most common approach of organizations whose program-maticists identified themselves as Exasperados.* We will discuss the reasons for this in more detail in Chapter 6.

The Operationalist Perspective

A second conception of programmaticist roles and responsibilities, which we will call the **Operationalist perspective**, is based upon a belief that programmaticists should be given a broader mandate for defining the operational plans of a project or program, and more responsibility for independently managing its operational uncertainty and complex-ity. Stakeholders who had an Operationalist perspective agreed with the Traditionalists' belief that a project management professional should, first and foremost, seek to deliver "contracted" project outputs on time, on budget, and to specifications. However, those with an Operationalist perspective also believed that programmaticists should be recognized as the organization's operational planning experts. They believed that the experience and knowledge of programmaticists about first-generation project management practices, processes, tools, and techniques should make them far more qualified to manage operational uncertainty and complexity than the executives who sit on their organizations' gover-nance committees. Stakeholders with an Operationalist perspective believed that programmaticists should be expected and empowered to negotiate agreements that resolve operational issues. They believed that program-maticists should independently manage stakeholder and organizational complexities whenever those complexities resulted from operational issues. Operationalists were prepared to more fully empower their pro-grammaticists to do so.

Operationalist stakeholders did *not* believe that programmaticists should assume primary responsibility for managing outcome-based or environmental uncertainty or complexity, however. In their judgment, the management of outcome-based uncertainty too often required unique subject matter knowledge or technical experience that generally was not (and often should not be) expected of a programmaticist whose training might have been focused on traditionally defined project and program management skills. They believed, for example, that program-maticists should not be held personally accountable for defining the best response to technical outcomes that did not match expectations, or for tracking environmental developments that might affect the strategy or priority of organizational endeavors. Operationalist stakeholders felt that outcome-based and environmental complexities were best managed under the watchful eyes of the organization's governance committees, since members of these committees were more likely to have knowledge and experience related to outcome or environmental complexities, and since outcome and environmental complexity were more likely to raise questions about the continued alignment of a project or program with the goals of the organization.

Stakeholders who subscribed to the Operationalist perspective asserted that the programmaticist's roles should be: (1) to manage the operational elements of his or her project or program somewhat autonomously, (2) to assume personal responsibility for managing operational uncertainty and solving operational complexity and for managing the stakeholder and organizational uncertainties and complexities that might be associated with operational uncertainty and complexity and (3) to facilitate the resolution of outcome-based or environmental complexities by organizational governing bodies. Thus, Operationalist stakeholders often suggested that a programmaticist's primary roles and responsibilities for complexity management were: to define and manage their endeavor so as to minimize any potential requirement for change; to monitor information that might signal a need for change; to manage any operational issues as they arose; to inform governance bodies of any need for change that might be triggered by unexpected outcomes or emerging environmental factors; to provide governance bodies with operational information and analyses related to their examination of the need for outcome- or environmentally-driven change; to recommend changes that are favored or proposed by members of the program or project team; and to implement operational changes that may be mandated after governance's review and response to outcome-based or environmentally driven change.

The Operationalist view of a programmaticist's "ideal" roles and responsibilities was most commonly held by stakeholders who sought to empower their programmaticists to respond agilely to operational challenges as they arose, and who thereby sought to optimize the operational efficiency of their organizations' programmatic management system. Stakeholders holding Operationalist conceptions of the programmaticist role seemed more often to be associated with projects or programs that had ready access to the pool of resources required to conduct operational activities. These projects and programs clearly benefited from having flexibility in how resources were assigned (and re-assigned) over time. (One example is a software development program with ready access to a dedicated pool of qualified programmers.)

The Inclusivist Perspective

A third conception, which we will call the *Inclusivist perspective*, is based upon a belief that a programmaticist's roles and responsibilities should be defined so as to provide the programmaticist with an even broader mandate—a mandate that made programmaticists more personally responsible for delivering the *expected benefits* from projects or programs, even if delivering those benefits required the realization of uncertain outcomes. Stakeholders who had an Inclusivist perspective believed that a programmaticist should be personally responsible for managing (or ensuring the management of) outcome-based, operational, stakeholder, and organizational uncertainties or complexities. (Some also believed that a programmaticist should participate in the management of environmental uncertainty and complexity.) Inclusivists generally believed that it is best to manage uncertainty and complexity holistically, because the various kinds of uncertainty and complexity are very often interconnected. Inclusivists felt that the programmaticist's role should be to manage them in the highly integrated and coordinated manner required for success.

Stakeholders who had an Inclusivist perspective were more likely to believe that their organizations' governance bodies are not inherently effective or efficient in managing outcome or operational uncertainty and complexity. They tended to believe that governance committees should focus principally on the management of environmental uncertainty and complexity. They felt that governance committees should principally serve an enabling function, supporting their organizations' project or program teams by providing an appropriate organizational environment; sufficient resources; and the benefits of their knowledge, experience, and insight. They sought to ensure that project or program teams were not overly encumbered by sometimes-intrusive governance committee reviews and frequent approval-driven intercessions triggered by outcome and operational complexity in two-party programmatic oversight systems. Inclusivists sought to empower programmaticists to create a high-performance team environment in which uncertainty and complexity could usually be managed by team members. In doing so, they sought to leverage the agility, creativity, and energy of their project teams, and to take advantage of their team leaders' and members' inherent professional "athleticism."

Stakeholders who endorsed the Inclusivist perspective tended to assert that the programmaticists' roles should be: (1) to autonomously manage both the *strategic and operational* elements of their projects or programs; (2) to assure that their teams sought out organizational support, knowledge, and experience that would be essential to project or program success; and (3) to assume personal responsibility for assuring that their teams effectively managed uncertainty and solved complexity related to outcomes, operations, stakeholders, and organizational processes, as required to deliver their project's or program's intended benefits or value. Thus, Inclusivist stakeholders suggested that an individual programmaticist's primary roles and responsibilities for complexity management were: to manage their endeavor with a continuous focus on the delivery of its intended benefits and value; to remain constantly vigilant about the possible need for change that is triggered by operational, outcome-based, stakeholder, or organizational uncertainty; to manage the uncertainty and solve the complexity that are often encountered while identifying, examining, and implementing change; and to thereby optimize the delivery of intended benefits and value from their projects and programs. Inclusivists promoted a much more independent vision of the programmaticist's role—especially when compared to the beliefs of stakeholders with a Traditionalist mindset.

Stakeholders who had an Inclusivist perspective recognized that programmaticists might need very different competencies to function in an Inclusivist programmaticist role—competencies that are not explicitly described in "standards" of project or program management. They might, for example, need education, skills, and experience that would enable the understanding and management of the uncertainty and complexity that are related to specific technical outcomes. In fact, during interviews, it was not unusual for Inclusivist stakeholders to assert (often, based on their personal experience) that specific technical knowledge and competencies might be of equal or greater importance to a programmaticist than the traditional project management competencies defined under "standard" first-generation programmatic systems.

The Inclusivist view of a programmaticist's "ideal" roles and responsibilities was most commonly held by stakeholders whose organizations sought to maximize their projects' or programs' abilities to respond quickly and agilely to outcome-based challenges as they arose. Stakeholders holding Inclusivist conceptions expected that by granting their project and program teams a high degree of autonomy they would enable those teams to be more responsive to emerging knowledge, more agile in responding to changing strategic and operational needs, and (consequently) more creative and innovative. Inclusivist stakeholders tended to work in fast-moving innovation-driven environments that benefited from rapid application of outcome-based learning, such as highly technical environments requiring rapid development and deployment of cutting edge products (see Table 5.1).

Table 5.1   Perspectives on the Programmaticist's Primary Roles in
Managing Each Type of Project or Program Complexity

Types of Uncertainty and Complexity to be Managed	Common Stakeholder Perspectives		
	Traditionalist	Operationalist	Inclusivist
Operational	✓	✓	✓
Outcome			✓
Stakeholder		✓	✓
Organizational	✓	✓	✓
Environmental			

ADOPTION AND VALUE

I have found during my interviews that many organizational stakeholders can more easily discuss and compare their views of programmaticist roles and responsibilities after having been introduced to the
Traditionalist, Operationalist, and Inclusivist definitions of stakeholder
perspectives. Most can quickly define how their own views align with
these definitions, and explain the specific reasons that they hold their
particular views. They can define and understand the alignment of views
held by other stakeholders, and more clearly discuss the possible reasons for their differences. The definitions seem to enable stakeholders
to engage in a more structured discussion of a programmaticist's "ideal"
roles and responsibilities within their organization's chosen programmatic system.

Perhaps more importantly, I have found that after considering these
three perspectives, many stakeholders find it easier to explain the conditions that would have to exist in their organizations for them to accept an
alternate definition of the programmaticist's role. (They might, for example, say that they could consider adopting a management system based
on the Inclusivist approach *if* their organizations hired programmaticists
with more advanced technical expertise.) There is great value in this.
Developing a language that enables organizations to easily discuss why
they might object to changing organizational definitions of programmaticists' roles is a critical first step toward aligning stakeholder perspectives
about the ideal programmatic systems for their individual organizations;
it enables clearer discussions about the ideal roles and responsibilities of
programmaticists working within their organizations. It is also a critical
first step in resolving the "identity crisis" that seems to exist within the

project management field. Moreover, it has immediate value to us as we further examine the emergence of the programmaticist Exasperados.

The Exasperados whom we identified in Chapter 4 have approached their roles with a decidedly Inclusivist mindset. They believed that the success of their projects and their careers depended upon their being enabled to assume greater personal responsibility for managing complexity of all kinds, and for delivering the outcomes and value (and not just the outputs) desired from their initiatives. When they became frustrated it was often because they had met resistance from individual (usually executive) stakeholders who expected or preferred that programmaticists perform in a more Traditionalist or Operationalist role. They were exasperated because their organizations' programmatic systems required them to perform in a role that limited their accountability for managing the complexity that their projects or programs were facing. They felt that they should be empowered to do something more—to be more accountable for delivering their endeavors' intended benefits. As "organizational athletes" they felt that they were qualified and ready to perform in that role. And they were frustrated not to have that responsibility. Sometimes they were even frustrated that other programmaticists didn't feel the same way. Why would that be?

In interviews with a large number of programmaticists it also became abundantly clear that programmaticists, as a group, had the same diversity of views about their ideal roles and responsibilities as the other stakeholders. Individual programmaticists could also be observed to define their own ideal roles and responsibilities according to the Traditionalist, Operationalist, or Inclusivist mindsets. Some project managers indicated that they preferred to operate according to Traditionalist assumptions. They accepted that managing adaptive change was not their strength, and they preferred that their success in managing or leading projects not be defined so as to require them to have that skill. These programmaticists often excelled when working within a command-and-control deliver-as-promised environment, and they were happy to have governance committees retain responsibility for managing adaptive change. They could argue (convincingly) that some of the best project managers are successful because of their single-minded Traditionalist focus on delivering project outputs—on time, on budget, to specifications.

Other project managers believed that they should assume the more adaptive and strategically focused roles of an Operationalist or an Inclusivist. They sought to assume greater responsibility for independently managing the complex issues that their projects and programs faced. They saw this as an opportunity to demonstrate their abilities—not only to manage their projects and programs, but to lead them.

The Operationalists among them accepted that they would or could not be given completely independent responsibility for managing outcome or environmental uncertainty. They often lacked the technical training that would be required of an Inclusivist role. They observed, however, that they could deliver much value in the management of operational uncertainty and complexity, and the stakeholder uncertainty and complexity that was often associated with it. They correctly noted that by managing operational complexity they would contribute significantly to the management of outcome and environmental complexity; managing outcome and environmental complexity often resulted in the need for operational change.

The Inclusivists among them felt that they should be independently responsible for managing their endeavors' uncertainty and complexity in a more holistic way. They felt that they could consult with appropriately experienced stakeholders (including their governance committees) at times when they required additional experience and advice. They felt that having the freedom to do so would enable them to manage their teams more efficiently and agilely. And they felt that the additional independence afforded to them would result in more creative and innovative results.

THE NEED FOR DIFFERENT KINDS OF PROGRAMMATICISTS

Interviews revealed that it was common for organizations to use two or three programmaticist mindsets when formally defining their programmaticists' ideal roles. Many organizations seemed to recognize that individual programmaticists may have skills and styles that make them better suited to functioning in either a Traditionalist, Operationalist, or Inclusivist role. To accommodate such differences, they had often adopted conventions for distinguishing programmaticist roles and responsibilities based loosely on job titles (see Figure 4.1): Greater responsibilities for managing uncertainty and complexity could be observed to be associated with titles that contained the word "senior" and/or "director," or that used "program" instead of "project." Sometimes the distinction was based on the use of the term "leader" instead of "manager." As a consequence, for example, organizations might be observed to use titles such as "program leader" or "senior director of program management" to reflect expectations that a programmaticist would have a more Inclusivist role, whereas a title of "project manager" might be used to suggest a Traditionalist role.

However, few organizations had been explicit in formally aligning titles with their specific expectations for managing the various types of project- or program-related uncertainty and complexity, and many programmaticists seemed to be only peripherally aware of the correlations of titles with their organizations' uncertainty-management expectations. In most organizations, the use of titles to distinguish the complexity-management expectations of a programmaticist did not result in clear understandings (or differentiation) of the intended roles and responsibilities of the programmaticist for managing project or program complexity.

During the course of interviews, executive stakeholders, programmaticists, and Exasperados all agreed that individual projects and programs may at various times have specific needs for a particular type of leader or manager. They believed that organizations should therefore recognize that Traditionalist, Operationalist, or Inclusivist programmaticists may each be better suited to managing certain kinds of projects or programs (or specific components of large and complex projects or programs). They even suggested that organizations should develop individual programmaticists to fill each of these roles specifically—perhaps as a first step toward addressing project management's identity crisis. (This is an intriguing possibility, which will be discussed in more detail in the second part of this book.) However, it could be recognized during interviews that many of today's organizations would find this to be a challenging exercise because of the differences of opinion that often exist among stakeholders from a single organization—stakeholders who might be responsible for oversight of the same projects or programs.

Line function executives who were members of a given project's governance committee very often disagreed with each other about the ideal role that should be assumed by that project's leader or manager. Managers on long-established governance committees would commonly have very different opinions as to what specific leadership behaviors should be considered to be sufficient versus insufficient, or acceptable versus unacceptable. It was very common, for example, that stakeholders would disagree on whether an individual programmaticist should assume a Traditionalist versus an Operationalist versus an Inclusivist role, even when the programmaticist's professional experience and capabilities were clearly understood. And it was also common that they were unaware of the striking differences in the opinions that they each held. As a result, a given leadership behavior exhibited by an individual programmaticist might be lauded by one line function manager as "appropriate and ideal," while simultaneously derided by another as being "inappropriate and undesirable." One was left to wonder whether the differences of understanding among organizational stakeholders about the ideal roles of a programmaticist might, in part, have resulted from their organizations' failure to clearly define when they would employ Traditionalist versus Operationalist versus Inclusivist approaches in the pursuit of their projects and programs.

It also became apparent during interviews that many modern organizations had experimented (somewhat intermittently) with management models that had encouraged programmaticists to embrace an Operationalist or Inclusivist leadership style. Organizations usually did so in an effort to realize the greater programmatic agility that they believed would result from those approaches. Many interviewees reported, however, that their organizations had reverted (consciously or unconsciously) to programmatic models that required more explicit endorsements of project or program change by their governance bodies— to programmatic models that reflected first-generation Traditionalist principles. When asked to explain the shifts in their thinking, executive stakeholders would acknowledge that they had quickly (almost reflexively) reverted to Traditionalist approaches when their organizations' project or program teams had struggled to resolve complex issues or (when acting more autonomously) had made poor decisions. Organizations (like parents of young adults) seemed to have trouble "letting go" of their oversight responsibility and allowing their project teams to learn (at least in part) by making mistakes. They found it difficult not to return to their previously acceptable directive behaviors when they saw that important decisions needed to be made.

It is perhaps understandable that organizations (and their executive stakeholders) would revert to the seemingly simple and ostensibly effective Traditionalist management systems. Traditionalist approaches ensure that complexity-management responsibilities and decision-making authority are retained within the well-understood hierarchical management structures that had been used to manage organizations since the Industrial Age. Those structures placed responsibility for adapting project strategies and plans in the hands of governing committees whose members are perceived to have more experience, and who were usually accountable for managing the current strategic direction and the operational efficiency of the organization. It would seem to be a natural response when issues arose.

One might even suggest that the frequent return of organizations to their traditional first-generation programmatic management models provides empirical evidence that Traditionalist models are (and will remain) the best of models for managing projects and programs (the frustrations of Exasperados notwithstanding). It is hard to dismiss that conclusion. But it does raise anew some fundamental and important questions.

Why do organizations that have used traditional first-generation programmatic management models continue to grow dissatisfied with them? Why do they find it necessary to explore the potential value of Operationalist or Inclusivist conceptions of the programmaticist's roles and responsibilities? At various times in the first five chapters of this book, we have noted that organizations often pursue second-generation programmatic approaches (and Operationalist or Inclusivist definitions of the programmaticist's roles) in an effort to improve the agility, flexibility, adaptability, efficiency, or creativity of their project and program teams. Why can't these benefits be realized using first-generation approaches and Traditionalist role conceptions?

We will explore these questions in more detail in the next two chapters, where we will examine how and why first-generation programmatic management systems typically (d)evolve in organizations as they grow and pursue projects or programs that are increasingly uncertain and complex.

CHAPTER 6

Modern Problems with Traditional Management Models

THE TWO-PARTY FULLY GOVERNED PROJECT OVERSIGHT MODEL

We observed in Chapter 2 that traditional first-generation project management systems were first adopted by organizations as a seemingly natural extension of Industrial Age management principles. We noted that these systems could provide a highly effective means for pursuing new organizational initiatives. Indeed, project management professionals and organizational executives generally agree that the project management principles, practices, tools, and techniques developed as part of first-generation project management systems have proven invaluable to organizations that have pursued their operational and strategic goals via projects and programs.

Over the years, many organizations have found that their project management needs could be satisfied by traditional first-generation programmatic systems. These systems were well-understood and commonly appreciated; they seemed to promise that any organization's projects could be pursued and managed with predictable professional consistency using repeatable standard practices. In most of these organizations, projects were defined and managed using a first-generation programmatic process that flowed something like this:

A governing committee of stakeholders or executives (often line function leaders) with responsibility for defining their organization's strategic direction would identify specific goals they wanted to achieve in order to move their organization in a desired direction. To achieve these goals, the committee would sanction the initiation and pursuit of a new endeavor—an organizational project.[1] The committee would then establish **enabling conditions** to support the project—organizational conditions that made it possible to pursue the project within the context of the organization. Enabling conditions might include, for example, access to organizational support in the form of resources (human and financial), infrastructure (technological and physical), and know-how (leadership, management, and governance). When establishing enabling conditions, the committee would often prioritize the project's work relative to the operational needs of the organization and the work being performed to support other (previously authorized) projects.

The governing committee would also enable the project by assigning a programmaticist—a project manager or leader (or someone who has perhaps unwittingly assumed that role) who would assume responsibility for assembling and managing a project "team." That team would generally be comprised of members from various line functions in the organization whose skills, experience, insight, and authority would be valuable to the project as it pursued the organization's goals. Together, the programmaticist and the project team would define a strategy and develop a precise plan by which the organization's (and the project's) goals could be achieved.

Defining the project strategy and plan would often require that assumptions be made about how best to pursue the project's goals and about how the outputs and outcomes of project activities would deliver the project's intended value. The process of defining and accepting these assumptions might be recognized as a first step taken by the project team toward identifying and managing any uncertainty and complexity associated with the project. When making assumptions about the timing or cost of a project activity, for example, the team would be establishing a benchmark of its expectations to thereafter be used when measuring and managing operational uncertainty. When making assumptions about the results that would be delivered, the team would be establishing a benchmark for measuring and managing outcome uncertainty. And obtaining organizational agreement on the operational- and outcome-related assumptions that the team had made would often be a complex

---

[1] We will refrain from discussing the differences between projects and programs until the second part of this book—where the definitions of projects and programs and the significance of the differences will be discussed in much more detail. For the purposes of this chapter and the next, we will refer to organizational initiatives as projects. It should be noted, however, that such initiatives might also be characterized as programs.

endeavor, requiring the understanding and management of stakeholder, organizational, and environmental uncertainties and complexities.

Under traditional first-generation programmatic management systems the project's proposed strategy and plan would require review and approval by the project's governing committee. Resources would be allocated to the project team upon the project's approval. The governing committee would then delegate primary responsibility for overseeing day-to-day management of the approved project to the responsible programmaticist, who would assure efficient and collaborative pursuit of the endorsed project goals. In most cases, when approving a project, the managing committee would also establish conditions of accountability whereby the project's leader or manager (or perhaps the entire project team) would periodically report to the governance committee on the progress of the project.

On paper, governance of a project according to a traditional first-generation programmatic management system looks simple: Projects were managed via a simple approach that we will refer to as the ***two-party fully governed project oversight model***. It was a "two-party" model based upon oversight by (1) a governance function that provides strategic authorization and operational enablement of a project, and (2) a project management function that provides operational oversight of that project (Figure 6.1). We refer to it as a fully governed model because the governing committee is expected to retain full responsibility for authorizing the project's strategy and its operational plan. Within the two-party fully governed project oversight model, projects would

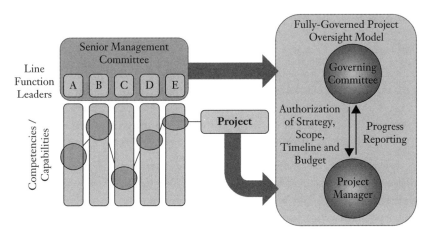

Figure 6.1   The two-party fully governed model of project oversight by a governing committee and project manager (programmaticist).

be conceived, authorized, and resourced under the authority of a single governance function, and that they would be operationally managed, precisely as approved, under the direction of a subjugate project manager or leader. Significant changes to a project's strategy or plans would require approval by the governance function before their implementation at the project level, since the acceptance of a new strategy was, in effect, a repudiation or replacement of the project's old (previously endorsed) one.

The two-party fully governed project oversight model is a familiar concept to almost all professional project managers and the stakeholders with whom they work. During interviews, the vast majority of programmaticists and executives agreed (at first) that it acceptably represented the managerial relationship between the governing and project management functions of their organizations.

Under traditional first-generation programmatic systems, where projects were expected to be managed according to the fully governed oversight model, it was generally accepted that project progress should be monitored, reported, and reviewed via formal and standardized processes. Executives and programmaticists noted that under the right circumstances (when projects were completed according to their plans and when they produced the expected results), project reviews could even be borderline-enjoyable experiences. Such reviews provided abundant opportunities for line function heads to marvel at the progress that was being made, the effectiveness of their staff, and the wisdom of the project's originators (themselves). Projects completed as planned were like athletic competitions won according to their original game plans. They would trigger high-fives on the field, on the sidelines, in the executive suites, and at happy hour in sports bars filled with enthusiastic stakeholders.

However, not all projects could be completed as planned. The project's strategic or operational assumptions might turn out to have been wrong. The uncertainties associated with a project's strategy, stakeholders, or environment might have a significant impact on that project's ability to deliver its intended goals.

Under a fully governed project oversight model, when projects could not be completed as planned, or when they did not produce the anticipated results, the project leader or manager would be expected to alert the governing committee as to the outcomes that had actually been achieved and the imminent need for change. The project manager might then be expected to re-evaluate the status of the project and the team's new perspectives about the impact of uncertainty on it. The leader or manager would then be expected to define options for changing the project's strategy or plans, to examine and propose solutions for the complexities associated with those options, and to make recommendations as to the specific changes that should be implemented to improve the project's ability to deliver its intended benefits and value. After considering the options for change, the governing committee would approve those changes that it deemed appropriate.

During interviews, some governing executives and programmaticists reported that their organizations were effective in using the two-party fully governed project oversight model along with Traditionalist definitions of the programmaticist's role. An interesting observation could be made from these interviews: Stakeholders who reported continued satisfaction with the model were more likely to work in smaller organizations, organizations whose governing committees had a small number of projects to focus on, or organizations whose governing committees oversaw projects that (by their nature) had a high probability of completion as originally planned (i.e., had little uncertainty). These stakeholders worked on projects whose uncertainty could be reasonably well understood and managed—either because their governing committees could afford to focus intensely on individual (albeit uncertain) projects, or because their larger portfolio of projects had only small amounts of uncertainty associated with it. These interviews suggested that the fully governed project oversight model was generally effective when its governing committee was able to focus intently on a "manageable" amount of uncertainty and complexity.

LIMITATIONS OF THE MODEL

Many other executives and programmaticists reported that their organizations were now struggling to use their fully governed project oversight models effectively, however. These stakeholders often worked in larger organizations, or in organizations whose governing committees dealt (in aggregate) with larger amounts of uncertainty and complexity (either from large numbers of projects, or projects with significant uncertainty). In interviews, these stakeholders would cite numerous examples of how issues with their fully governed project oversight models had negatively impacted their projects. And while the examples were different in their specific details, they seemed to have one thing in common: *Their governing committee members seemed to have become less responsive to their project teams' needs and simultaneously more reliant on their project managers for project information and perspective.*

Programmaticists who reported that their organizations were struggling with their project oversight models often felt that their committees were having trouble keeping up with and responding to their projects' needs. They believed that their committees had reached the limit of how much uncertainty and complexity they could efficiently manage.

Perhaps we (and they) should not be surprised by this observation. When one re-examines the responsibilities of a governing committee under the two-party fully governed project oversight model, it becomes apparent that the model requires governance committees to assume a long list of responsibilities that span the entire lifespan of a project. The model requires that governing committees stand constantly ready to examine and endorse a new project's strategies and plans, to monitor and allocate resources for its support, to assess its outcomes, to analyze its options, and then to consider and approve any strategic or operational changes that may be required. The model requires that the governing committee be ready and able to contribute to the analysis and optimization of strategies and plans that are often complex and uncertain. These are substantive responsibilities that would require a governing committee to be intimately familiar and intensely engaged with the projects (and the project teams) that they sponsor (see Figure 6.2).

And usually, stakeholders noted, the model requires still more: It requires that the governing committee remain aware of the needs of *all* the other projects under its direction *all* of the time. Governing committee

Governing committee:
- Defines strategic direction
- Authorizes projects
- Establishes "enabling" conditions and priorities
- Endorses project strategies and plans
- Approves resource allocations
- Delegates responsibility & accountability
- Assesses results
- Analyzes options
- Authorizes change

Project manager:
- Defines project strategy, plan, and assumptions
- Oversees the efficient, collaborative completion of work
- Manages project uncertainty and complexity
- Alerts governance to the need for and recommends change

Figure 6.2   Responsibilities of the governing committee and the project manager under the two-party fully governed project oversight model.

members and project managers frequently observed that projects sponsored by any given governing committee were often interconnected. Individual projects commonly supported strategic goals of the organization that were related and interdependent. Projects also frequently depended upon resources (human and budgetary) that needed to be shared in a balanced, efficient, and highly choreographed way. The decisions made for one project by a governing committee might therefore have profound effects on the other projects under the committee's direction. As a result, governing committees needed always to be prepared to consider the potential impact of their decisions on each of the projects that they were sponsoring (even the most predictable and routine of them).

Given these circumstances, stakeholders observed that any organization's governing committees would have a finite "capacity" for efficient and effective review, analysis, and oversight of its projects. It seems logical to expect that under the two-party fully governed project oversight model a governing committee's capacity for effective oversight could become strained and eventually exceeded. And it seems obvious that a committee would be at higher risk for this to happen when it assumes responsibility for overseeing larger numbers of uncertain and complex projects, and when its members assume responsibilities for simultaneously managing bigger line function organizations.

PROBLEMS WITH BACKGROUND DOCUMENTS

Let's examine the specific stories that led stakeholders to observe that their governing committees were becoming less responsive to their project teams' needs and more reliant on their project managers for information and perspective.

One of the most commonly mentioned sources of programmaticist concern emerged during discussions about the purpose and length of the "background documents" that project managers were usually required to generate prior to review meetings with governing committees. Programmaticists usually acknowledged that background documents had initially served an important purpose in their organizations: They had historically been used to provide managing committees with timely updates on their project's progress, summaries of newly emerging information about project outputs or outcomes, and analyses that supported the team's recommendations and decisions. (One programmaticist referred to them as "press releases" that communicated results and perspectives in advance of project review meetings.) Programmaticists generally agreed that background documents could contribute to the success of meetings held under the two-party fully governed project oversight model because they provided new information that was critical to the decision-making process. They indicated that the "return on investment" for creating such documents could be high, because providing new project information to executive stakeholders in this way enabled them to proactively raise and address critical issues and questions. Background documents enabled executives to be better prepared to participate in an efficient decision-making meeting. Moreover, programmaticists observed, the act of writing such documents often helped to clarify the team's thinking about a given question or issue.

It became apparent during interviews, however, that not all programmaticists retained a positive view about the value of background documents. Many thought that the return on investment for creating them had decreased over time. And interestingly, those who felt this way were more likely to be using a fully governed project oversight model in large organizations, pursuing large numbers of projects, or managing projects that were highly uncertain or complex. These programmaticists often complained that their governing committees expected too much from their background documents. The committees expected that background documents would include extensive descriptions of the projects—descriptions that included (for example) summaries of a project's established strategy and plans, its logic and assumptions, its history and progress, its timing and budget, its analyses and recommendations, and (in the words of one interviewee) "anything else they might want to refer to before, during, or after the latest committee meeting." Programmaticists reported that their committees seemed to be relying on background documents to remind themselves of previous discussions and agreements—using them more as standalone "reference" documents than as "press releases" with emerging news. And programmaticists often doubted that their committees were diligent in reading these documents: Why else would they also be asked to present summaries of the documents as part of their project's review meetings?

When programmaticists were asked why they felt that their documents had become so burdensome, they gave varied answers. Each answer, at its heart, seemed to suggest that it was primarily due to a dilution of their managing committee's focus. It was due to their managing committee's need to "manage too much" in an expanding two-party fully governed project oversight system. In their opinions, governing committees requested lengthy background documents in order to use them to "catch up" on a project before critical decisions needed to be made. They were remedial. They used them as a means "to re-learn what they should already know" (to quote one particularly exasperated programmaticist).

Many programmaticists lamented that their organizations' increasing reliance on background documents provided a good example of how, as their organizations had grown, the nature of the programmaticist's job had changed. Programmaticists were spending more and more time creating documents (which were project outputs only indirectly related to the "parent" project goals) so as to increase the likelihood of efficiently getting appropriate governing committee decisions (which were project outcomes indirectly related to the parent project goals). Programmaticists felt that they were, in effect, focusing more of their energies managing document-and-presentation-writing subprojects within their parent project. And they felt that their performance was too often being judged by how well they managed their documentation and presentation sub-projects, and not often enough by how well they managed their parent projects. *They were being judged increasingly by how well they enabled their managing committees to function, instead of by how well they enabled their project teams to function.* As organizational athletes, they wanted to spend more time worrying about those in the game, and less time worrying about those on the sidelines.

During discussions about background documents, many stakeholders (programmaticists and executives alike) had stories (sometimes long stories) about steps they had taken to ease the burden. Many of their organizations had spent a lot of time (and money, if they had used consultants) trying to streamline and improve their project documentation requirements. And many stakeholders reported that their organizations had made progress in doing so. Surely it was important that they had; documentation is critical to any project, and managing it effectively is vitally important. However, none of the stakeholders felt that their organizations had completely resolved the issue. The most positive of them seemed to feel that the problem was "less bad," and that "less bad" was the best that they could expect. But is it?

I have spent considerable time in this chapter on the subject of project background documents. I chose that subject because almost every stakeholder I met with had an opinion on it and a story to tell about it. (I presume the same is true for those who would read this book.) Each of those stories, it seemed, ended with a stakeholder expressing a degree of understanding about their organization's needs for background documents and their overall importance. Each of them seemed to end in the same way—with a tone of resignation (not unlike conversations we might have about the importance and the exasperation associated with paying our taxes). Each of the stories seemed to focus on a problem that was, in the end, not completely solvable.

PROBLEMS WITH OPERATIONAL DECISION MAKING

Having talked to many (probably too many) of my colleagues about "the problem of background documents" I cannot help but conclude that it may remain forever unsolvable—at least, that is, if we continue to think of it as the *problem*. But after hours of discussions, I have now come to believe that most of us are thinking of it in the wrong way. It is not so much a problem, as it is a *symptom*. It is a symptom of a much bigger problem that the managing committees in most organizations are more reluctant to acknowledge or to discuss (or to entrust to the care of consultants). The real problem, it would seem, is this:

> As organizations using the two-party fully governed project oversight model grow and as they pursue increasingly uncertain and complex projects, their senior managers find it increasingly difficult and eventually impossible to stay abreast of all the project-related information that is critical to their ability to make good decisions.
>
> Moreover . . .
>
> When the senior managers who sit on governing committees cannot stay abreast of project-related information that is critical to decision making, the two-party fully governed project oversight model becomes very inefficient.

To an athletic programmaticist, this can be very exasperating.

It is easy to identify examples of managing committee inefficiency within the two-party fully governed project oversight model. They can be found in the many stories told by programmaticists and executives from modern organizations—stories that revealed several other "symptoms" of this same problem. Each example appears to have emerged as busy managing committees struggled to fully govern their growing portfolios of uncertain projects using a two-party oversight model. Let us consider a few more of these symptoms as expressed in stakeholder interviews. (They will become important in subsequent chapters.)

During discussions, many stakeholders reported that as their organizations had begun to support more numerous projects, larger projects, and projects facing a significant amount of operational uncertainty, their managing committees were finding it increasingly difficult to make operational decisions and implement operational changes in response to project team recommendations. According to some stakeholders, their "managing committees had become indecisive," and that was a problem. But was it *the* problem?

Pressed to examine issues with operational (in)decision making, stakeholders observed that the analyses of a project's operational strategy, plans, and options were often quite complex. The best of these analyses, even when presented in the clearest of ways, were often difficult to adequately understand during the course of a governing committee meeting. Such analyses might have been exquisitely described in the project's background document, but it was rare that background documents could be written in such a way as to satisfy all of a committee's informational and interactive needs. Adequately detailed analyses of operational issues often required the combined use of data-filled background documents and well-crafted presentations that together supported the discussion and consideration of a room full of perspectives. Presentations of these analyses required the production of a well-staged event, choreographed to produce a common conclusion that was satisfactory to (almost) everyone. They required the employment of programmaticists who were more specifically focused on the development of advanced writing, presentation, and meeting-management skills for success.

But even in the best of organizations, project presentations most often focused on a carefully prepared (albeit complicated) examination of what would be "ideal" for the project at hand. This was only half of the picture that needed to be considered by stakeholders who sat on a governing committee. Stakeholders observed that the conversations in governing committee meetings quickly expanded into discussions of what would be "ideal" for an organization trying to balance the needs of many other projects and its other operational commitments—each with their own needs and assumptions and strategic considerations. And as project numbers and uncertainty expanded linearly, the operational complexity of these considerations seemed to expand more exponentially.

Governing committees—even those with advanced capabilities for tracking operational information—could easily become overwhelmed with the factors to be considered for each decision. And the result (as attested to by many stakeholders) could have profound effects on an organization. Sometimes managing committees (much like trial judges) would indicate that they would take additional time to consider the implications of their decisions before "rendering judgment." At other times, they would indicate that they needed to consult with other stakeholders who might be impacted, usually in follow-up committee meetings that made the decision-making process a more iterative than linear process. And at other times, the governing committee might elect to make a decision, only to reconsider it at a later time (when they became more aware of its unintended consequences).

The net result, most stakeholders agreed, was a reduction in the overall efficiency of the two-party fully governed project oversight model. The real problem, it seemed, was that an increase in the number of projects sponsored by a governing committee, and an increase in the uncertainty associated with each of those projects had resulted in a dramatic (exponential?) increase in the operational complexity being managed by the organization. Identifying the best operational strategy and plan for the project and for the organization had become a highly complex task that would benefit from the expertise of a professional with specific talents and training in the optimization of operational efficiency. Under the two-party fully governed project oversight model, where project managers were typically expected to follow Traditionalist definitions of a programmaticist's role and responsibilities, and governing committees assumed responsibility and authority for approving operational change, it was not always clear who was best prepared to fill that role.

It could be observed from the input gathered during stakeholder discussions that as organizations had grown larger, as they pursued more projects, and as their projects had grown more complex, programmaticists had assumed more responsibility for ensuring that their organizations' governing committees were adequately prepared to govern—and this had itself become an increasingly complex task. The nature of the relationship between the project manager and the governing committee had changed; in a seemingly ironic reversal of roles, programmaticists had become responsible for enabling their managing committees to function effectively. Increasingly, programmaticists reported that they were expected to demonstrate professional skills befitting an Operationalist programmaticist while being professionally constrained to function in a Traditionalist role. They were expected to demonstrate advanced skills in facilitating the management of operational uncertainty and complexity, while not empowered to assume authority in managing the same. Along the way, the purported efficiency of the two-party fully governed project oversight model seemed to have suffered, and pro-grammaticists become dissatisfied with their organizations' recognition of their professional roles.

PROBLEMS WITH STRATEGIC DECISION MAKING

The stories told by stakeholders about issues they encountered with their two-party fully governed project oversight models were not limited to examples of *operational* inefficiency. They also revealed evidence that as organizations had grown, and as they began to support more numerous projects, larger projects, and projects facing a significant amount of strategic uncertainty, their governing committees had found it increasingly difficult to make timely *strategic* decisions. In particular, stakeholders suggested, governing committees seemed less capable of agreeing to strategic changes that became necessary as a consequence of newly emerging project outcomes. During interviews, programmaticists commonly observed that their *governing committees had become less agile in responding to project outcomes*. They had, in the words of one, become "only periodically engaged" in monitoring and managing the strategies of their individual projects. And as a result, they were having more difficulty coming up to speed when their teams needed quick responses. That (by itself) was a problem. But there was more. Some programmaticists went further; they went so far as to indicate that their *governing committees had become less capable of responding insightfully to their projects' outcomes and strategic oversight needs*.

Let's examine their comments on the engagement and agility of governing committees that use the two-party fully governed project oversight model.

When asked to discuss their governing committee's strategic oversight of projects within this model, many stakeholders indicated that the *initial* strategies and plans of their projects were usually predicated upon the approval of carefully examined strategic assumptions. They observed that their governing committees' reviews of these assumptions were most often based on the collective wisdom (knowledge, skills, experience, and insights) of committee members, team members, and a sometimes-large group of external advisors with whom they may have consulted. They generally felt that this first review was thorough. It included careful consideration of how best to manage the outcome and (sometimes) environmental uncertainties and complexities that might be expected to be associated with their projects.

As projects proceeded, however, programmaticists reported that it was common for governing committees to be only intermittently engaged in monitoring and managing their strategies. Committees seemed to presume that a project strategy could be managed with much less consultation; they presumed that the strategy was (in the words of one interviewee) "stable and fixed." Programmaticists observed, however, that for uncertain outcome-based projects (or projects being pursued in an uncertain organizational or external environment) this was too often not true. As uncertain projects proceeded, their project teams often learned information that led to changes in their strategies. Sometimes they were big changes.

Under fully governed project oversight models it is the project team's responsibility to report on new project outcomes, to monitor whether the original project assumptions are still reasonable, and to call for re-analysis of a project's strategy whenever it is appropriate. And it is important for governing committee members to remain aware of any factors that might influence the project's strategy, so as to be prepared to respond to them. The model requires that governing committee members stand ever at-the-ready to contribute their wisdom and to agilely re-engage with the project team and with advisors whose insights they may have previously considered.

Programmaticists observed, however, that as the oversight responsibilities of governing committees expanded and their attention was divided among more projects, and as the functional groups of managing committee members grew to demand more of their managerial attention, it became much more difficult for them to quickly re-engage with projects when new outcomes were achieved. Their attention could be harder to command, and they weren't always at-the-ready. That presented challenges. Adapting a "game plan" during a game is much more difficult than formulating the plan before the game has begun. It requires much greater speed and agility, and a superior degree of athleticism. And it requires readiness.

Organizational stakeholders generally observed that efficiently examining new project strategies became much more difficult for their governing committee members as their organizations grew and they sponsored larger numbers of projects, each of which might require attention at a moment's notice. It also became much more difficult as the uncertainty associated with each of those projects increased. They reported that their governing committee members had trouble remembering the nuanced assumptions that had been made when authorizing the strategies of each of their projects. They began to overlook the fervency of input that they had received from colleagues or consultants who had previously advised them. And as a result, governing committees could (once again) be observed to depend more and more heavily on their programmaticists to "remind" them of that which was critical for effective strategic decision making.

The observations that stakeholders made about their governing committees' "capacity" for retaining and considering critical strategic information were reminiscent of the observations described above for operational information: As governing committees sponsored more and more projects, or as they sponsored projects that were more and more uncertain, they began to rely more and more heavily on their programmaticists to support them. Programmaticists became more directly responsible for enabling their governing committees to function effectively. Governing committees increasingly found that they needed their programmaticists to have the professional skills and focus of an Inclusivist, even though they were organizationally constrained to function in a Traditionalist role. Some members of governing committees began to expect their programmaticists to demonstrate more advanced insights about the management of outcome and environmental uncertainty and complexity, even though this might not have been a skill set that was emphasized for traditional project managers working in a fully governed project oversight model.

In this context, it is easy to understand why individual committee member perspectives on the ideal roles and responsibilities of a programmaticist would shift further (and become less consistent). Their individual views on the ideal roles and responsibilities of a programmaticist would be significantly influenced by their individual needs for strategic or technical support from their programmaticists.

It was common for programmaticists to observe that the expansion of their governing committees' project oversight responsibilities had dramatically diminished their committees' efficiency in managing uncertainty and complexity that resulted from project outcomes; the oversight-by-committee models used by most organizations were neither agile nor responsive. Their common reliance on background documents, formal presentations, and bureaucratic committee-based processes for making decisions was inherently slow even under the best of conditions, when decisions could be made after a single governance meeting. And, programmaticists reported, the committees were often unprepared to make decisions in a single meeting. Too often, committees felt that they needed more time or more information. And when that happened, decision making was turned into an iterative multi-meeting process that could slow projects to a crawl. Athletic programmaticists became all the more exasperated by that. Their "game clocks" were ticking.

Each of these concerns is clearly significant. However, the additional opinions expressed by some programmaticists (albeit a smaller number) were perhaps even more worrisome.

UNSATISFIED NEEDS FOR EXPERTISE

Some of the more vocal programmaticists whom I had the opportunity to interview believed that their governing committees had also become "less capable" of responding insightfully to their projects' outcomes and strategic oversight needs. They opined that as their organizations had become comfortable with the two-party fully governed project oversight model, they had begun to use it to oversee a wider variety of initiatives—often under the supervision of governing committees whose membership was expanded (to reflect the greater breadth of its responsibilities) but whose backgrounds were less specific to the subject matter of any given project. These programmaticists expressed concern that in an attempt to achieve greater "bureaucratic efficiency" by collecting project oversight responsibilities under larger, commonly administered committees, their governing committees had evolved to have a more "generalist" culture. The governance committees had more often sponsored projects where only a small fraction of the committee had project-specific subject matter expertise, or where the technical, strategic, and environmental insights of committee members were limited. As a result, they lamented, the burden that programmaticists carried for "enabling" their committees to function effectively was increased all the more, and it became much more difficult to assure that their management-by-committee process would result in the approval of the ideal project strategy.

During the course of my interviews, it was interesting to solicit opinions from governing committee members about the above-mentioned perspectives (which were voiced most adamantly by programmaticists). Most committee members considered the perspectives very thoughtfully. And after doing so, it was common for them to acknowledge that their increasing reliance on programmaticists, their shifting views of the programmaticist's role, and the inherent inefficiency of their two-party fully governed project oversight models were important points for further discussion. However, they often objected to the suggestion that *their* committees were not capable of effectively overseeing the projects that they sponsored. (One might understand why they would!) They observed that they were responsible for defining and sponsoring their organizations' projects, and for authorizing their continued support. They felt that their high-level professional skills, knowledge, and experience were critically needed by their organizations' projects, and they were often reluctant to agree that their governing committees should exert less control over the strategic or operational direction of their sponsored projects.

Committee members would often acknowledge that they were not experts in the subject matter of every project that they sponsored. However, they noted that they actively sought external input when they felt that they needed additional technical, strategic, and environmental expertise. They felt that they were effective in garnering important insights, sometimes by establishing additional organizational processes and controls that supported their fully governed project management model. (We will discuss these processes and controls, and the impact of their introduction, in much greater detail in the next chapter.)

Interestingly, numerous committee members eventually observed that (in the traditions of Industrial Age organizations) members of their respective oversight committees were "principally" responsible for managing their organizations' line functions. They viewed that as their "full time" job. Many had ascended to their positions by virtue of their abilities to effectively guide and manage technical and operational matters related to their line function responsibilities. As their organizations had grown, that had become a more full-time job. And in moments of candor, some went so far as to indicate that they were not interested in becoming more personally accountable for managing the cross-functional strategies or the cross-functional complexities that were the focus of their organizations' projects. They were satisfied with assuming "advisory" or "supervisory" roles in the management of cross-functional strategy and complexities. Tellingly, many committee members also noted that projects are by definition temporary endeavors. They viewed their line function roles as more permanent—and (also in the traditions of Industrial Age organizational models) as providing a firmer foundation for their long-term professional security and success.

These views of managing committee members are completely understandable. In the historical context of the traditional, first-generation, two-party fully governed project oversight model, one might agree that they are natural and predictable. But they do raise another question:

> Could problems related to the scalability and overload of the two-party fully governed project oversight model be addressed?

The answer, of course, is "it depends"—this time on one's definition of success.

A SEARCH FOR SOLUTIONS

During interviews with governing committee members and program-maticists, I had the opportunity to discuss many examples of processes and controls that had been introduced by organizations to improve their two-party fully governed project oversight models. The examples were similar in nature, though they varied in the details of their implementation. And both groups acknowledged that to varying degrees, *many of these processes had been successful in addressing the specific needs for which they were introduced.* Moreover, most of the people I had interviewed expressed willingness to introduce new processes that might further enhance the oversight of projects.

Yet over the course of many interviews, it was hard to find stakeholders from modern organizations who believed that their needs had been fully satisfied, or that their managing system was now "optimized." It was hard to find large, modern organizations whose roll-call of pro-grammaticists did not still include significant numbers of Exasperados. If these new processes and controls were effective in resolving the issues that they were intended to address, then why should so many organizations (each filled with smart and highly motivated people) report that they continue to be dissatisfied?

As I interviewed these stakeholders, I could not help but to think about crown vetch (*Coronilla varia*).

Crown vetch is a low-growing perennial vine introduced to the United States from Europe in the 1950s. It was valued for its ability to prevent erosion by establishing a dense network of roots within the soil, and for its summer-long production of pleasant pink, rose, or lilac flowers. It was held in high regard by government transportation agencies, who planted it along the nation's roadsides to (1) stabilize the soil, (2) beautify the highways, and (3) reduce the cost of roadside maintenance. It served those purposes very well.

The crown vetch vine also grows well in other parts of suburban America, spreading readily via its underground roots, surface rhizomes, and seeds that remain viable for up to fifteen years. Homeowners soon observed that it happily spread to garden areas that were already stable and attractive, and that otherwise required little maintenance. Once there, it (1) destabilized the horticultural environment and (2) displaced indigenous plants that were often more beautiful. (Apparently, what looks pleasant at 65 miles per hour looks scruffy at backyard speed.) Because crown vetch becomes so strongly rooted, it is extremely hard to get rid of. In the suburbs, crown vetch cannot quite be considered a scourge (on the scale, for example, of kudzu), because it can be held at bay when it is important to do so. It just takes (3) a lot of maintenance. Thus, the three unintended consequences of planting crown vetch may be perversely opposite to the three intended consequences. Yet, because it satisfies specific needs, it continues to be introduced in various environments.

To assess the *overall* impact of crown vetch, one must consider the complex implications of *all* of its more local effects. The value that one perceives crown vetch to have depends very much on his or her individual point of view, and his or her definition of success.

I dislike crown vetch (and know far too much about it) because it has now completely overtaken a beautiful garden that I had spent years carefully cultivating and that, because of its steep terrain and densely blooming but fragile flowers, was very hard to weed. Crown vetch has now completely overrun that garden, and its small lilac blooms, while pleasing to some, are merely a reminder to me of the better result that I had really been seeking.

The organizational lesson to be learned from crown vetch is simple: The net benefits of new processes or controls depend upon one's current and longer-term needs. Within a larger "environmental system" they should be measured holistically, based on a broad assessment of their intended and unintended consequences.

We will observe in the next chapter that the seemingly simple processes and controls that had been introduced to enhance the oversight of projects via first-generation two-party fully governed programmatic systems were often effective in addressing the specific issues for which they were introduced. However, they often had other (unintended) effects on the oversight and management of projects within organizations.

CHAPTER 7

Adaptations of the Traditional Two-Party Fully Governed Project Oversight Model

STAKEHOLDER STORIES

I found it curious that in discussion after discussion, executives and programmaticists were very quick to state that their organizations used a two-party fully governed model to oversee their projects. The principles and assumptions of the two-party fully governed model often seemed to define their programmatic mindset—the model provided a seemingly common frame of reference that they applied "by default" when talking about the respective roles of their governing committees and programmaticists. As those discussions wound on, however, it became clear that many of their organizations' project oversight systems, while *derived* from the two-party fully governed project oversight model, were actually quite *different* from the relatively simple model that we described in the previous chapter. Their oversight models had evolved significantly over the years. I have had the opportunity to discuss the evolution of their models with many organizational stakeholders, and their stories are interesting.

The stakeholders' stories often began with a description of the presumably unique problems that were being faced by their organizations as they sought to manage projects using the two-party fully governed project oversight model. Often, their stories were about how their models seemed to have "failed" them in some way—about how their models had not sufficiently ensured that project-related decisions would be made in a consistent and appropriately informed manner. Each of their stories went on to describe how their organizations had introduced changes to the model—usually in the form of new processes and practices that their project teams would be required to follow. Most of the stories ended with the confirmation that benefits had been realized from the changes, and that their organizations' specific needs had been effectively filled.

If one probed and then listened carefully enough, however, it was clear that the stories had not ended completely. Almost as a footnote, stakeholders would often observe that their organizations were now dealing with new and different problems. And, if one examined these problems closely enough, it was clear that many of them were actually unanticipated and unintended consequences of the changes that had been made previously. Stakeholder stories had sequels; they led to more stories that may or may not yet be complete. Each of these stories, in its details, seemed at first to be unique. Yet most of them, in their plot-lines, were actually quite similar.

Most of the stories told by organizational stakeholders were about how, over time, their organizations had expanded their "two party" project oversight models to include additional project reviews. They were stories about how project teams were now required to have their results, analyses, needs, options, and proposals pre-reviewed by what we will call *secondary governance or review committees* before those teams would be allowed to present them to their "primary" governing committees (as defined in the two-party project oversight model). And usually, they were stories about how executive managers (and project teams) had increasingly relied on the results of these pre-reviews to help them examine the operational and strategic implications of project team proposals, or to provide some assurance that the project teams had considered *all* the perspectives of the line function stakeholders and *all* the implications of the project team's recommendations.

The stories about pre-reviews were rich with details about the organization's use of newly defined processes for managing project operations and strategy. Many of these processes became important to the eventual success of project teams and their organizations. (As we will soon discuss, meetings held with secondary governance and review committees can provide a good forum for working through issues related to operational, outcome, or stakeholder uncertainty and complexity.) However, I also found these processes to be interesting for a different reason: When observed through the lens of Chapter 6, they were recognizeable as stories about the most common adaptations of the two-party fully governed project oversight model. They were stories about adaptive changes that were often triggered by the need to more effectively manage uncertainty and complexity in organizations that were (1) growing significantly, (2) pursuing larger numbers of projects, or (3) pursuing projects that are increasingly large, uncertain, and complex.

When seeking to advance one's understanding of programmatic systems it is especially helpful to examine organizational changes through the lens of these three factors. Doing so provides valuable insights about how the relationships between governing committees and the programmaticists who manage their programs may change as organizations grow under a (presumed) two-party fully governed project oversight model.

ORGANIZATIONAL GROWTH

The Benefits of Growth

Executives and programmaticists are clearly happy to talk about the growth of their organizations. As a group, they point proudly to that growth as a sign (even as proof) of the success of their business strategies and their organizations' current processes for managing ongoing projects. They view organizational growth as a key component of success, according to a simple logic:

Success in managing projects has contributed (or led) to the success of their organizations; success of their organizations has led to organizational growth; organizational growth has enabled the pursuit of more and bigger projects; and the pursuit of more and bigger projects can be expected to further stimulate success of the organization. See Figure 7.1.

In interviews and discussions, many executives confirm that they welcome the progressive expansion of their functional groups. They observe

Figure 7.1   Project success's impact on organizational success.

that the expansion of their functional groups has (historically) improved their groups' abilities to support both project-based and operational activities within their areas of responsibility. They believe that expansion has increased the value that their group delivers to its organization, and they note that it has enabled their group to advance its core technologies and capabilities, and its readiness for its future. It was unusual to meet a leader who was opposed to expanding his or her functional group's "empire." After all, expansion of their groups had the additional advantage of increasing their groups' "footprint" and prominence within their organizations.

Responding to Growth-Related Challenges

Line function leaders were keenly aware of the challenges that group expansion had presented. They commonly observed, for example, that their larger groups' involvement in more work activities had made managing work schedules and resource allocations significantly more complicated. It had also resulted in the need to establish bigger, more bureaucratic, often-layered, and somewhat "compartmentalized" management hierarchies within their departments.

It was interesting to explore with line function leaders how these hierarchies had evolved; most line function leaders were happy to describe (in sometimes excruciating detail) the successive changes that they had implemented and the results of those changes. Their descriptions seemed logical, understandable, and (to a former executive) hauntingly familiar. Most often, executives would explain that their organizations had managed growth by developing, within each group, extensions of the bureaucratic management systems common to many Industrial Age organizations. They had organized their groups into hierarchically "nested" subgroups, each reporting to the one above. The creation of subgroups served two primary purposes: (1) it broke large groups into smaller units that could each be more easily monitored and managed by individual leaders or managers, and (2) it grouped together professionals with common specialties or complementary areas of expertise, to enhance their professional capabilities, development, and learning (see Figure 7.2). Executives reported that the creation of such subgroups had enabled line function leaders to manage the progressive expansion of their groups in a highly scalable way.

The growth of organizational line functions had in most cases been managed by applying traditional Industrial Age organizing principles— the same principles that had provided a foundation for first-generation

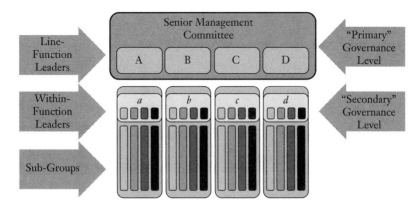

Figure 7.2   The organization of line functions into subgroups.

programmatic management systems, the two-party fully governed project oversight model, and Traditionalist notions of the programmaticist's role. It is understandable that it would be managed this way given organizations' previous success with that approach. Industrial Age management systems were familiar to executives and programmaticists alike. Programmaticists had developed a formal means of "mapping" the responsibilities of subgroups (and their members) as part of their project monitoring and control processes, using what were commonly referred to as "organizational breakdown structures."

In discussions and interviews, most line function executives reported that the formation of these subgroups was highly valuable to them. It enabled them to bring together staff with common interests, training, and responsibilities, and it helped them to manage staff development and work completion in a highly focused and efficient way. Moreover, it enabled them to establish more formal "within function" support and oversight structures responsible for monitoring the operations, strategy, performance, training, compliance, or safety of the line function's growing numbers of employees. Most importantly, it enabled them to delegate certain responsibilities for oversight of line function activities to newly created review committees that assumed responsibility for monitoring the activities and commitments of their line function organizations (see Figure 7.3).

Many line function executives indicated that this was a critically important step for them, because it enabled them to "assign" responsibilities for certain elements of project oversight to other leaders within their functional organizations: It enabled them to delegate some of the project oversight responsibilities that they needed to satisfy under

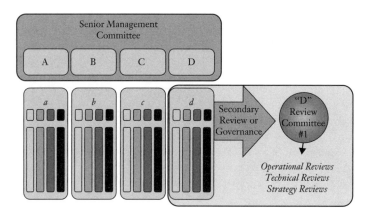

Figure 7.3   The emergence of line function review committees.

the two-party fully governed oversight model. Delegation of these responsibilities relieved them of some of their burden for monitoring and managing project-related activities whithout requiring them to give up decision-making authority over those activities. Line function executives reported that delegation of responsibilities provided a solution to their governing committee "overload" issue.

This was an important development. It was the "crown vetch" that, once planted and well-established, addressed many of the problems that had been associated with growth of their organizations. It provided a solution they needed; as the size of their line function groups had increased, line function leaders reported that they needed to spend more time on oversight and management of within function activities, and proportionately less time on the oversight of cross-functional projects. The ability to delegate certain elements of project review and oversight to line function subcommittees helped line function leaders to manage the expansion of their workload.

Operational, Technical, and Strategic Review Committees

It was interesting to explore how line function leaders delegated elements of their project oversight responsibilities. Line function review committees reportedly served up to three purposes relating to the management of uncertainty and complexity:

Many line function leaders had created *operational review committees* to help manage the scheduling, staffing, financing, and conduct of line function work activities. Operational review committees were expected to manage *operational uncertainty and complexity* associated with the work being conducted by their departments. They were also expected to provide a venue for managing any *stakeholder uncertainty and complexity* that might arise as members of their departments balanced their needs to support both project-related activities and everyday operations. Operational review committees tended to be focused on managing uncertainty and complexity related to the efficient generation of expected line function *outputs*.

Line function leaders often also formed *technical review committees* to help monitor, review, and manage the delivery of intended benefits and value from line function activities. Line function committees with technical review responsibilities focused more specifically on managing *outcome uncertainty and complexity*. They also provided a mechanism for managing any *stakeholder uncertainty and complexity* that might arise as department members assessed the suitability of outcomes, particularly in relation to their needs to be responsive to *environmental (external) uncertainty and complexity*.

Finally, line function leaders sometimes also formed *strategic review committees* responsible for defining and prioritizing the strategic goals of the line function. Strategic review committees tended to focus on the management of *environmental uncertainty and complexity* relating to the strategic decisions being made by members of the line function. They sometimes focused, for example, on the department's need to develop new "core competencies" important to several projects, for filling the needs of other organizational groups (such as finance or human resources), or for ensuring the continued growth of line function capabilities.

During interviews and discussions with line function heads, many reported that their departments had initially formed single review committees to conduct a blend of operational, technical, and strategic reviews. However, many executives observed that the committee members who were charged with conduct of these three kinds of reviews might need to have quite different skills, knowledge, or experience. Individual committee members were sometimes more appropriately suited for one but not the other types of reviews. Many executives reported that, as a consequence, as their line functions had continued to grow and as the workload in each area had expanded, they had found it beneficial to form more than one review committee—each to fulfill a specific purpose (or a selected combination of purposes). Executives from large organizations reported that it was common for departments in their

organizations to establish two, three, or more secondary review committees within a given line function. Each might be principally responsible for monitoring and managing different areas of responsibility and
different types of uncertainty and complexity. Line functions in large
organizations had, in a sense, become organizations in and of themselves—essentially, they were in the business of running an organization
within an organization.

When asked to comment on the effectiveness of their review committees, line function leaders usually responded quite positively. (It is understandable that they might, since they were personally responsible for their
committee's effectiveness, and since it was within their power to make any
changes that were necessary to improve committee performance.) They
reported that the specialized expertise that their committees had developed for overseeing their line functions' operations were critical to their
groups' abilities to assess, monitor, and resolve uncertainty and complexity
on a larger scale. And they acknowledged that they relied on the review
committees to provide line function leadership with department-specific
perspectives on project-related issues (see Figure 7.4).

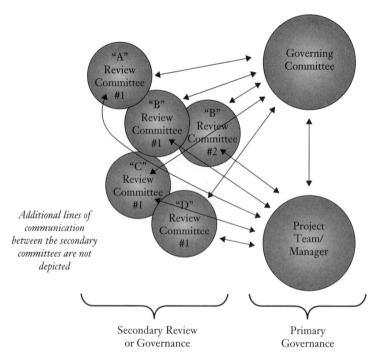

**Figure 7.4   Lines of communication between a project team and its pri-
mary and secondary oversight and review committees.**

Their comments made it clear that line function executives depended heavily upon their line function review committees for support in their roles overseeing cross-functional projects as part of their organization's two-party project oversight models. Line function review committees, like the programmaticists we discussed in Chapter 6, were important enablers of the line function executives who had decision-making roles on the primary governance committees responsible for project oversight. Like crown vetch, they were effective in serving their intended purpose. And for that reason, we would be wise to examine their potential unintended or undesirable consequences.

The Unintended Consequences of Review Committees

The best perspectives on the unintended and undesirable consequences of the line function review committees were voiced during interviews and discussions with organizational programmaticists. They often noted that the introduction of such committees had significant impact on the processes that project teams were asked to follow, and also on the dynamics of their teams' interactions with organizational stakeholders and governing committees.

Programmaticists commonly observed that to support line function leaders in their governance of projects, line function review committees needed to review a project's strategy, status, outcomes, and recommendations well in advance of decision-making meetings with the project team's primary governance committee. Only then would review committees have sufficient time to inform their line function leaders of the results of the review, their own perspectives on the issues at hand, and their recommendations. Programmaticists often noted that preparing for these reviews was a process-focused endeavor that significantly increased their teams' workload; in large organizations, project teams often needed to schedule, prepare for, and participate in several review meetings with the subcommittees of the line functions that supported them. Each of these meetings had specific and unique requirements for background documents and presentations. Each might require pre-meetings or rehearsals with additional line function stakeholders. And as a result, programmaticists commonly reported that their teams might be asked to spend weeks presenting their views and recommendations in numerous line function venues before their teams' "official" meetings with their primary governance committees. It was common for programmaticists to complain that line function review committee processes had grown to be increasingly (and unnecessarily) onerous.

It was not lost on programmaticists that these review meetings could also be very helpful to their teams. The meetings could provide the teams with guaranteed access to line function stakeholders whose knowledge and insights were important to the team's final recommendations or decisions. They could afford teams opportunities to uncover and examine elements of uncertainty that the team needed to face, and to (hopefully) find solutions for some of the team's complex issues. However, programmaticists reported that too often these meetings involved a bigger group of stakeholders than was necessary, each with different degrees of interest, knowledge, influence, and preparedness. Keeping such a group informed of project-related information and issues further increased the workload of project managers and leaders. To many, the benefits of their interactions with line function review committees seemed to come at an unacceptably high cost of their time, energy, and resources.

But programmaticists also had another, larger concern.

Programmaticists universally noted that line function review processes had significant and usually underappreciated effects on the dynamics of decision making within their organizations. They observed that over time, senior line function executives came to rely on their review committees more and more to participate in the decision-making process. Executives who sat on primary governance committees began to expect—and even to require—that project teams would attain endorsement and approval of their recommendations from the line function review committees. Programmaticists observed that over time, line function executives who sat on governing committees became increasingly reluctant to approve project team recommendations over the objections of their review committees. This had profound effects on the dynamic behaviors of the committee members and stakeholders responsible for decision making within their fully governed project oversight models.

The first and perhaps most obvious effect that this had on the decision-making process was that it changed the organization's fully governed project oversight model into something more than a two-party model. It enabled line function review committees to assume (in practice) a *governance* role that was independent of the primary governance committee. (If review committee endorsement was necessary for a governance committee member's endorsement, and that endorsement was necessary for a governance committee decision, then the review committee was, in essence, acting as a governance committee.) The two-party model, whether by explicit intent or as an indirect consequence of executive leadership's behavior, was functioning as a *multi-party fully governed project oversight model*, in which the approval of several independent review committees was required if project teams were to get their recommendations approved.

Programmaticists observed that the shift to a multi-party project oversight model often occurred slowly. It was, in a sense, an evolutionary change that occurred as line function review committees' independence and influence grew, as their organizations grew, and as the line function leaders who had authorized them came to rely on them more for decision-making advice. The change occurred in an environment that allowed independent development of diverse committee structures and processes. Line function leaders responded differently to the unique needs of their individual groups; they adaptively changed their organizational structures in the ways that best enabled them to survive and to thrive.

Given the gradual appearance of line function review committees in many organizations, it is understandable that programmaticists and line function executives alike would remain comfortable in their *beliefs* that their organizations were still following the two-party fully governed project oversight model. After all, project proposals were still presented by project teams and officially approved by their primary governance committees. But in fact, their management models had slowly evolved into something that was quite a bit different and much more complex. Their organizations had transitioned into the use of a multi-party fully governed project oversight model, in which secondary review committees had (wittingly or unwittingly) assumed the role of secondary governance committees.

Impact on Decision Making and Programmatic Complexity

The *de facto* emergence of secondary governance committees profoundly affected the dynamics of complexity management and issue resolution relating to projects. Programmaticists noted that under the original tenets of the two-party fully governed project oversight model, they might expect that emerging issues could be brought to primary governance committee meetings for timely discussion and rapid resolution. Each of the stakeholders involved in the meeting would have been expected (indeed, required) to be knowledgeable about the perspectives of colleagues who worked within their line functions and about the potential impact of any decisions that might be made. Each would be expected to work together in the primary governance committee meeting to examine the issues at hand and the options for their resolution, and to dynamically negotiate and compromise in whatever ways were necessary to find solutions. Under the two-party system, decision making was expected to occur at a discrete time: when a project and its executive sponsors (its governing committee) came together for that purpose. The engagement of stakeholders—and the effective management of stakeholder uncertainty and complexity—was largely accomplished through dynamic interactions between individual stakeholders before and during the governance meeting.

With the advent of review committees and their subsequent assumption of the role of "secondary governance committees," programmaticists reported that there were dramatic changes in how issues were resolved within their organizations. Each line function review committee meeting, held in isolation, became an "event" that had the potential to end with the establishment of assumptions and stakeholder agreements that were specific to a given committee's perspectives at a particular moment in time. The outcomes of review committee reviews were subject to uncertain (sometimes unknowable) group dynamics that unfolded unpredictably during each review "event." These events were more difficult to manage (control) than interactions with individual stakeholders. Programmaticists reported that they often felt that they could not wield enough influence in the review committee environment to assure that a cross-functional project's needs were prioritized appropriately to achieve its desired outcomes. Line function review committees were more likely to prioritize decisions that optimized line function (versus cross-functional) performance. They seemed to be occurring within functional "silos."

Programmaticists also observed that additional issues arose when the assumptions and agreements from review committee meetings were communicated formally (for example, to line function heads who were members of the primary governance committee) as part of updates and minutes. Programmaticists observed that these updates frequently took the form of committee positions or conclusions that appeared (too often) to be final. In practice, however, such agreements more often needed to be viewed as part of an ongoing (though interrupted) dialogue. They could only become part of a complete cross-functional solution after they were integrated with the knowledge, assumptions, and agreements of stakeholders from other line functions—and their respective line function review committees. After obtaining such input changes were often necessary.

In discussions, programmaticists observed that the sequential nature of line function review meetings also affected the dynamics of project decision making. Project teams seeking the input and agreement of several line function review committees were constrained to obtain such agreements via review meetings held over a sometimes protracted time period, in a rigid sequence that they usually could not control. They reported that it could be exceedingly difficult to resolve project issues via these review meetings because iterative discussions were often required for the resolution of complex issues. In a sequential meeting format, each new review had the potential to raise questions about (or even to reject) the conclusions reached in the one before, and issues raised in later reviews often needed to be addressed by committees responsible for the earlier reviews. Programmaticists observed that issues could not be resolved agilely via processes that constrained teams to interact with line functions via sequential reviews; agile issue resolution usually required dynamic discussions with individual (or small groups of) stakeholders.

It was interesting to observe the reactions of programmaticists as they discussed the impact of secondary line function review committees on the management of project uncertainty and complexity. They often experienced both "Aha!" and "Oh no!" moments of clarity (sometimes simultaneously). They were struck by the realization that line functions' introduction of review committees to facilitate the management of operational, outcome, stakeholder, or environmental uncertainty had unintentionally (and paradoxically) resulted in an increase in organizational uncertainty and complexity. And, as their organizations had grown, it had become the programmaticist's responsibility to manage it. The introduction of secondary governance committees had had unintended consequences that were clearly (crown) *kvetching*.

Programmaticists noted that their successfulness had become increasingly dependent on their abilities to manage *organizational* uncertainty and complexity. As a consequence, their organizational roles and responsibilities had changed. They were spending increasing proportions of their time ensuring that their governance committees (both primary and secondary) were well informed—not only of the their project teams' needs, but also of each other's opinions, perspectives, and positions. In an effort to manage organizational uncertainty and complexity, they were spending more and more of their time trying to ensure effective communication of information between the functional "silos" that now seemed (with increasing significance) to compartmentalize their organizations. And, as line function review committees assumed a role of increased prominence, programmaticists reported that they had less time available to remain personally engaged in the resolution of the other kinds of uncertainty and complexity. They, much like the line function heads who sat on their projects' primary governance committees, found that they were becoming progressively more dependent on their organizations' bureaucratically endowed line function review committees to help them manage operational, outcome, stakeholder, and environmental complexity. And many of them found that to be exasperating.

Growth in the size of line function groups had had profound effects on programmaticist roles and responsibilities in many different organizations. But this was not the only growth-related factor that programmaticists cited as a significant influence. They also reported that they were affected significantly by their organizations' pursuit of larger numbers of projects.

PORTFOLIO EXPANSION

The Benefits of Pursuing Larger Numbers of Projects

When discussing organizational growth, it was common for executives and programmaticists to proudly observe that their organizations were now in a position to pursue a larger number of projects. They were usually pleased to enumerate the initiatives that they were pursuing and the value they expected each to provide. As a group, they observed that pursuing more projects provided their organizations with several great advantages: It enabled them to pursue bigger and more diverse goals; it provided opportunities for expanding their business, their capabilities, and their influence; it made it possible to balance their pursuit of shorter- and longer-term objectives; and it sometimes enabled their organizations to pursue more than one approach for attaining their most important goals. To most stakeholders, the ability to pursue larger numbers of projects was another sign of their organizations' past successes, current strength, and future promise.

Programmaticists enjoyed their organizations' pursuit of more projects for another reason: It provided them with direct professional benefits. It stimulated the growth of their project and program management groups, and enabled the hiring of colleagues with more diverse experience and capabilities. This often resulted in additional career opportunities. The formation of bigger project and program management departments elevated their profession to the status of a "line function" and increased the likelihood that they would be represented on organizational governance committees. In many organizations, it enabled the development of advanced infrastructure that expanded project management's capabilities. For example, it might have led to the introduction of enterprise-resource and project management (ERPM) systems and enhanced professional educational opportunities. In some organizations it led to the establishment of project (or program) management offices (commonly referred to as PMOs) whose purpose was to support and advance programmaticist capabilities, and to ensure that their skills were fully leveraged within their organizations. And, programmaticists observed, with the establishment of formal project and program management departments and the broader recognition of their professional capabilities, organizations began to more frequently ask programmaticists to lead or to manage their strategic initiatives. Most programmaticists welcomed these opportunities, and most organizations appreciated their programmaticists' contributions to them. It is easy to understand why many organizational stakeholders would embrace an increase in the number of projects that they support.

Responding to Portfolio-Related Challenges

However, as organizations increased their numbers of projects and programs they found themselves facing new challenges—challenges that once again affected the performance of their two-party (or sometimes now, multiple-party) fully governed project oversight models. We introduced one of those challenges earlier in this and the preceding chapter—the challenge faced by governance committee members who needed to remember the detailed operational plans and strategic assumptions of each of the projects in their organization's portfolio, so as to ensure that the decisions they made for one project would not have unintended or unappreciated harmful effects on another. That challenge, we noted, seemed to stimulate their organizations' formation and dependence upon line function review committees. But there were also other effects.

Stakeholders noted that the pursuit of more projects sometimes led to unexpected resourcing issues; their projects were much more likely to face issues related to several projects' simultaneous need for limited resources (whether human, physical, or budgetary) because of unfortunate timing coincidences. Competition between projects for specific resources at critical and particular times meant that projects were sometimes unable to pursue planned activities (and thus unable to deliver their outputs or outcomes as promised). To avoid such issues, stakeholders observed, necessitated that organizational leaders carefully monitor, coordinate, and prioritize resource use.

In interviews and discussions, stakeholders frequently observed that coordinating and prioritizing resource use became increasingly complex as the number of organizational projects grew. Two projects that did not have conflicting needs for the resources of one line function might produce significant competition for the resources of another. As a result, project plans that might have been readily endorsed by one line function review committee might be summarily rejected by another. Communicating and coordinating the scheduling needs of numerous projects to each line function review committee could become a formidable task (see Figure 7.5).

Effective operational planning became even more difficult when one needed to anticipate the aggregated effects of operational uncertainty in numerous projects, not only because the volume of activity increased,

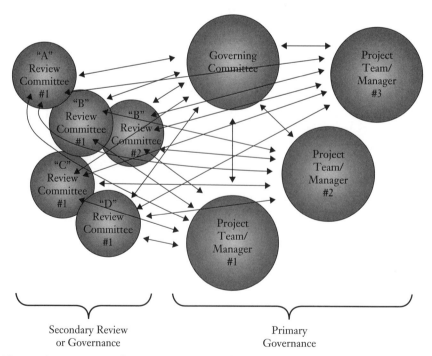

Figure 7.5 Lines of communication that arise as a consequence of pursuing increased numbers of projects.

but also because the inconsistency of resource estimates. (Different teams tended to use different conventions and assumptions when estimating their project's uncertainty.) Monitoring operational uncertainty became significantly more difficult when the events that affected operational estimates were spread across different projects *and* different line functions. As the number of projects grew, it became increasingly difficult for members of an organization to understand and manage operational uncertainty and to identify solutions to their increasingly complex operational issues.

Stakeholders also noted that the *increased operational uncertainty and complexity resulted in an increase in outcome uncertainty and complexity.* Operational uncertainty affected projects' timelines for achieving their targeted outcomes. Perhaps more significantly, however, operational uncertainty and constraints resulting from an increased number of projects sometimes influenced the strategies that projects were authorized to apply when pursuing their goals. Stakeholders reported that as project numbers increased, some projects experienced greater pressure to choose "resource light" approaches for pursuing their outcomes, despite the potential negative impact of that decision.

Finally, interviewees (particularly programmaticists) observed that *increasing the number of projects dramatically increased the stakeholder and organizational uncertainty* that they needed to manage. As programmaticists sought to resolve each of their projects' operational and outcome uncertainties, and as they sought to resolve the complex prioritization issues that arose as a consequence of those uncertainties, they found it increasingly important to engage with their organizations' individual stakeholders and line function review committees. Programmaticists observed that the views, assumptions, and recommendations of each stakeholder or committee could be influenced by their personal perspectives about certain projects and their needs to simultaneously manage the efficient use of resources within their own groups. As a result, programmaticists noted, stakeholders often used different (more personal) criteria as a basis for granting or withholding resources requested by individual projects. As the numbers of projects in the organizations' portfolios grew, programmaticists found that they needed to more carefully monitor the diversity of views and assumptions of stakeholders and line function review committees about those projects, and to more frequently manage the complex issues that arose when those views were not aligned with those of their project teams.

In interviews and discussions, programmaticists and line function stakeholders both generally concluded that the pursuit of *more* projects

by their organizations had made the pursuit of *all* projects more complicated. As their organizations sponsored larger numbers of projects—
even projects that (in isolation) seemed uncomplicated—the uncertainty
and complexity associated with the management and governance of each
project rose significantly.

The issues which arose as a consequence of larger numbers of projects were somewhat different from those that were the focus of line
function review committees; the issues caused by a larger portfolio of
projects were best addressed by individuals (or committees) who could
simultaneously examine the operational needs of the many projects
being supported by an organization, and who were focused on managing
their organization's portfolio of projects in a manner that was consistent
with high-level organizational strategy and priorities. Those were not
necessarily the responsibilities or the strengths of department-specific
line function review committees (discussed earlier in this chapter), or of
the programmaticists who were responsible for leading and managing
individual projects.

As discussed in Chapter 6, under the two-party fully governed
project oversight model, project prioritization was the responsibility
of the primary governance committee that sponsored and supported
(resourced) an organization's projects. It is understandable that it would
be. In traditional (Industrial Age) organizational models, the line function heads who comprised senior management committees "owned"
their functional resources. They owned the estimates of how many
resources would be required to complete a given task and of what would
or would not be achievable by their departments. They were charged
with primary responsibility for ensuring that those resources were used
with maximum efficiency. And historically, they had been rewarded for
their control over resource allocation, and for effectiveness in managing their line function's portfolio of work. Within their domains they
had long been the resource and portfolio managers, and they had been
successful at it.

Unfortunately, organizational executives and programmaticists
agreed, as organizations grew and sponsored more projects, they faced
issues similar to those that resulted from departmental growth and expansion. It became increasingly difficult for line function leaders (who were
often the same executives who were members of the primary governance
committees) to remain aware of all the information required to inform
project resourcing and prioritization decisions. Larger numbers of projects had resulted in the scheduling of greater numbers of independently
managed activities with the potential for conflict, an increased number of

scheduling scenarios to be considered as part of options analyses, and a greater diversity of perspectives from important stakeholders. Members of primary governance committees once again found that their capacity for retaining and analyzing information became increasingly strained as their organizations grew. They needed support.

The line function review committees discussed earlier in this chapter were not always capable of providing the kind of support that governing committee members needed. Line function committees faced the same difficulties as their executive leaders when they tried to examine the cross-project resourcing issues within larger project portfolios— they needed to access and analyze a large amount of cross-project and cross-functional planning information that was not readily available to them. While line function review committees could be highly effective in examining the within-function consequences of project recommendations, they were not as effective in examining their cross-function implications.

In interviews and discussions, stakeholders frequently observed that the resourcing or prioritization recommendations made by line function review committees too often minimized or overlooked the needs of other line functions. And as a consequence, programmaticists reported, recommendations made by line function committees were too often incomplete, misaligned, or untenable. The need to manage inconsistent recommendations sometimes resulted in organizational confusion; it increased the organizational uncertainty and complexity that programmaticists needed to manage, and even the best of programmaticists reported that it could be difficult to resolve the resultant confusion. Indeed, programmaticists themselves faced the same issues as their governing committee members; they also found it difficult to remain consistently aware of the needs and priorities of projects that they weren't responsible for managing. Resolving issues that arose as a consequence of a growing number of projects usually required specific knowledge and insights about the many projects being supported within the portfolio.

Mixed-Function Review and Governance Committees

When responding to this issue, diverse organizations with clearly different types of projects had often implemented similar solutions.

Discussions with line function executives and programmaticists revealed that many of their organizations first sought to address resource and prioritization issues and to increase collaboration between line function review committees by expanding the membership of their line function review committees to include members of other line functions. These organizations formed what might be called *mixed-function review committees*. The logic to this change was straightforward: By expanding the membership of their review committees to include members of other line functions, their committees would be able to anticipate the needs of those line functions better. Consequently, the committees' abilities to identify acceptable solutions for resourcing and prioritization issues would improve. Indeed, programmaticists and executives reported that the formation of such committees did sometimes help. The introduction of mixed-function review committees could improve planning and increase interdepartmental collaboration. Interviewees reported that mixed-function review committees could be especially beneficial when they were staffed by influential stakeholders whose line functions had specific reasons to work closely together (for example, research and development with engineering departments working on new product design issues, or packaging with marketing departments as they sought to satisfy customer preferences).

However, programmaticists and executives also observed that the formation of mixed-function review committees could have negative impacts on organizational programmatics. The formation of too many mixed-function review committees sometimes resulted in the creation of committees with overlapping responsibilities. That caused confusion over the intended authority and responsibility of each; the reciprocal involvement of two line functions in each other's mixed-function review committees sometimes led to confusion as to which meetings were intended to provide the more definitive guidance to project teams. It sometimes led to confusion over the responsibilities of mixed-function committees (which might be recognized as secondary governance committees) versus the responsibilities of the primary governance committees (whose composition might also be considered to be "mixed function").

The formation of mixed-function review committees also made meeting preparation more complex for programmaticists. Programmaticists reported that the diversity of attendees at mixed-function review committee meetings created a need for project teams to produce secondary committee presentations and background documents with a broader scope.

Programmaticists also observed that the introduction of mixed-function review committees led to increased confusion over the authority and responsibility of the project team for managing cross-functional collaboration. Before the introduction of mixed-function committees, cross-functional collaboration was expected to occur principally within the project team. After the introduction of such committees, the primacy of the project team was less clear.

In interviews and discussions, executive stakeholders and program-maticists both noted that the formation of too many mixed-function secondary committees sometimes resulted in greater uncertainty about who would be present when project issues were reviewed and discussed. In their experience, the proliferation of mixed-function secondary com-mittee meetings too often led to inconsistent attendance by key line function representatives, or to delegation of attendance to colleagues that were less influential or effective. Over time, mixed-function review committees had difficulty in assuring the sustained attendance of cross-functional members (who typically viewed attendance at their own department's meetings as more important).

In general, stakeholders agreed that the establishment of mixed-function review committees provided a solution to some of their resourcing and prioritization challenges, but that it was a partial and often imperfect solution. They were almost unanimous in observing that the introduction of such committees to help reduce specific elements of organizational complexity sometimes had a paradoxical effect of increas-ing other elements of organizational complexity—by creating some-times redundant organizational venues for the discussion and resolution of cross-functional project issues.

Business Governance Committees

Many other organizations had pursued another approach when seeking to improve their management of cross-functional issues relating to project resourcing and prioritization. They had formed *additional* (new) second-ary review committees—*portfolio review committees* and/or *resource review committees*—to support the analysis of issues that crossed the boundaries of individual projects and line functions. These committees, which we will refer to as *business governance committees*, were intended to support the governance of projects via their organizations' two-party (and commonly now, multi-party) fully governed oversight models. The decision-making powers (versus advisory responsibilities) granted to such committees var-ied from organization to organization. However, in each organization their purposes were similar: They were intended to satisfy three critical needs of their primary governance committee(s).

First and foremost, stakeholders reported, business governance com-mittees were expected to compile and maintain accurate information about the current and expected future resource needs of organizational projects.

Business governance committees would be a good source of information for stakeholders seeking to fully understand the within-project, across-project, and line function–specific implications of any resourcing or prioritization decision that governing committees needed to make. In this role, business governance committees proved themselves to be valuable; as organizations increased the numbers of projects they sponsored, they found it increasingly difficult to access cross-project planning and resourcing information. The bureaucratic departmental structures previously created by organizations and the assignment of project management responsibilities to individual programmaticists had unintentionally resulted in the segregation of that information into department- and project manager–based "silos."

Second, stakeholders reported that their business governance committees were expected to support organizational stakeholders in providing cogent analyses of project-related information (and in some cases, provide independent analyses of the same). In this role, business governance committees could provide critical assistance to stakeholders. They helped identify options for resolving operational or prioritization issues. Stakeholders agreed that identifying the best options for resolving issues required collaboration between programmaticists, their project team members, and other (primary and secondary) governance committee members—but that each of them could make better contributions when they were provided with common access to the important information and analyses provided by business governance committees. The assistance provided by business governance committees recognizably improved stakeholder decision making.

And third, stakeholders reported that their business governance committees were expected to support and reinforce the use of their organizations' preferred methods (practices, processes, or measures) for prioritizing project work and allocating organizational resources. Business governance committees were expected to provide consistent guidance to organizational stakeholders regarding the decision criteria to be used when examining and resolving resourcing or prioritization issues. Business governance committees in one organization might, for example, guide stakeholders to apply decision criteria that assured optimal engagement of the organizational workforce (thereby promoting resource-leveling strategies), while those in another organization might guide stakeholders to maximize the progress of high-priority projects by quickly re-assigning budgetary or human resources to them whenever it was necessary (thereby promoting resource-prioritization strategies).

As a group, stakeholders agreed that business governance commit-tees (like mixed-function review committees) could provide significant support to organizations that had become overwhelmed by the volume of project information generated by additional projects and programs. Such committees could be highly effective in providing appropriate information and analyses to programmaticists and governing committee members who needed to manage resourcing and prioritization issues (see Figure 7.6). They served their intended purposes; business governance committees reduced operational uncertainty by enabling centralized access to planning data. Moreover, they might reduce outcome uncer-tainty by ensuring that an organization remained focused on achieving its most important outcomes, and they often reduced stakeholder uncer-tainty by providing authoritative guidance and support to stakeholders who needed to address resourcing and prioritization issues. However, stakeholders also observed that the introduction of business governance committees (like the introduction of line function review committees, and crown vetch) could have unintended and undesirable consequences.

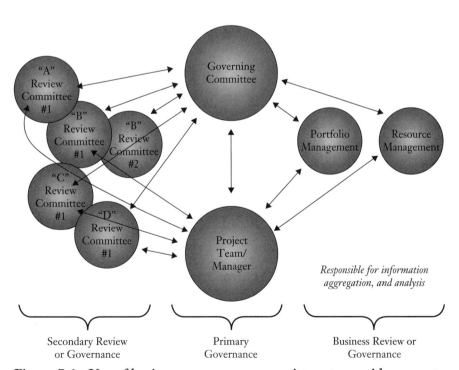

Figure 7.6   Use of business governance committees to provide access to aggregated resource and portfolio management information.

More Unintended Consequences

When prompted to cite the "problems" with business governance committees, one group of stakeholders quickly observed that business governance committees could only be effective when they had access to large amounts of accurate information, and that this information— on the resource needs, the timing, and the importance of operational activities—needed to come from the line function departments and project teams who "owned" it. The stakeholders pointed out that providing this information and maintaining its accuracy required significant time and energy investment (resources), because project plans changed frequently and asynchronously as a consequence of their operational, outcome, and environmental uncertainties.

These stakeholders frequently complained that it took too much effort to collect such information, and they questioned whether the value obtained from its intermittent use in support of decision making justified the effort required to continuously maintain it. Many of these stakeholders worked in organizations whose data collection and aggregation systems were still immature, however (meaning labor-intensive and manually executed). Based on the reported success of other organizations in improving data collection and management (using enterprise resource management systems, or by adjusting the scope, timing, and processes for data collection), it seemed that this problem became more manageable as organizational capabilities matured.

Another group of stakeholders expressed doubt about the analyses provided by their business governance committees. They often questioned their organizations' use of recommendations that emerged from the pre-ordained analyses that business governance committees routinely relied upon (estimates of project value, selections of "optimized project portfolios," and computer-generated recommendations for "optimal resource distribution," for example). As a group, these stakeholders questioned the accuracy of such estimates because they relied on the aggregation of large numbers of data points, and they were subject to the accumulated influence of the uncertainty associated with each. This stakeholder group expressed a preference for decision-making processes that relied more on focused data collection, applied strategic insights, and the "gut instinct" of influential and highly successful stakeholders. They considered the "dispassionate" computer-based resource analyses to be just one of many elements to consider in the decision-making process. The problems that this group of stakeholders focused on were often related to a perceived negative impact of the business governance committee on the dynamics of decision making in their organizations. They cited examples of analyses that had produced misguided recommendations or that had resulted in "analysis paralysis" in their organizations. This group of stakeholders tended to believe that their organizations' introduction of new processes and systems for collecting and analyzing business data had resulted in a decision-making process that was too often slower and more bureaucratic.

It was difficult to determine from interviews whether the introduction of business governance committees was generally perceived to have had a net positive or net negative effect on the dynamics of governance and decision making within organizations. The capabilities provided by business governance committees seemed to have value; however, the high level of anxiety that was often expressed about them revealed a persistent underlying basis for stakeholder dissatisfaction with them.

Based on interviews with programmaticists, however, one thing was very clear: *The creation of business governance committees had also led to the need to establish new avenues of organizational communication*—this time between the various business review committees and organizational line function review committees, primary governance committees, and project teams. In most organizations, the burden of responsibility for managing these communications was borne by programmaticists. Operational data needed to be provided or validated by programmaticists and their team members, and the results of business analyses needed to be vetted with them. Decision options that emerged from such analyses needed to be communicated with stakeholders on their project teams and in their organizations' line functions. Conclusions and recommendations needed to be incorporated into project team documentation and presentations. Programmaticists needed to actively manage the organizational uncertainty and complexity that grew more significant as a result of their teams' need to interact with an expanding group of independently functioning primary and secondary governance committees.

Programmaticists consistently reported that their organizational roles and responsibilities had changed further as a consequence of the creation of business governance committees. The introduction of business governance committees (in response to their organizations' sponsoring greater numbers of projects), like the introduction of line function and mixed-function review committees before that, had resulted in a further increase in the organizational uncertainty and complexity managed by programmaticists.

Increased Project Size, Uncertainty, and Complexity

The Benefits of Large and Uncertain Projects

In the course of discussions, senior executives and programmaticists frequently observed that as their organizations had grown in size, they had also begun to pursue projects that were larger, more uncertain, and more complex. As organizational stakeholders, they usually expressed a degree of pride in this. In their views, the ability to pursue bigger and more challenging projects was additional evidence of their organizations' past success, their current competitiveness, and their probably bright future. For the most part, the stakeholders I interviewed believed that to build on their legacies of success their organizations needed be innovative. And, they believed, being innovative more often than not required that their organizations be ready, willing, and able to pursue projects that were larger, more uncertain, and more complex.

In fact, executives and programmaticists were usually quite eager to discuss their organizations' pursuit of large and complex projects in the name of innovation. They observed that big and complex projects usually sought to solve big and important problems, and in doing so they made big differences and valuable contributions. As a current academician, former programmaticist, and onetime organizational executive, I found it exciting and inspiring to talk to them; they were truly invigorated by the importance of their work. But I also noticed that when I spoke to them about the challenges they faced in managing such projects, their tones often changed. It was easy to see that the pursuit of larger, more uncertain, and more complex projects had presented new challenges to my interviewees' organizations. Good examples of such challenges were sprinkled especially generously in the stories told by Exasperados. Many interviewees observed that their organizations had struggled (or were still struggling) to define how best to manage such large and complex projects under their current project oversight models. They were not yet convinced they had "gotten it right." And when we discussed the steps their organizations had taken while trying to improve project oversight, it could be observed that their organizations, though highly diverse, had (once again) responded to their challenges in somewhat similar ways.

For example, the pursuit of *larger* projects had commonly stimulated the introduction of more sophisticated approaches for organizing project work. Many organizations had responded by (re-) organizing their large projects into more manageable components—other (smaller) projects or workstreams—each of which was charged with delivering a particular output or outcome. By these approaches, large parent projects were effectively broken down into smaller daughter projects that were more easily managed because of their smaller scale. (Some daughter projects had even given birth to granddaughter and then great-granddaughter projects!) Many organizations had, in essence, developed advanced *within-project infrastructure systems* to improve their management of larger, more complicated projects.

The pursuit of more uncertain and complex projects had stimulated changes in the oversight of projects. In many organizations it had resulted in the introduction of new secondary review and oversight committees—*specialty review and governance committees*—responsible for examining the outcomes delivered by the parent project and its offspring. Specialty review and governance committees were generally made up of stakeholders who had knowledge, skills, insight, and experience about how outcomes being delivered by a project would be used to achieve the project's intended goals and benefits.

It will be valuable to examine the adoption of these changes by organizations in a little more detail, so that we might better understand how they also affected an organization's use of two-party (or multi-party) fully governed project oversight models and the roles and responsibilities of the programmaticists responsible for them.

Establishment of Within-Project Infrastructure

It is easy to understand that managing very large projects would pose significant challenges to organizations, if only because of the scale of their requirements: Large projects might be composed of many hundreds, thousands, or even tens of thousands of tasks, each with its own scope, budget, resource requirements, timeline, and specifications. Each of these tasks needs to be scheduled deliberately, after carefully considering when they could or should be started, what activities they need to wait for, and what activities would (in turn) need to wait for them. Defining and optimizing an operational plan for a very large and complicated project should be recognized as a daunting detail-driven endeavor.

Within the traditional two-party project oversight model, responsibility for the detailed planning of large projects lies principally with the project management function. In interviews and discussions, most senior executives expressed relief that it does; understanding and making sense of the enormous amount of information required to effectively plan large projects is usually beyond the responsibility, interest, and capacity of executive stakeholders who sit on primary governance committees. Executives are usually grateful to work with a project management group that assumes responsibility for managing project details.

Managing project details is a strength that has been honed by project managers since the early Industrial Age, when practices and processes for managing complicated engineering, construction, and manufacturing projects were first developed. During that time, project managers introduced approaches for breaking down project work into "tranches" that were more easily managed. These took several forms. Larger groupings of work related by their pursuit of clearly identifiable and common goals, the relatedness and (co-) dependencies of their tasks, and the benefits that could be realized by managing them as a group, were often defined and managed as separate and distinct projects-within-the-project (see Figure 7.7). This enabled the naming of a manager or leader who would focus on that particular grouping of work, and who would be particularly well suited for

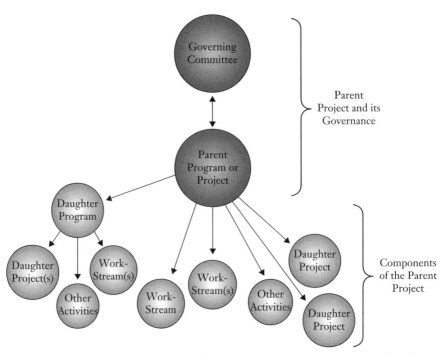

Figure 7.7 The breakdown of a large project into component daughter projects, workstreams, and related project activities.

managing it. Other groupings of related work, usually of smaller scope or duration, might be managed as workstreams. These might alternatively be overseen by either full- or part-time project managers or members of the project team who agreed to act (essentially) in that role.

The relationship of each of these work groupings to the primary project's plan was often displayed in an aggregated project plan that hierarchically presented the project as a collection of daughter projects, workstreams, and groupings of activities, according to what project managers referred to as a "work breakdown structure." Such a display might be expected to capture each grouping of work as a component of the primary project, and (conversely) to show that the primary project was, in fact, a rollup of its (sometimes multitudinous) major and minor components. The approach was a logical extension of the decomposition/re-composition managerial approach that had proven to be the strength of traditional (first-generation) project management practices, and to lead to success in the Industrial Age.

It was a beautiful thing. The plans for large projects could thereby be represented as successive groupings of interrelated activities, richly layered within the project, assigned to their owners and splayed over time (much like a piece of symphonic music may be represented as successive lines of music and groupings of notes to be played by unique instruments, streamed over time, and layered harmoniously over one another). Framed in this way, a well-executed project (like a well-played orchestral piece) could produce a result that could not be achieved by any one of its contributors, but whose richness and complexity could be appreciated by all. Project management's highest-level role was to act as the conductor.

The beauty of this approach seems to lie in its simplicity. It enables large projects to be pursued and managed in a manner that seems entirely consistent with the principles of project oversight via the two-party model. The rollup of project planning responsibilities to a single point of integration—the programmaticist responsible for overseeing the project—seems to enable even the largest and most complicated projects to be effectively managed by the project management and primary governance functions responsible for the two-party model. It seems to enable the semi-autonomous management of daughter projects and workstreams by contributors who might be organizationally dispersed, while simultaneously ensuring that the programmaticist retains responsibility for coordination and control of those activities at the primary project level. And it reinforces the importance of the programmaticist in ensuring effective communication between the primary governance committee, the project, and those responsible for its component activities. Unfortunately, however, the beauty of the approach too often does seem to "lie" in its simplicity.

The Unintended Consequences of Within-Project Infrastructure

When asked to discuss the effectiveness of this approach for managing complicated projects within the two-party project oversight model, senior executives and programmaticists both quickly agreed that managing such projects was, in reality, a more complex endeavor than might be implied by a neat diagram or a breakdown chart of project components. They commonly observed that difficulties arose—usually from the need to manage each project component within the context of an organizational structure that had (as it had grown) created the secondary project oversight mechanisms that we have previously discussed (line function and business review committees). Stakeholders observed, for example, that it was common for a daughter project or an individual workstream to become the principle responsibility of a line function group. It seems natural that it would; daughter projects and workstreams often focused on work that required the unique technical expertise of a specific line function.

However, the assignment of daughter projects to individual line function groups led to organizational complications. It led daughter projects to be managed more directly (and independently) by the line function review committees we discussed earlier in this chapter. It led to requirements that daughter projects have their strategies and operational requirements approved by their line function review committees. And when they did, stakeholders observed that daughter projects or workstreams became accountable to two entities—to the programmaticist (and project team) responsible for managing the primary project, and to a line function review committee responsible for allocating resources and providing technical expertise.

Under these circumstances, stakeholders reported, line function review committees often assumed the responsibilities of a governance committee—they provided strategic and operational oversight to the daughter projects. They became capable of exerting a governing influence on the primary project by insisting on the pursuit of specific strategies or approaches. And when they did, the organizational roles, responsibilities, and authority of the programmaticist changed in ways that were not described by the two-party project oversight model. Programmaticists responsible for parent projects observed that they now needed to manage the interactions of their teams (and their daughter project subteams) with more than one "governing" committee. Thus, the fragmentation of large projects into component daughter projects and workstreams often resulted in an unintended expansion of the "two" party project oversight model into something more. And in doing so, project fragmentation further increased the organizational uncertainty and complexity faced by programmaticists responsible for collaboration and communication between the components of their projects.

During interviews, programmaticists also observed that organizational complexity grew even more when the scope of responsibilities of daughter projects extended beyond the domain of one line function. When a daughter project's responsibilities involved several functional domains, it was common for it to require interaction with several line function secondary review committees and with mixed-function review committees. And as they did, programmaticists reported, the number of committee-based interactions requiring management by programmaticists grew even more dramatically.

Perhaps most importantly, however, programmaticists made this observation: The organization of a parent project into daughter projects and workstreams made it much more difficult for a programmaticist to function as the primary point of contact between a project and its governance committee members (as would be expected under the traditional two-party project oversight model). Programmaticists observed that the secondary review committees that became responsible for overseeing daughter projects and workstreams were often commissioned by the same line function leaders who comprised their project's primary governance committee. In fact, the secondary committees were sometimes *chaired* by the members of their project's primary governance committee. As a consequence, line function stakeholders often had two means for governing or influencing organizational projects—through the primary governance committee, exerted as one member of a parent project's primary governing committee, and through a secondary governance committee, exerted as an individual executive who retained substantial influence and control over daughter projects and project workstreams (see Figure 7.8).

Programmaticists observed that the existence of these parallel influences affected them significantly. By enabling secondary committees to assume more of a governing role, the relationship between those committees and the parent project's programmaticist to manage parent projects according to traditional two-party principles, and the organizational

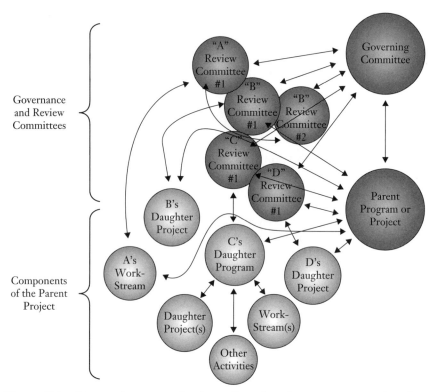

Figure 7.8 Lines of communication when daughter programs, daughter projects, and workstreams are managed by line functions with independent review committees.

uncertainty and complexity associated with the management of large projects increased dramatically. To paraphrase one programmaticist, "To ensure continuous communication and alignment of my project with the wishes and constraints of all of the governance and review committees that can influence it has become a full-time job."

Many programmaticists believed that managing projects comprised of independently managed daughter projects was a fundamentally different endeavor than managing projects that were more simply organized. They correctly observed that these projects were more properly identified as "programs." (The Project Management Institute defines a program as "a group of related projects, subprograms and activities that are managed in a coordinated way to obtain benefits not available from managing them individually.") And they were quick to stipulate that "program management" requires different skills than "project management."

However, many programmaticists were unsure of how the designation of an endeavor as a "program" was expected to influence its
governance or management. They observed that their organizations
did not have a clear or consistent understanding of how their two-party
fully governed project oversight model might need to be adapted to
enable the more effective management of programs. And they had difficulty explaining how defining any given endeavor as a program should
lead their organizations to have different expectations of its programmaticist's roles and responsibilities. This led many programmaticists to
express additional confusion (sometimes exasperation) about their roles
and responsibilities when managing programs (or very large projects)
under their two-party oversight models. (We will discuss this point and
the significant differences between programs and projects in much more
detail in a Chapter 10.)

In discussions, some programmaticists and executives offered an
additional perspective on how the roles and responsibilities of a programmaticist changed when he or she became responsible for a program.
They focused less on the use of daughter projects to manage a large
project's *size*, and more on their use to manage a large project's *scope*.
These stakeholders often observed that the most compelling reason for
creating daughter projects was to ensure that critical elements of a project's scope were effectively monitored by stakeholders (usually line function experts) with the most appropriate subject matter knowledge. They
believed that it was easy for programmaticists to become consumed by
the operational challenges of managing a large project. They opined
that by forming daughter projects that were managed under the guidance and support of line function or mixed-function review committees
and by assigning daughter project leaders with specific subject matter
expertise they could better ensure that the *outcomes* required by a large
project would be effectively monitored and delivered. As one executive
explained, "Project managers do not always have sufficient subject matter knowledge about the outcomes that might be achieved in subprojects.
It would be unrealistic to expect that they would."

In discussions and interviews, stakeholders generally agreed that
the delegation of governance responsibilities to line function and mixed-
function review committees was driven by needs that were not satisfied
within their two-party project oversight models—the need to facilitate
the operational oversight of very large projects and the need to oversee the delivery of outputs and outcomes from those projects. There
was general consensus that the effectiveness of large projects in delivering their desired outputs and outcomes was often improved by the

creation of within-project systems for managing daughter projects and workstreams.

One might conclude that within-project infrastructure systems served their desired purposes by improving the management of operational and outcome complexity in large projects. But they did so via a mechanism that (once again) increased organizational complexity. It was, in the eyes of many stakeholders, a necessary tradeoff.

But was it sufficient?

Based on further discussions with executives and programmaticists, the answer would seem (once again) to be: "It depends." Most stakeholders agreed that the introduction of line function review committees and of operationally focused business governance committees (which we have previously discussed) provided programmaticists and their project teams with sufficient access to information and insights required for the management of *operational* uncertainty. They indicated that additional forms of support for the management of operational uncertainty were not usually required. Their bigger challenge, it appears, was to manage the stakeholder and organizational complexity that grew with the introduction of new committees to improve operational complexity. They shuddered at the thought of doing anything that would further increase that stakeholder and organizational complexity.

However, many stakeholders reported that these approaches did not always satisfy their needs for management of *outcomes*. Their organizations sometimes needed to introduce additional mechanisms to improve their management of *outcome*-based uncertainty and complexity. They had sometimes needed to also establish specialty review and governance committees.

The Establishment of Specialty Review and Governance Committees

In discussions and interviews, a number of stakeholders noted that the outcomes realized by uncertain and complex projects sometimes had ramifications that extended well beyond the scope of the project itself. Outcomes achieved within one project could sometimes have a very profound influence on other projects, or even on the broader strategy of the organization. They might, for example, result in the acquisition of new knowledge about an organization's core capabilities and technologies, or affect its relationships with important external stakeholders (partners, customers, regulatory agencies, or the government). The detailed review and assessment of such outcomes was sometimes beyond the technical capabilities of the members of existing review committees (whether they were primary governance, business governance, line or mixed-function review committees). And consequently, stakeholders observed, their organizations had often taken additional steps to enable their rigorous review: They had formed *specialty review and governance committees.*

Specialty review and governance committees usually had scopes of interest that were much broader than those of any secondary committees we have previously described. They were staffed by individuals with special knowledge, expertise, insight, or responsibility for managing specific elements of an organization's strategic plan. Most often, they were staffed by high-level executives who had responsibilities for significant portions of their organizations' business and its strategy, and who were more specifically focused on those responsibilities than the group of executives who made up the project's primary governance committees. Sometimes they also included external advisors or consultants with unique expertise or perspective (see Figure 7.9).

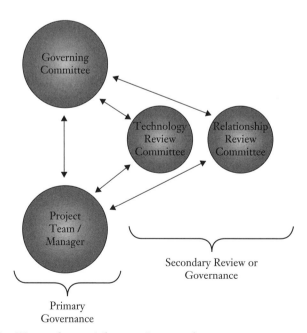

Figure 7.9 Use of specialty review and governance committees to improve oversight of core capabilities, technologies, and key organizational relationships.

There were many examples of specialty review and governance committees to be found in the stories told by senior executives and programmaticists. Some were focused externally—on managing their organization's relationships with customers or collaborators, or its understanding of an external environment. Interviewees from the aerospace and defense industries, for example, indicated that their organizations had often created specialty committees to manage interactions with specific government agencies or customers. Interviewees from the manufacturing or consumer goods sectors could identify specialty committees responsible for oversight of their organizations' relationships with their largest clients, distributors, and retail groups. Stakeholders from healthcare industries indicated that their organizations used specialty committees to manage interactions with healthcare providers, payers, and patient advocacy groups. And representatives from various industries reported that their organizations relied on specialty committees to oversee their business alliances, research collaborations, and investors.

Other specialty review and governance committees were focused internally. Interviewees from research-based organizations indicated that their organizations had used specialty committees to oversee the development and use of "platform technologies" intended to support several projects. Information technologists used specialty review committees to oversee their needs for new hardware, software, user training, and support. And many stakeholders reported that their organizations used specialty committees to manage their corporate brands, their use of social media, and their advertising.

Finally, interviewees sometimes indicated that their organizations also used specialty review and governance committees to manage uncertainty and complexity that was specific to a given phase of a project's or program's lifecycle. Pharmaceutical research and development organizations, for example, commonly formed separate specialty committees to help with decision making for early-phase and late-phase development programs. Stakeholders from manufacturing or information technology organizations often reported that they had formed specialty governance committees to oversee the transfer of new technology from their development environments to their operations groups.

After review, executives and programmaticists often observed their large organizations had formed more specialty review and governance committees than they had realized. It was common for them to note that their larger, more uncertain and complex projects often interacted with one or more specialty review or governance committees regularly. And when they were asked to comment on the effects that such committees had on the management of their programmatic endeavors, executives and programmaticists provided perspectives that were familiar: They indicated that specialty review and governance committees had both positive and negative effects. The committees had produced effects that were both intended and unintended.

Often, stakeholders reported, their organizations realized an immediate and recognizable benefit from the introduction of specialty review and governance committees. They observed that these committees were effective in gathering experienced stakeholders into groups that benefited the organization and its projects. These groups became "knowledge centers" or "think tanks" that were uniquely capable of analyzing project outcomes and recommending adaptations to their organization's direction, strategy, and vision. They stimulated their organizations to muster (and to master) the skills required to manage outcome-related uncertainty and the complex issues that result from it.

The Unintended Consequences of Specialty Review and Governance Committees

Stakeholders also reported that introducing specialty governance committees resulted in unintended consequences similar to those discussed for other secondary review and governance committees, however: It created an organizational environment where conclusions were reached and recommendations were made by organizationally segregated groups. In doing so, it created a need for programmaticists to assume responsibilities for weighing and balancing the views of their specialty committees alongside those of their projects' other review and governance committees. And sometimes it resulted in further uncertainty about the intended roles and authority of each of those committees.

Stakeholders reported that it was not always clear whether specialty governance committees were expected to provide insight or oversight—whether they were advisory or supervisory. And following through on the recommendation of such committees was not always easy, because they did not usually control allocation of the resources that would be required to implement those recommendations. (Resource allocations were more often controlled by individual line function leaders, line function review committees, or business governance committees.) Most programmaticists and executives agreed that the introduction of specialty review and governance committees had therefore resulted in an unintended (and by now, perhaps familiar) further increase in the organizational uncertainty and complexity that needed to be managed by their organizations' programmaticists. They observed that their specialty governance committees served very important roles within their organizations, but (once again) it had come at a price.

Challenges Ahead

Congratulations may be in order for those who have made it through this unexpectedly long chapter. When I set out to characterize how organizations had adapted their two-party fully governed project oversight models I did not fully appreciate the richness of the topic. The broad array of adaptive responses that were captured in those discussions was both surprising and enlightening.

By asking stakeholders to discuss the "evolution" of their organizational systems I sought to collect information in a narrative form that would be easily recounted. The diverse stories told by stakeholders revealed that their organizations' project oversight systems were currently at different points on a common "evolutionary curve" that was defined and influenced by their organization's size, its maturity, and the nature of its programmatic endeavors. Few stakeholders were able to trace the entire history of their organization; however, from the timeframes of their individual observations a common evolutionary storyline could be recognized. The stories that were told could be pieced together in a process that might be described as "organizational archeology."

The storyline told to this point (like any archeological interpretation) is likely to have imperfections; it relies on assumptions and it might, over time, be subject to modification based on additional observations by independent observers. I have found, however, that most organizational professionals find that the story it tells "just makes sense." They report that it has provided them with valuable perspectives on issues being faced by each of their organizations.

During the course of interviews and discussions, stakeholders commonly reported that examining their organizations' adaptation of the two-party fully governed project oversight model has enabled them to better understand the nuanced behaviors of their organizations' professionals and the oversight committees that most stakeholders interact with. It has provided them insight on the effects that those behaviors have had on the management of projects and programs, and on the simultaneously evolving roles and responsibilities of their organizations' programmaticists. Often, it has led to concurrent "Aha!" and "Oh no!"

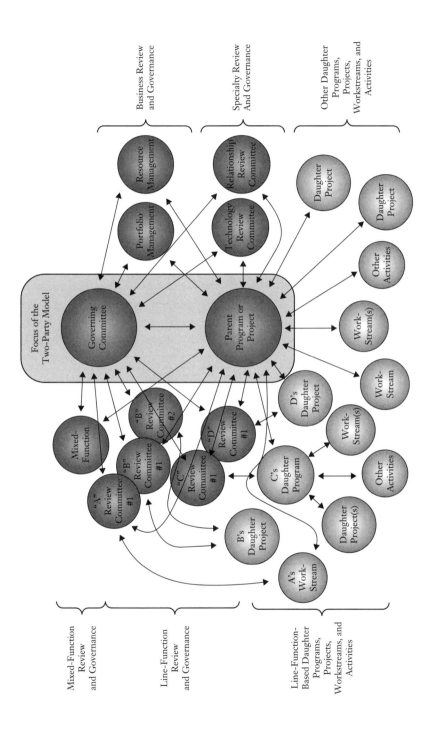

Figure 7.10 The interactions of primary governance committees and project teams with secondary review and governance committees of many modern organizations.

reactions, as stakeholders came to better understand the issues they were facing, and to recognize that the continued success of their organizations would probably also lead to additional challenges.

In particular, stakeholders working in modern knowledge-based organizations expressed concern over the growth of organizational complexity in their programmatic environments, and the clear impact that it has had on the management of their projects and programs. They frequently observed that the "solutions" that they have implemented in response to issues caused by operational and outcome complexity had too often left them mired in organizational complexity that was paralyzing. One needs only to consider the "map" of communications that must be maintained to support such a system to realize the magnitude of the problem. It is displayed graphically in Figure 7.10—in a simplified form that does not begin to capture the lines of communication that exist *between* the many secondary committees that are displayed, or the influence that each may have upon the other.

Understanding how the complexity-management roles and responsibilities of a programmaticist must change as an organization evolves has led many to a better understanding about why successful and experienced programmaticists (and some of their supervising executives) have, over time, become increasingly exasperated. The definitions of their roles and responsibilities, as originally framed using assumptions of the two-party project oversight model, focus upon only a small part of the universe within which they must work. These definitions do not by themselves define the relationships that programmaticists should have with the various other "systems" that their organizations have come to rely on; neither do they clearly define the programmaticist's individual roles and responsibilities for managing the operationally driven and outcome-based complexities that triggered the creation of such systems.

Most stakeholders would agree that the management of uncertainty and complexity within their organizations has too often become (to use the words of systems thinking and operations research pioneer Russell Ackoff) "a mess." In interviews and discussions, many have expressed a yearning for new thinking that might point to a better path going forward.

CHAPTER 8

Moving Forward

OTHER APPROACHES

My discussions with executives and programmaticists about their organizations' project oversight models (described in Chapter 7) provided me with opportunities to explore their thinking about alternative responses to growth and complexity—responses that did not focus so specifically on adaptation of their organizations' two-party project oversight systems. Such responses were prompted by simple questions: "What other steps have your organization considered (or taken) to address issues with project oversight or project management?" Or, "If you could introduce a more dramatic (or disruptive) change to address these problems, what would it be?" Their responses provided additional insights about modern organizations' search for better programmatic systems.

DOWNSIZING THE ORGANIZATION

When prompted to identify alternate solutions to programmatic issues associated with organizational growth and increased numbers of projects, a fraction of interviewees made seemingly flippant observations that growth- and portfolio-related problems could be addressed by "downsizing the organization." It was a casual comment that might be summarily dismissed by others. (Organizational growth and increased project numbers are signs of strength, aren't they?) But several interviewees insisted that it was a serious proposal that warranted sober consideration. They observed that thought leaders in their organizations were adamant that smaller, more focused organizations were inherently more agile, creative, and innovative than large and broadly focused ones. They often observed that nimbleness had become much more important in knowledge-based environments. They noted that the most successful of their peers often had reputations for being agile and adaptive innovators in their fields. And they pointed to the success of certain startup companies and small "tech" companies as evidence that "smaller is better."

These interviewees could cite examples of organizations that had broken themselves up into smaller separately managed business units, and subsequently increased the efficiency, innovation, and success of their projects and programs. They observed that making those organizations smaller had reduced organizational and operational complexity, and it enabled the appointment of governing stakeholders who were more experienced in managing the specific kinds of outcome uncertainty and complexity faced by their endeavors. These interviewees had concluded that the creation of smaller organizations was a viable mechanism for reducing project and program complexity.

There were, however, dissenting views. Other executive and programmaticist interviewees cited examples of organizational downsizing that they had considered to be failed (and costly) experiments. This group observed that reorganizing into smaller business units had resulted in the further segregation of business expertise into "organizational silos," and that it had sometimes led to inefficient resource deployment among business units whose needs might vary significantly over time. They observed that many organizations did not have enough experienced executives to staff their newly created business units, and that distributing experienced executives among organizationally dispersed units reduced the quality of governance and leadership within the units. This group also observed that the separation of organizations into distinct business units may limit a programmaticist's access to stakeholder expertise and specific resources important to their projects' operational needs. They often reached a conclusion that was opposite to the first group: The creation of smaller units had not sufficiently improved their organizations' ability to manage the uncertainty and complexity associated with projects and programs.

Is downsizing an organization an effective approach for reducing complexity? Does it lead to an improved ability to manage projects and programs? It would seem that the most prudent answer to both of these questions is (once again): "It depends." The notion of placing project governance responsibilities in the hands of a smaller group of stakeholders did seem valuable to most people interviewed. However, stakeholders agreed that dividing and downsizing per se was not an approach that could be casually applied by most modern organizations. (What works for amoebas does not work for more specialized organisms.) It was far too disruptive to be considered a natural response to increasing complexity.

For any given organization, the benefits that would be realized and the costs that would be associated with such significant disruption were difficult to know. Executives and programmaticists generally observed that the approach was far too risky for most of their established (bureaucratically organized) organizations to accept.

TRANSFERRING GOVERNANCE

A number of executives and programmaticists observed that their organizations had sought to improve their management of a given project's uncertainty and complexity by fully transferring project oversight responsibilities to specialized governance committees as a project progressed through its various phases. By doing so, the organizations sought to ensure that projects were governed as directly as possible by a governance committee that was most precisely focused on (and uniquely capable of) managing the uncertainties and complexities being faced during a specific phase of the project lifecycle. Projects reporting to specialized governance committees would ideally be less dependent upon the input of other secondary governance and review committees—and thereby less likely to be encumbered by excessive organizational and stakeholder complexity. Limiting the number of secondary governance committees was one means of preserving the two-party intent of an organization's project oversight systems.

There were many examples of "governance transfer" to be found in the experiences of executives and programmaticists whom I interviewed. Some involved the transfer of oversight authority for a project from its primary (original) governance committee to another (perhaps previously a secondary) governance committee during a period when a specific and critical issue was being addressed. When that phase was completed, oversight responsibilities might be returned to the original primary governance committee. This approach might be used, for example, by organizations seeking to develop a specific product by first developing a new supportive technology and then applying it.

Other examples involved the sequential transfer of governance responsibility to committees that were responsible for (and uniquely qualified in) managing definable, successive phases of a project's lifecycle. Stakeholders observed that this approach could be valuable for projects in research, product design, and software development. These were projects that were routinely managed in sequential phases—when projects had clearly elaborated goals and well-defined progression criteria, and when there was recognizable value in ensuring the engagement of stakeholders with experience in managing complexity that was specific to particular project phases. It did not work as well in projects (or programs) that simultaneously pursued goals that were diverse and independent.

When stakeholders were asked whether they had significant concerns about governance-transfer approaches, they expressed reservations that were reminiscent of the concerns expressed about organizational downsizing. They were concerned that newly named governance committees were difficult to staff—this time with executives who had appropriate (high-level) influence, authority, and access to resources. It was also important that each governance committee executive be aware of the project's highest-level mandates. Committee executives needed to know how the project was expected to contribute to the organization's broader strategy and goals, so that perspectives of the original governance committee would be considered, understood, and reflected in subsequent decisions.

As my discussions with executives and stakeholders about alternate approaches progressed, it could be observed that there were similarities to be recognized in the downsizing and governance-transfer approaches. Both approaches were grounded in the notion that *modern-day projects benefited when oversight responsibility for them was placed in the hands of a smaller group of highly accountable and competent stakeholders*. This was an important observation because it suggested that organizations were finding it necessary to address those issues that had arisen as unintended consequences of "fixing" their two-party project oversight systems. They were now actively seeking to reduce the organizational and stakeholder complexity that had resulted from the introduction of secondary committees, and they were seeking to do so in ways that would preserve the strengths of their secondary review and governance committees in managing operationally driven and outcome-based complexity. My discussions with stakeholders indicated that some of these approaches had been partially successful. It seemed, however, that none had proven completely adequate.

The critical question became: "How else might this be achieved?"

REDEFINING THE ROLE OF A PROGRAMMATICIST

Operationalist Approaches Re-Examined

When pressed to examine further how programmatic complexity could be better managed, many executives and programmaticists turned their attention to the critical roles of programmaticists. They observed that the advanced complexity-management skills of programmaticists had sometimes contributed significantly to their organizations' critical complexity-management capabilities. Certain programmaticists had earned reputations for their abilities to resolve organizational and stakeholder complexity. They seemed to have already embraced and embodied the "programmaticist's credo" that was proposed in Chapter 4: To manage the uncertain, solve the complex, and deliver the value.

Many executives and programmaticists told stories, for example, of having worked with project management professionals who demonstrated exceptional understanding and insight about operational planning and the management of operational uncertainty. They observed that these professionals had demonstrated an extraordinary ability to solve their projects' complex operational challenges by identifying solutions that "made sense." Programmaticists such as these were recognized as "operational savants." They had become "masters" (in the context of Figure 4.3) of their projects' operational uncertainty and complexity.

Project or program managers who were recognized as operational savants were incredibly valuable to their organizations. They were able to aggregate operational information, to understand the operational constraints that their organizations faced, and (understanding the diverse perspectives of the stakeholders responsible for operations) to identify common grounds for managing operational uncertainty and resolving operational complexity. The best of these savants established highly functional and collaborative peer relationships with the leaders of their projects' operationally focused secondary review committees. And when they did, they were well positioned to manage the operational uncertainty and complexity that might otherwise have befuddled either their teams or those committees.

The respect and credibility that operational savant programmaticists earned, both from individual stakeholders and their projects' secondary review and governance committees, made them highly effective in managing not just operational complexity, but also the stakeholder and organizational complexity that was often associated with it. In discussions and interviews, executives and programmaticists both observed that operational savant programmaticists seemed much less likely to encounter show-stopping issues related to operationally driven organizational and stakeholder complexity.

It was valuable to learn about the roles and responsibilities of these project managers in various organizations. Executives and programmaticists noted that the operational savants in their organizations had been granted greater authority and autonomy in managing the operational elements of their projects; they were assigned roles and responsibilities befitting the "Operationalist" programmaticists we described in Chapter 5. They were entrusted to assume personal responsibility and accountability for managing operational uncertainty and complexity. All of this was possible because they had accepted and adopted a new definition of their leadership roles. They had assumed the role of an "Operational Integrator."

What exactly did that involve? They often assumed personal responsibility for collecting and amalgamating project-related operational knowledge, for identifying operational issues, and for defining options by which they might be resolved. They expected themselves to understand and examine the sometimes widespread implications of those options and to negotiate agreements with their organizations' stakeholders and secondary governance and review committees. They expected themselves to find solutions that resolved operational issues (and solved operational complexity) and, while doing so, to assume responsibility and accountability for simultaneously managing the associated stakeholder and organizational issues that inevitably arose. *They viewed their abilities to simultaneously manage operational complexity and the stakeholder and organizational complexity associated with it as a unified indicator of their effectiveness.*

The input from executives and programmaticists alike suggested that a highly effective Operationalist project manager could and should be expected to reduce programmatic complexity. *Developing (or hiring) operational savant project management professionals and placing them in an Operationalist role (where they would act as Operational Integrators) was a viable means of placing oversight responsibility for projects "in the hands of a smaller group of accountable and competent professionals" and thereby reducing programmatic complexity.*

Interviewees also observed, however, that doing so was not always easy. It required that bureaucratically endowed organizational stakeholders accept that some of their control over line function operations must be ceded to their Operationalist project managers. Sometimes that was a hard sell. Many stakeholders did not want or trust project managers to assume such a role. It was interesting to probe the reasons for that with executives and programmaticists. After all, the technical (project management) knowledge required by Operationalist project managers was the same technical knowledge that had been taught to project managers who had supported traditional first-generation programmatic management systems for decades.

In discussions, executives and programmaticists both observed that effectiveness in the Operationalist role required that project managers understand more than just the tools and techniques of their trade. It required soft skills that could not be taught in the same way as tools and techniques—skills that were not tested during Project Management Professional (PMP) certification. Project managers needed to have good communication, negotiation, and influencing skills; they needed to be sensitive to others' perceptions and motivations; they needed to interact with stakeholders in an emotionally intelligent way. *They needed to be perceived as leaders who were capable of functioning at the same level as their organizations' managing executives.*

Executives and programmaticists observed that professionals in project management were very inconsistent in their mastery of these skills, however. In executives' opinions, project managers too often focused too intently on their tools and techniques. In the words of one executive, "When I take my car to a specific repair shop, it is because I trust that its mechanic will understand my problem, and I trust his ability to do good work when fixing it. It is not because I believe that he has good tools; I have never asked to look at his toolbox. It is *how and when* he uses his tools that really matters." Being effective in an Operationalist role was more about the programmaticist's *behavior*.

Stakeholders observed that many project managers needed to develop higher levels of behavioral competency—better leadership skills—before being qualified for the Operationalist's role. And they often lamented that many of the large and complex projects that their organizations currently relied upon were supported by project managers who did not have such competency. It was an issue that would need to be addressed if project managers were to be expected to assume the Operationalist's role in managing operational complexity and the stakeholder and organizational complexity that come with it.

Many project management professionals indicated they would accept and embrace such a challenge. They noted again, however, that various executives in their organizations were not prepared to allow it. For many executives, it was not something that was intended under their organizations' traditional two-party fully governed project oversight models. And while adopting Operationalist philosophies might arguably reinforce the two-party nature of the model (by nudging operational planning responsibilities back toward the organization's project management function) it seemed (to some executives) to erode the fully governed aspect of the model. Project management professionals frequently observed that proposals to use Operationalist definitions of a project manager's roles and responsibilities had been received less than enthusiastically.

Why did line function executives have such tepid reactions? They often made comments reminiscent of our earlier discussions—about their need to maintain tight control over their groups' operations and their "principal" responsibilities for ensuring the efficient completion of line function work (in the traditions of Industrial Age organizational principals). But as the conversations progressed, another concern emerged. It came principally from executives whose organizations were pursuing complex, knowledge-based projects and programs that depended upon the delivery of uncertain outcomes. *Executives feared that the adoption of Operationalist approaches (which allowed project managers and their teams to have greater autonomy in managing operations) might unintentionally diminish their organizations' diligence in monitoring project outcomes.* Stated differently, improving their organizations' management of operational complexity (and its associated stakeholder and organizational complexity) via Operationalist approaches might unintentionally result in the deterioration of their abilities to manage outcome complexity (and its associated stakeholder and organizational complexity).

These executives observed that to be highly effective in independently managing a project's operational plans, Operationalists needed to also be highly effective at anticipating and responding to that project's outcomes. To be effective in managing a project's operational complexity, a project manager needed to anticipate and respond to that project's outcome uncertainty and complexity. *To effectively pursue complex projects, projects needed to balance the skills and focus of an operational savant with those of a corresponding professional: a professional who focused on the realization of uncertain outcomes—an "outcome sage."*

But who should fill such a role?

Discussions about the potential role of an outcome sage programmaticist inevitably turned into discussions about Inclusivist conceptions of the project or program manager's role, and how Inclusivist programmaticists might also contribute to the reduction of programmatic complexity. Assigning an Inclusivist to a project (or program) is another way to place responsibility for it in the hands of a "smaller number" of competent and accountable stakeholders.

Inclusivist Approaches Re-Examined

Inclusivist programmaticists, as defined in Chapter 5, were project or program managers or leaders who were expected to assume personal responsibility for managing (or ensuring the management of) all types of uncertainty and complexity that a project or program might face. An Inclusivist programmaticist might be expected to simultaneously and somewhat autonomously manage the delivery of the outputs and outcomes required from a project or program. He or she would assume responsibility for simultaneously managing both operational and outcome complexity, and also for managing the stakeholder and organizational uncertainties and complexities that were associated with them. It might therefore be expected that the assignment of an Inclusivist programmaticist to a project or program would diminish the need for that endeavor to be overseen by their secondary committees; such an assignment might enable review and governance committees to assume a role that was more advisory and less supervisory in nature. It was quite interesting to discuss with executives and programmaticists whether they believed that adoption of an Inclusivist conception of the programmaticist's role might further improve their organizations' management of complex projects or programs.

Executives observed that in theory the adoption of an Inclusivist approach could be extremely valuable. It could provide organizations (their executives, their governance and review committees, and their assorted other stakeholders) with a single authoritative point of contact for a project or program—a combined operational (output) savant and strategic (outcome) sage—who would assume personal responsibility for aggregating project information, for engaging project stakeholders and their committees, and for managing programmatic complexity in an integrated holistic manner. In theory, such a programmaticist would be well positioned to address issues that were commonly encountered when managing complex projects and programs. By serving as a single authoritative point of contact for his or her project or program, an Inclusivist programmaticist might also be expected to turn an organization's project oversight system back into something that more closely resembled the two-party system that most stakeholders were familiar with.

Was this the direction that modern organizations should pursue to improve how they managed their large and complex projects and programs? Was it a viable means of resolving the issues that had arisen as project oversight systems had expanded through the years? Would it truly improve their management of programmatic uncertainty and complexity?

Executives and programmaticists responded cautiously.

They observed that their organizations had already tried to adopt more "inclusive" definitions of a project or program manager's roles and responsibilities. That was, after all, the basis for many of the second-generation programmatic approaches discussed in Chapters 2 and 3. Those approaches had shown promise—but only when applied to specific types of projects, under uniquely defined circumstances. None were universally applicable or generally acceptable for broad use in the management of uncertain and complex projects or programs. And none had provided a unifying view of how the roles and responsibilities of project and program managers could be better defined. In fact (as discussed in Chapter 3) one might reasonably argue that second-generation approaches had the opposite effect; they had triggered a project management identity crisis.

When considering the above questions, many executives and programmaticists also noted that our description of an Inclusivist programmaticist's roles and responsibilities most closely resembled the roles and responsibilities of individuals who were designated as project or program "leaders" in their organizations. When I explored use of a project or program leader title, however, the roles and responsibilities of those called leaders varied widely. Their association with the organization's governance versus project management functions was inconsistent.

Sometimes the title of project or program leader was used to identify the programmaticist most responsible for a project's success. He or she was the individual responsible for actively managing (or even directing) the endeavor's daily pursuit of its goals and objectives. These programmaticist-leaders might indeed have roles and responsibilities that resembled our definition of an Inclusivist. At other times, however, stakeholders indicated that the title of project or program leader referred to an individual executive who had agreed (based on their interest, expertise, and organizational responsibilities) to serve as that endeavor's executive sponsor. Sponsor-leaders usually served as an executive advisor to the most senior "manager" responsible for a project or program, and often they served as a member of the project's or program's primary governance committee. That role is somewhat different than what we had described for an Inclusivist (or programmaticist-leader). A more detailed investigation of project leader roles and responsibilities under various project oversight systems would be an interesting area for further research.

I heard multiple stories about programmaticists who were clearly identified by executives and programmaticists as Inclusivists. Among them were examples of individuals who were reported to be exceptionally successful in acting as both operational savants and outcome sages. They seemed to be equally capable of adopting the full-speed-ahead command-and-control mindset that was sometimes most effective for ensuring efficiency in the generation of outputs, and the more learning-oriented pause-and-consider learn-and-adapt mindset that could be more effective in ensuring the delivery of uncertain outcomes and benefits. More importantly, they seemed keenly aware of how to balance those mindsets.

The stories told by executives and stakeholders indicated that these exceptionally talented individuals were uniquely dexterous in managing programmatic complexity. They were masters at balancing the management of operational and outcome-based complexities, and in presenting solutions in ways that minimized stakeholder and organizational complexity. They were operational savants and outcome sages whose presence was recognized to increase the probability of success of every project or program that they worked on. And when one examined their behaviors, it was easy to conclude that they functioned as Inclusivists.

They were exceptionally talented, but unfortunately, they were exceptionally rare. One executive observed that, "They were as rare as unicorns." I prefer to think of them as centaurs—noble and rare creatures with the strategic perspective and insight of man, and the horsepower required to ensure that work would get done.

When I pressed my interviewees into discussions about the knowledge, skills, and behaviors that led these particular programmaticists to be so successful, I did not learn of any secret tools or techniques. (I wished that I had.) Instead, stakeholders told stories about the uncommon ability of these individuals to work holistically as they solved programmatic complexity. These were programmaticists whose individual understanding of operationally driven and outcome-related complexities allowed them to absorb the most complex of operational and strategic information in an unfettered way. Their personal understanding of the issues that their projects faced enabled them to understand not only the nature of their challenges, but also the likely responses of organizational stakeholders and their committees to them. This knowledge enabled them to independently and successfully explore diverse options for responding to project or program complexity. They depended less on their organizations' bureaucratic committee processes to negotiate solutions to issues. They had earned their stellar reputations because of their unique abilities to solve operational, outcome, stakeholder, and organizational complexity in a completely integrated way. And they were recognized for being able to contribute to every aspect of the work at hand.

I believe that these "centaur stories" provide clues about an alternate approach for managing exceptionally complex projects and programs—an approach that does not necessarily require that we search for programmaticists (whether unicorns or centaurs) that were so exceptionally rare that in the minds of some, they were mythical.

My interviews had led to evidence that Inclusivist approaches might indeed improve the management of projects and programs by placing responsibilities for managing project or program complexity in the hands of a single accountable and competent programmaticist. They had revealed that this might be achieved by a "centaur," of sorts, who is half–operational savant and half–outcome sage, and who is wholly capable of managing programmatic complexity. *Wouldn't it then be possible to design new (and improved) approaches for managing programmatic endeavors using a system that was based on joined-at-the-hip operational savant and outcome sage programmaticists?* In the absence of a real-world source of ready-and-able centaurs, it would seem to be a very practical solution. Pursuing such a system would be a significant departure from the two-party mindset that had defined (and perhaps limited) our views on project oversight systems. It would enable consideration of a three-party system that we will explore in much more detail in the second part of this book.

Is there a precedent for such a thing?

Building a Centaur

As it turns out, during discussions with executives and programmaticists, several stories had emerged about their organizations' flirtations with the use of three-party systems to manage complex projects and programs. In the most common scenarios, three-party management systems were introduced by host organizations that had recognized a need to ensure the rigorous management of their projects' or programs' operational plans while simultaneously managing highly uncertain and complex technical outcomes. There were a number of examples of such systems being tried in the pharmaceutical industry, for example, where complicated drug development plans depended on the precise conduct of many hundreds of operational activities (on time, on budget, and to specifications), and where incredibly high outcome uncertainty and complexity led to project success rates in the neighborhood of 5 percent. The three-party approach used by most of these organizations was reasonably straightforward. It was based on the assignment of two types of programmaticists to each project or program team.

The first type (and often highest ranking) of these programmaticists was usually a technical expert who assumed principle responsibility for delivering a project's (or program's) intended outcomes. That programmaticist would be responsible for oversight of the strategy by which a project or program team would pursue its desired outcomes. He (or she) was usually tasked with monitoring outcomes—assessing their contributions to the delivery of benefits and overseeing the adaptation of strategies or plans based on lessons learned. This expert was often selected for his knowledge, skills, or experience related to the desired project outcomes. In the examples shared by executives and programmaticists during our interviews, that programmaticist might serve in his role on either a full- or part-time basis. He might report to either his original line function department or to a project or program management executive. He might even retain some professional responsibilities within his original line function. But often, he was considered to be the project's "programmaticist-leader."

The second of these programmaticists was usually a project management professional who assumed responsibility for the oversight of a project's operational plan. He (or she) was usually tasked with the conduct, management, and oversight of a project's operational activities, as might typically be expected of project managers working in a more traditional (first-generation) programmatic system. This programmaticist was usually selected for his knowledge, skills, and experience in the practices, processes, tools, and techniques of a professional project manager. He was usually a full-time project manager, and he might have responsibilities for managing more than one project concurrently. Most often, these programmaticists were recognized as project or program managers within their organizations' programmatic systems.

It was valuable to explore the experiences of my interviewees with three-party systems; there were numerous lessons to be learned. Were the interviewees successful? What issues did they face? How had their organizations adapted or responded to the three-party system?

Executives and programmaticists whose organizations had employed three-party systems usually viewed their systems as having had mixed success. They sometimes began with stories of projects that were poorly managed under such systems. They would provide long lists of issues that those projects had faced—difficulties that they seemed to never overcome. It could be observed that the list of issues and difficulties could be divided into two categories: Those that were also common to two-party systems and those that related to the newfound challenges of their three-party system.

The former list was a familiar one. It contained observations (and complaints) about the difficulty of simultaneously managing their projects' operations and strategy, and of delivering outputs and outcomes. It contained stories about the difficulty of working in a large organization that was pursuing a big portfolio of uncertain and complex projects. It contained anecdotes about misbehaving stakeholders and committees, and the issues they raised. And it contained stories of exasperation over an unclear understanding of the roles and responsibilities of programmaticists and secondary review and governance committees. Same old, same old; the list might suggest that nothing had changed.

The second list was less familiar, but (in hindsight) perhaps unsurprising. It mostly contained stories about leader-programmaticists, manager-programmaticists, and executives from their governance committees who had not quite figured out how to work together. It contained examples of misplaced assumptions about who would do what and who had what authority. It contained stories about two programmaticists focused on managing the same project complexity while another complex issue went unattended—stories, for example, about a leader (outcome)-programmaticist being taken to task for a subpar result that was a manager (output)-programmaticist's responsibility, or about the issues that could be triggered by Inclusivist programmaticist behaviors in an expectedly Traditionalist environment. The most novel of issues seemed to relate to newfound organizational complexity that was based on the "twist" of sometimes having a technical leader-programmaticist who reported bureaucratically to a line function organization. This list clearly suggested that roles and responsibilities of each of the parties within the three-party system needed to be more clearly elaborated.

This much seemed clear: There were still many questions to be answered about the potential value of a three-party programmatic oversight system. There was far less information available and experience to be tapped about organizational applications of such systems. Indeed, several organizations had flirted with the development of three-party systems for the management of uncertain and complex projects and then, faced with these newfound issues and the continued presence of old ones, retreated to the familiarity of two-party systems (despite their well-known problems). In particular, it could not be determined whether some organizations' disappointment with these three-party oversight model "experiments" should be considered as proof of the system's inability to add value in particular circumstances, or if it should be considered a misleading result from a trial that was poorly or naively designed. There did not seem (at least to this programmatic scientist) to be enough data to know.

I returned again to questions of whether there was enough evidence that it could or should work—whether there was enough "reason to believe"—to make it worth re-examining whether organizations had, in fact, conducted experiments that were appropriately designed to test the hypothesis. Was there evidence, whether theoretical or practical, to suggest that three-party systems could be highly valuable to (some) organizations for the management of complex projects and programs? We will discuss the theoretical basis for believing that the answer is "yes" in Chapter 9, but was there practical evidence?

In my discussions with executives and programmaticists, there were several stories about exceptionally complex projects or programs that were recognized to have been managed exceptionally well using a three-party project oversight system—stories that leveraged the complexity management skills of operational savant–and outcome sage–programmaticists working together in a collaborative environment. The executives and stakeholders who told those stories often believed that the success of those projects was directly related to the use of a uniquely functional three-party project oversight system. I asked them to speculate on what characteristics were most important in making that system effective. It was interesting to observe the consistency of their responses.

Each of them noted that the roles and responsibilities of each party in the system had been clearly defined: An operational savant–programmaticist had assumed primary responsibility for managing operational uncertainty and solving operational complexity; an outcome sage–programmaticist had assumed primary responsibility for managing outcome uncertainty and solving outcome complexity. The primary governance committee had assumed principal responsibility for managing and solving environmental complexity, and all three parties assumed collective, joint responsibility for managing stakeholder and organizational uncertainties and complexities (see Figure 8.1).

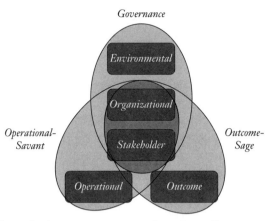

Figure 8.1   Complexity-management domains of governance members, operational savant–programmaticists, and outcome sage–programmaticists in the three-party project oversight model.

Each of them also noted that success of the three-party system depended heavily on collaboration between the parties. Each success story was about how the three parties worked together in an exceptionally collaborative manner to satisfy their projects' needs for appropriate skills, knowledge, and experience. Specifically, the combinations of operational- and outcome-focused programmaticists worked exceptionally well together. It was critical that they did; the issues that arose in their highly complex projects and programs usually required that the endeavor's operational and strategic approaches be modified simultaneously.

Their stories also emphasized the unique skills that could be brought to bear when operational- and outcome-focused programmaticists worked together. They observed that each had unique knowledge, skills, and insights that would be difficult to find in a single programmaticist. In successful projects, the collaboration between operational- and outcome-focused programmaticists was usually so seamlessly integrated and complete that they had in essence begun operating as a "centaur of excellence" in programmatic leadership.

The stories of executives and stakeholders seemed to support the notion that the management and leadership of complex projects and programs could be improved using a three-party programmatic oversight system based on the collaborative sharing of leadership responsibilities by an operational savant–programmaticist, an outcome sage–programmaticist, and a primary governance function. The challenge that remained was to define in more detail how such a system should operate.

An appropriate starting point might be to define what success looks like. What should we seek to achieve when defining an improved project or program management system?

ELEMENTS OF AN IMPROVED PROJECT OVERSIGHT MODEL

The insights of executives and programmaticists suggest a number of goals that are worthy of pursuit. They suggest, for example, that an ideal oversight system should:

- Improve the abilities of organizations to manage their complex programmatic endeavors (using what we will call a third-generation programmatic approach), and still. . .

- Fully embrace the use of first- and second-generation approaches when they are most appropriate.

- Clearly define the roles and responsibilities of the programmaticists under every generation of programmatic systems, and also. . .

- Clearly define the relationships that should exist between programmaticists and governance committees—regardless of the numbers of "parties" in their oversight model.

- Minimize the amount of organizational complexity that needs to be managed, and thereby. . .

- Address the pain and suffering of programmaticist-Exasperados.

In the second part of this book we will explore how the development of a new three-party management model and a "third-generation programmatics" mindset provide a framework whereby each of these goals can be achieved.

Part 2

The Promise and Practice of Third-Generation Programmatics

CHAPTER 9

Leading Complex Endeavors

THE JOURNEY SO FAR

In the first part of this book we explored how an organization's growth, pursuit of more projects, and pursuit of projects that are inherently more uncertain and complex all result in changes that can make the management of projects and programs more difficult. We examined how organizations have responded to these challenges by expanding their review and governance systems and we observed that this expansion, while at times improving the management of some kinds of uncertainty and complexity (those that were operationally driven or outcome based), too often had the unintentional effect of increasing other kinds of uncertainty and complexity (stakeholder and organizational). We also observed that expansion of governance systems very often had profound effects on the roles and responsibilities of programmaticists—as perceived both by programmaticists and the stakeholders with whom they worked. This had frequently resulted in confusion and exasperation and, ultimately, the emergence of Exasperados.

The narrative told in the first part of this book was pieced together in a somewhat archeological fashion, by gathering snippets of information and insight from many programmaticists and executives, and arranging them on a timeline of "organizational evolution" that highlighted the common experiences in their individual journeys. It is an imperfect narrative when viewed from a historical perspective, but it is a valuable one. Upon hearing their stories retold in the context of the others', programmaticists and executives have been enthusiastic about the perspectives they have been afforded. Many of them expressed gratitude for the perspective that it gave about their organizations' past actions and present challenges. Others were interested anticipating problems they were likely to face in the future. Most expressed comfort in learning that their experiences are shared; it is not that they are "lost" on their journeys or that they are not moving in a rational direction, it's just that they haven't yet "arrived" at the place they need to be. The challenge for all those who are still facing obstacles is to understand where to go next.

Unfortunately, here is where their roadmaps become more vague. There seem to be paths forward, perhaps still narrow and winding, forged by programmaticist and executive trailblazers among us. Some of those paths are extensions of paths that we might be familiar with—further explorations of the limits of second-generation programmatic approaches, for example (agile, lean, complex, or extreme approaches to project and program management). Others venture into areas that are less traveled.

The stories of sojourns down those new paths suggest that some of the paths forward can lead to new vistas and horizons. Others are more cautionary; they sometimes suggest difficult travels that too often reach dead ends. The challenge seems to lie in telling the difference, and for many, in knowing when to forge forward and when to turn back (or jog sideways, perhaps). For many organizations there is still a need to find a new path forward—to find a better place.

At the conclusion of Chapter 8, we reached a crossroad that revealed a somewhat new direction. I suggested a path that embraces what we have learned in our journeys to date, but that might take us forward to places we've yet to fully explore. I also suggested the development of more advanced three-party systems for managing and leading complex projects and programs. But this is a road less traveled. The stories told by those who have scouted in that direction have been mixed. They leave one to wonder: How strong a reason is there to believe that this path will be promising? Is there a reason to suggest that the engagement of two different types of programmaticists in a three-party project oversight system would provide advantages over the two-party systems we have more traditionally employed? Is there a "science" that we might use to guide us in choosing the right path forward? Could that path lead to a new organizational model for managing complex projects and programs—the "centaur piece" of a new programmatic oversight system?

In fact, the literature reveals that there are "scientific" reasons to believe that a three-party model might be more effective for the management of complex projects and programs. Perhaps the most relevant of these is based on the insights of "complexity leadership theory," which explains that several (notably, three) *different* kinds of leadership are critical for resolving complex problems and (thus) for the management of complex endeavors. It will be beneficial to briefly explore the key observations made by complexity leadership theory, and to examine their implications for the management of complex projects and programs. (For a much more detailed review, I encourage readers to examine the books and articles listed in the "Suggested Reading" section near the end of this book.

LEADERSHIP THAT RESOLVES COMPLEX PROBLEMS

Complexity leadership theory proposes that highly complex problems are best resolved by bringing together key stakeholders in an environment that allows them to leverage not only their individual knowledge, but also their individual leadership capabilities and styles.

One relevant observation of complexity leadership theory is that the resolution of highly complex problems (like it or not) usually requires the initiation of also-complex activities. It requires that teams be enabled and encouraged to interact together in ways that are messy, unstructured, and unpredictable, so as to stimulate the spontaneous unimpeded exchange of information and perspectives. Complexity leadership theory proposes that the unstructured and unpredictable interaction of stakeholders within these groups stimulates adaptive thinking—which is the most reliable source of new insights and ideas—and innovative solutions to truly complex problems. It refers to these groups as "complex adaptive systems."

A second relevant observation of complexity leadership theory is that traditional, top-down, bureaucratically based organizational systems can impede the formation of complex adaptive systems (and hence, the resolution of complex problems). The theory opines that the penchant of bureaucratic systems to rely on detailed, predefined, fully governed action plans promotes a culture that focuses on order and control more than messiness and change. As a consequence, bureaucratic systems diminish the likelihood that complex adaptive systems will be formed, that they will function freely enough, and that their outputs will be embraced.

It is interesting to discuss the perspectives of organizational stakeholders about these first two observations; they are consistent with our earlier discussions.

The label of "complex adaptive systems" was new to many executives and programmaticists—but the concepts of how such systems might contribute to innovation, creativity, and problem solving were not. During the course of our discussions, it was common for these stakeholders to affirm their beliefs that complex adaptive systems could be very valuable in solving complex problems. They observed that the most creative solutions identified by their teams were often born during spontaneous and unstructured "problem solving" discussions (sometimes arguments) that fit the description of a complex adaptive system. They frequently cited business examples that seemed to validate their views— examples of large companies and small (like Google Inc. and a gaggle of entrepreneurial startups from diverse industries) whose success seemed to be based on their use of complex adaptive systems to resolve tough problems and generate new ideas.

These stakeholders also agreed that top-down bureaucratic management systems seemed to impede the formation of complex adaptive systems. The examples they provided to support their beliefs were reminiscent of the discussions described in Part 1 of this book. Sometimes they recounted stories about how difficult it was to champion adaptive changes within formal multi-party project oversight systems that contained deeply layered governance committees. At other times, they observed that their secondary review and governance committees were stifling when they acted as governing bodies, but effective when they acted more intuitively and messily, as complex adaptive systems.

Thus, executives and stakeholders generally agreed with these first two observations made by complexity leadership theory.

A third observation of complexity leadership theory is perhaps the most intriguing: Complexity leadership theory proposes that the leadership required to resolve complex problems should not be expected to come from a single person; it should arise through the dynamic interaction of people with diverse behaviors and disparate interests, as each of them influences the thoughts and contributions of the others within a group (the complex adaptive system). The theory proposes that the leadership required to solve complex problems is often a product of the tension generated when people with diverse and disparate interests are brought together. And it proposes that there are three specific kinds of leadership actions required as part of that process: administrative leadership, adaptive leadership, and enabling leadership.[1]

Complexity leadership theory observes that *administrative leadership* is reflected in the actions of stakeholders whose role is to manage the completion of work. Administrative leaders are often managers in organizations who ensure that work is planned, coordinated, resourced, and completed in a way that efficiently delivers outputs and outcomes under the constraints that exist in the organization. Administrative leaders work to resolve conflicts that might otherwise hinder or prevent the complexion of work.

Adaptive leadership is reflected in the actions that must be taken to adjust to new learning or tension. Complexity leadership theory does not propose that adaptive leadership comes from a single person (we will revisit this later, however). It proposes that adaptive leadership most often results from people's interactions within a complex adaptive system, as they respond to new learning, tension, or conflict, and as they seek ways to respond. It proposes that adaptive leadership emerges from groups of people—as a result of their collective attempts to realign strategy, operational plans, and activities.

Finally, complexity leadership theory posits that *enabling leadership* is reflected in the actions of stakeholders who support administrative and adaptive leadership, and who ensure that the expression of administrative versus adaptive leadership is appropriately balanced. An important role of enabling leadership is to manage the tension that sometimes arises between administrative leadership (which seeks to efficiently pursue work plans) and adaptive leadership (which might be expected to more continuously question the validity of current strategies and previously established plans). These three kinds of leadership are summarized in Figure 9.1.

Complexity leadership theory proposes that all three types of leadership are critical to the resolution of complex problems. Complex adaptive systems function best when they bring these three types of leadership together to collectively contribute to the resolution of complex problems.

This third observation—about the types of leadership required to solve complex challenges—is vitally important to our discussions about the science of managing complex projects and programs. We might, for example, observe that it provides a reason to ask whether it would be

---

[1] See Uhl-Bien et al., Complexity leadership theory: Shifting leadership from the industrial age to the knowledge era. Leadership Quarterly 18:298–318, 2007.

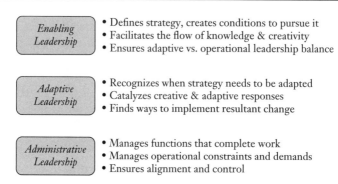

Enabling Leadership	• Defines strategy, creates conditions to pursue it • Facilitates the flow of knowledge & creativity • Ensures adaptive vs. operational leadership balance
Adaptive Leadership	• Recognizes when strategy needs to be adapted • Catalyzes creative & adaptive responses • Finds ways to implement resultant change
Administrative Leadership	• Manages functions that complete work • Manages operational constraints and demands • Ensures alignment and control

Figure 9.1   Key foci of enabling, adaptive, and administrative leadership.

unwise to assign sole responsibility for managing complex projects or programs to an individual leader—whether it would be unwise to expect that a Inclusivist programmaticist should be used to provide single-leader solutions to the many complex problems that are faced by an organization. Complexity leadership theory posits that complex challenges that require adaptive thinking are more effectively solved by *groups* of responsible stakeholders having diverse leadership skills and foci.

We might also observe that the theory enables us to better understand the emergence of Exasperado programmaticists: Exasperados, as we discovered, are often responsible for managing the completion of operational (administrative) project work *and* the adaptation of project strategy in response to newly emerging outcomes. *They are often responsible for ensuring that their endeavors have two forms of leadership that are expected to have tension between them* because of their disparate focus and interests. Sometimes, Exasperados are personally responsible for providing both types of leadership. They might be recognized as programmaticists who have (to some degree) internalized their endeavors' tensions. Other times, Exasperados are responsible for managing teams whose members are providing that leadership—perhaps in a very messy way. Those Exasperados might be recognized as being responsible for resolving tensions that they cannot completely control. In light of complexity leadership theory, the exasperation of both kinds of Exasperados becomes more understandable.

In fact, we might speculate that the theory would *applaud* the emergence of Exasperados. It gives us reason to believe that the tension experienced by Exasperados is good and perhaps necessary, because tension contributes to the dynamic exchange of information within complex adaptive systems—and that exchange stimulates innovation and creativity. It is the reason that "Oh no!" moments born from exasperation turn into "Aha!" moments. It might be painful to *be* an Exasperado, but complexity leadership theory predicts that it could be very valuable to *know* one.

Perhaps most importantly, we might observe that this third observation of complexity leadership theory provides us with a framework for further examining the commonly accepted roles and responsibilities of organizational programmaticists, executives, stakeholders, and their committees. It enables us to ask: "Who should be expected to provide what kind of leadership within the programmatic management systems that our organizations employ?"

The answers that various stakeholders have provided to that question are also revealing.

CRITICAL LEADERSHIP ROLES

In discussion after discussion, interview after interview, organizational stakeholders had similar perspectives about two (of the three) kinds of leadership defined by complexity leadership theory. They commonly acknowledged that their project oversight systems can be viewed as high-level complex adaptive systems. Within those systems, they believed that project management professionals (and especially Traditionalist project management professionals) serve principally in an "administrative leadership" role; project management professionals are responsible for aggregating and acting upon relevant administrative (operational) information on behalf of their teams' complex adaptive systems, and for ensuring alignment and control of those activities. The only objection to this characterization came from professional project managers who felt that the term "administrative leadership" under-represented their roles and responsibilities. They agreed with the assignment of administrative leadership responsibilities, but they preferred that the term be changed to "operational leadership." (In deference to their views, I will use this term going forward.)

Stakeholders also concurred that their governance committees serve principally in an enabling leadership role. Governing committees enable the pursuit of operational activities by defining their organizations' goals and the strategy for pursuing them via projects and programs; they provide resources and they establish organizational conditions to make pursuit of projects and programs possible.

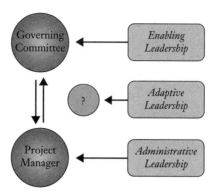

Figure 9.2   Alignment of leadership types with commonly accepted roles and responsibilities of the governing and project management functions, as defined in two-party project oversight systems.

There was consistency in stakeholder perspectives on the "primary" responsibilities of the governing executives and project managers within the two-party project oversight system.

However, stakeholders were often flummoxed by the conception of adaptive leadership as presented by complexity leadership theory (see Figure 9.2). They readily accepted that adaptive ideas flowed from complex adaptive systems (groups of people, or teams) who came together to solve complex problems. They could also accept that those ideas were often a creation of the group—a unique consequence of melded ideas formed in response to the actions and reactions of many contributors. But they had trouble accepting that adaptive leadership could not in many cases also be attributed to individuals who (in their experience) showed exceptional skills in catalyzing those actions and reactions.

In fact, many stakeholders went so far as to name individuals who, within their organizations' various incarnations of complex adaptive systems, could be relied on to stimulate their groups' synthesis of new, adaptive, innovative, and creative ideas. Sometimes they were executives who stimulated adaptive thinking while participating in their organizations' governing committees. Other times they were programmaticists who were exceptionally capable of enhancing their teams' creative and innovative processes. And some were team members who exhibited these same skills. Each of them, stakeholders opined, could be considered to contribute much more significantly than others to the emergence of adaptive leadership. In the minds of the stakeholders whom I interviewed, they were all clear examples of fully embodied adaptive leaders.

And yet, stakeholders acknowledged they could also understand "disembodied" conceptions of adaptive leadership. The emergence of adaptive leadership did not always require that special leaders be present. Stakeholders agreed that adaptive leadership could also be a "pure" product of other participants in complex adaptive systems— attributable not to a single individual, but only to the group, because it was truly a consequence of the dynamic interactions of members of the group.

Stakeholder perspectives on adaptive leadership implied that the source of adaptive leadership required to solve a given complex problem would be difficult to predict. Stakeholders agreed that it could come from individuals, from groups, or even from circumstances. Nonetheless, they remained (as evidenced by their stories) quite willing to name specific stakeholders or groups of stakeholders (committees) that they felt they could count on as a "source" of adaptive leadership. They insisted that there were certain stakeholders who consistently assumed responsibility for catalyzing the adaptive behaviors of projects or programs, and they observed that those stakeholders might be found on programmatic teams or on various governing committees.

To explore this notion, I sought out a number of experienced project management professionals and asked them to identify the various (primary and secondary, review and governance) committees with which their projects or programs interacted. I then asked them to define to what degree they would consider their projects' relationships with those committees to be enabling, operational (administrative), or adaptive in nature. I also asked them to assess the leadership focus of their own project teams.

Together, we explored their responses.

The interactions of project or program teams with their various primary and secondary review committees were rarely characterized one-dimensionally (see Figure 9.3). While project managers differed in their estimations of how much each committee focused on each of the three leadership roles, they very rarely indicated that any one committee assumed *only* one role. For example, line function review committees were commonly thought to have roles related to enabling, adaptive, and operational leadership. Project managers were not surprised by such a finding. After all, line function review committees might need to assume an enabling demeanor when they supported line function executives who served in an enabling role, or when managing operational activities within their own departments. However, they might need to contribute

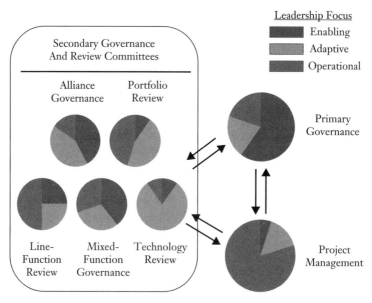

Figure 9.3   Leadership foci of various governance and review commit-tees, as assessed by an individual project manager.

adaptive perspectives when responding to issues that emerged as they managed their departments. Their adaptive contributions, in turn, would need to be informed by their operational leadership perspectives and capabilities. In the operational leadership role they would also be respon-sible for the efficient completion of departmental work.

The complex nature of stakeholder (and committee) roles, respon-sibilities, and relationships could result in an equally complex intersec-tion of leadership needs under various circumstances. Project managers interacted with many committees—primary and secondary, review, and governance. The sources of various types of leadership were spread broadly across their organizations.

As the opinions of project managers were examined at an organiza-tional level, however, a new question arose—one that takes on increasing significance (especially in light of our earlier discussions): *Who was responsible for ensuring effective integration of the leadership responses of each of these committees?* Most stakeholders agreed (based on their benchmark of a two-party fully governed project oversight system) that a primary governance committee should assume principle responsibility for ensur-ing the integration and assimilation of the enabling leadership perspec-tives within its domain of responsibility. Most stakeholders also agreed (based on the same benchmark) that a project management function should assume principle responsibility for ensuring the effective integration and assimilation of operational leadership perspectives. But there was little agreement on how organizations could best ensure that adaptive leadership responses did not stagnate within their individual governance and review committee silos. The stakeholders I interviewed could quote case studies that provided insight about how such responsibility *had been* assumed; however, few could identify overriding principles that defined how it *should be* assumed.

The three-function nature of complexity leadership theory made it apparent that a gap might exist in organizational management models built upon two-party leadership systems. In many organizations, there was no formal recognition of who would (or should) be responsible for integrating concepts that emerged as a consequence of adaptive leadership. It seemed (once again) to suggest that a three-party model—in which adaptive leadership responsibilities are more clearly assigned—might be better for the management of complex projects and programs.

During discussions and interviews, stakeholders generally agreed that complexity leadership theory provides a useful framework for better understanding the types of leadership required to manage complex projects or programs, and for examining the expectations for each kind of leadership within any given organizational context. Several have since reported that they found value in using it to examine and more explicitly define the expected roles and responsibilities of their organizations' primary and secondary governance committees. Most of them also agreed that in each of these respects it had contributed significantly to their understanding of programmatic science. (It is for those reasons that I have described it in some detail in this chapter.)

However, complexity leadership theory also seems to highlight a sometimes unfulfilled need for adaptive leadership in organizations that pursue highly uncertain outcome-based initiatives. When the outcomes of programmatic activities are uncertain, the pursuit of their goals becomes much more complex. When the pursuit of goals is complex, the need for adaptive leadership rises.

Many executives and programmaticists report that their organizations have struggled to ensure the growth of adaptive leadership. They would like to assign some measure of accountability for it to a specific organizational stakeholder or group. Many interviewees report that they have already concluded that the development of "outcome sage" programmaticists who embody the adaptive leadership described in complexity leadership theory would improve their organizations' abilities to manage complex projects or programs.

ADAPTIVE LEADERSHIP AND THE OUTCOME SAGE–PROGRAMMATICIST

As described in Chapter 8, an outcome sage–programmaticist might be envisioned as a leader who assumes primary responsibility for managing outcome uncertainty and solving outcome complexity. We have proposed, based on the complexity management framework described in Chapter 8 and Figure 8.1, that to fulfill such a position an outcome sage–programmaticist would need to embody or stimulate adaptive leadership as described in complexity leadership theory. Let's consider the skills that might be required from such a leader.

To be effective in his (or her) role, an adaptive leader would be highly aware of the assumptions that his teams have made when defining how programmatic outcomes are expected to contribute to a team's delivery of benefits. He (or she) would need to be adept at measuring the delivery of those outcomes and at identifying results that signal the need for a shift in his team's strategic or operational approaches. He might be personally capable of quickly identifying or recognizing new approaches (strategic or operational) that would improve the subsequent delivery of desirable outcomes and benefits, or to be uniquely effective in stimulating others to do the same. He might be uniquely capable of stimulating members of his project or program teams, members of primary or secondary review or governance committees, and any other loose confederations of organizational stakeholders to contribute enthusiastically (as complex adaptive systems) to the synthesis and emergence of adaptive leadership responses.

To possess these competencies, an adaptive leader might be expected or required to have a unique understanding of the sometimes technical options that his (or her) team is pursuing and manage the complex problems that might arise as a consequence of outcome uncertainty. He (or she) should stimulate the dynamic interactions of stakeholders to catalyze the emergence of options for solving complex problems. He should clearly communicate such options to the many organizational groups who might (as independently organized complex adaptive systems) contribute to the improvement or adoption of those solutions. He would consequently need to exhibit exceptional skills in the communication and negotiation of sometimes technical proposals. He would be highly sensitive to how an individual's personal motivations and context are likely to affect his views during decision making. And finally, as an embodiment of an adaptive leader, or as one who is responsible for integrating the unembodied adaptive leadership contributions of individuals in organizationally dispersed complex adaptive systems, he would need to work seamlessly and collaboratively with those who are principally responsible for the operational and enabling leadership functions of his organization.

In the eyes of many, that is quite a tall order.

CHAPTER 10

A New Perspective on Programs and Program Management

FROM ADAPTIVE LEADERSHIP TO PROGRAM MANAGEMENT

We ended Chapter 9 with a two-paragraph description of the competencies and skills that might be essential to an adaptive leader. It was a conceptual list, built on the foundation of complexity leadership theory. But it might also be viewed as a pragmatic list, intended to be valuable when defining the skills, knowledge, and experience that might be required of a programmaticist who embodies or evokes the adaptive leadership role—an outcome sage–programmaticist.

I laid versions of that description before executives and programmaticists after discussing their organizations' approaches for managing complex projects or programs. Some of them responded with looks of befuddlement. They questioned the role of a programmaticist in interpreting project outcomes and in assuming more active (and more "expert") responsibility for leading organizational committees in their review and analysis of those outcomes. These stakeholders did not believe that a programmaticist should be expected to have the technical knowledge required for such tasks. They observed that placing programmaticists in charge of such reviews and analyses would require that programmaticists interact with high-level leaders almost as peers. They often opined that, "that is not really the job of a project manager." For the most part, these were the stakeholders who preferred more operational (administrative) conceptions of the programmaticist's role.

But other stakeholders responded with grateful recognition. They expressed relief to read a narrative about programmaticist competencies that went beyond that which was "traditional" and operationally focused.

They were pleased to receive a description of programmaticist roles that focused on outcomes more than outputs. They believed that the true success of their complex projects or programs depended on the delivery of benefits through outcomes, and they felt that programmaticists needed to become more involved in managing benefits. These were stakeholders who saw the value in having an "adaptive programmaticist." A few of them mused that the descriptions before them might be the missing piece to a programmatic puzzle that they had been struggling to solve; a couple asked if they could keep their copies of the description.

The two frames of reference reflected in stakeholders' responses seemed to confirm that complexity leadership theory could provide valuable insights about the practice of project and program management.

They also seemed to provide important context for understanding research that has been conducted in the "programmatic sciences"; these two frames of reference are also well represented in published research-based literature on project and program management.

The operational perspectives represented by the former group of stakeholders are reflected in the large body of publications about traditional project management processes. These publications focus on the pursuit of project goals (and sometimes, project strategy) by breaking down projects into manageable pieces (activities) and pursuing them through rigorous command-and-control-oriented processes. They focus principally on advancing an operational (administrative) role for project management, whereby project managers are held responsible for delivering preplanned outputs in a traditional bureaucratically based project oversight model. They tended to be based on fundamental assumptions that efficiently completing work according to plan is the mission of a project management professional because completing work is the primary means by which a project manager contributes to the delivery of a project's inherent value.

The adaptive perspectives represented by the latter group of stakeholders are reflected in a different wave of publications—a wave that has emerged much more recently. These publications are based on research that has focused on the approaches and competencies required to deliver benefits from programmatic endeavors that are uncertain (and usually, much more strategic) in nature—endeavors that are fraught with uncertain assumptions and that (as a result) might be exceptionally complex to manage. These publications focus on the kinds of initiatives commonly sponsored by modern organizations working on knowledge- or learning-based subjects; they focus on complex endeavors whose value is uncertain because it is based on assumptions about results that have yet to be realized.

This latter wave of recent publications focuses specifically on the management of endeavors that are labeled as "programs" (or "programmes"[1]) and that (from the points of view of the authors) need to be recognized as quite different from traditional projects. The research contained in this new wave of literature shares an important theme: It highlights that the leadership and management skills required of a program(me) manager are quite different from those required of a project manager.[2] The leadership required of a program manager must be much more outcome-focused and adaptive in nature. It emphasizes that a program manager needs to have a learn-and-adapt management and leadership style, which is quite different from the command-and-control leadership style more often required of a project manager. This new wave of publications presents research that links program leadership requirements to the adaptive leadership competencies that are described in the previous chapter.

As a former organizational programmaticist (and current academic and advisor in the field), I find it quite interesting to observe that the more recently published practice-based studies of "program management" focus on skills that might best be described as adaptive leadership, whereas practice-based studies of "project management" focus on skills that are associated with operational (administrative) leadership. It seems to validate our earlier observations about the importance of two types of programmatic leadership because it strongly suggests that the fundamental roles of project management and program management might best be defined by their respective abilities to satisfy the operational and adaptive leadership needs of complex programmatic endeavors. And it leads to a suggestion that project management and program management should indeed be viewed as *qualitatively* different organizational

---

[1] It should be noted by readers who prefer American English that much of the new research and literature on the nature of programs has been conducted by researchers from the United Kingdom. My habit is to use the American spelling of program. To examine the rich literature in the field, however, it is necessary that literature searches also include "programme."

[2] For important examples of literature on the differences, please see "Distinctions between projects and programs, project management and program management" in the "Additional Suggested Reading" section near the end of this book.

roles—roles that (according to complexity leadership theory) are so sufficiently separate and distinct as to allow (and even encourage) tension to arise between them.

The emerging literature supports the notion that the leadership competencies of both project and program management are required for the effective management of complex projects and programs. It suggests a basis for joining them together (under the umbrella of "programmatic science") to fill separate and critical roles in the pursuit of complex endeavors. And in so doing, it should embolden us to investigate clearer, more distinct definitions of projects and programs, and of the ideal roles and responsibilities of program and project managers within our organizational systems.

What Is a Program, Really?

For years now, I have begun the first lecture in my courses on program leadership with a simple question: "What is a program?" I had once presumed that students who were taking such a course as part of an executive master's degree program and who were (for the most part) professionals in the field would have a strong sense of what they were about to study. I was often surprised to learn, however, that most students had difficulty answering the question directly. Most of them described programs in relation to projects using descriptors of scale. "A program is bigger; it is longer; it has a bigger budget; it is more complicated, more difficult, and more strategic." Their responses hardly suggested that they might be prepared to consider that programs were *qualitatively* different from projects.

We had interesting discussions about the nature of programs based on these initial responses. Their suggestions that programs were larger, longer, or more expensive than projects led to unwinnable debates about thresholds and cutoffs that might distinguish projects from programs. Suggestions that they were more complicated or more difficult or more strategic led to impossible discussions about how best to measure such things—and even more difficult debates about thresholds and cutoffs. None of these discussions led to agreements on a precise definition. It was easy to identify exceptions to any of the criteria that my students offered.

Students who had already studied project management (and especially those who were certified as Project Management Professionals®) were seemingly more prepared. They would usually cite definitions based on the published "standards" of program or project management. The most commonly cited definition came from "The Standard for Program

Management," published by the Project Management Institute. In its third edition, that standard defines a program as "a group of related projects, sub-programs, and program activities managed in a coordinated way to obtain benefits not available from managing them individually."[3] It is a widely accepted (hence, standard) definition, grounded in the recognition that organizational initiatives commonly recognized as "programs" are usually comprised of several project-like components, and that managing them together in a coordinated way can be beneficial. Upon close examination, however, it can be recognized as an imperfect definition.

Perhaps the most obvious reason that it is imperfect is that it does not by itself provide an obvious reason to believe or to consider that there might be qualitative differences between projects and programs, or that there would be significant differences between the skills and the competencies required of those who would manage programs versus projects. To those who participated in the discussions from our previous chapters, that does not feel right.

The Standard's primary assertion that a program is an aggregation of projects applies a distinctively bureaucratic and traditional project management mindset. In doing so, it invites questions about whether programs are really *that* different from "big projects." Otherwise, why couldn't a big project be turned into a program by compartmentalizing its workstreams into more formally defined subprojects? Students in my classes who were program managers objected: "There is more to a program than that." Students who were project managers began to wonder if they had learned of a way to justify the purchase of new business cards. Many of my students eventually agreed that the "standard" definition of a program was somehow incomplete. They wondered aloud, however, "Why would that be true in a newly published Standard for Program Management?"

The answer is reasonably simple.

Writers of the Standards (this author being one) face an inherent conundrum. Standards must focus on that which has come to be accepted as "standard." It is important that they do; it is a requirement that assures users that their content has become widely accepted and that it is valuable. As a consequence, however, it takes time before newly proposed perspectives make their way into Standards—they must first become widely accepted, no matter how valuable they may be. And so,

---

[3]The Standard for Program Management, 3d ed., Project Management Institute, Newtown Square, Pennsylvania, 2013.

Conceiving

Testing

Refining

Accepting

Adopting

Publishing

Figure 10.1   The natural evolution of standard perspectives.

it should be recognized, the timeline associated with conceiving, testing, refining, accepting, adopting, and (eventually) publishing those new perspectives in Standards is usually long (Figure 10.1).

Literature on the more qualitative differences between project and program management and on emerging insights about a program manager's adaptive leadership role is relatively new (especially when compared to the historical literature espousing traditional views of project management). Many of the literature's new teachings have not made their way into the available Standards. In part, that is because the best ways for adopting those insights in an organizational setting are not yet well understood. (We will discuss that challenge in the following chapters.) We might also expect that it will take time, and perhaps the publication of more "nonstandard" books (like this one) to disseminate such ideas. For now, we should accept that the various new concepts that have been introduced in recent years are still in the testing, refining, and accepting stages.

Through the years, I have invited my students to examine a broad range of literature on the management of projects and programs. I have required that they read the works of authors considered to be leaders in the field; it is an essential part of their study of the "programmatic sciences." One publication that has made significant contributions to our understanding of the differences between programs and projects, and to the practice of program management, is *Managing Successful Programmes*.[4] In that publication (which characterizes itself as a "guide"), a program(me) is defined as "a temporary, flexible organization created to coordinate, direct, and oversee the implementation of a set of related projects and activities in order to deliver outcomes and benefits related to the organization's strategic objectives."

---

[4]Managing Successful Programmes, The Stationary Office, Norwich, UK, 2011.

Students generally agreed that this definition goes beyond the Standard definition because it includes an indication of the intended scope of a program (*benefits* related to the organization's *strategic objectives*), its primary deliverables (*outcomes* and *benefits*), and its nature (a *flexible organization*). Its focus on outcomes and its emphasis on flexibility bespeak a management approach that differs from the historically accepted output-focused approach of traditional project management. And its characterization of a program as an organization seems to imply that it will be comprised of people with different leadership roles. *Managing Successful Programmes* emphasizes that programs deliver value that is derived from outcomes, and that programs can be viewed as a means for managing change—concepts consistent with the more recently published program management literature and our proposal of the adaptive leadership role of a program manager.

My students agreed that the program definition suggested in *Managing Successful Programmes* represents a "step in the right direction." However, they (and I) still felt that there was room for improvement. They observed that it does not provide a description that is sufficiently clear in defining the qualitative difference(s) between programs and projects—differences that necessitate which programs should be managed in qualitatively different ways. Unfortunately, a review of program definitions offered by other Standards and publications revealed similar issues and questions (see the Suggested Reading section near the end of this book).

Why should it be so difficult to write project and program definitions that provide a clear basis for their distinction and that highlight the differences in how they should be managed? Could we propose new definitions that would be more understandable not only by professional programmaticists, but also by the various stakeholders with whom they work? To try to answer these questions, I conducted a test. I asked students and clients in classrooms and workshops to quickly fill in the blanks in the following statements with either "project" or "program."

Cleaning the basement is my latest_____.

I've gotten too heavy; I need a weight loss_____.

I'm planting a garden; it's my springtime_____.

To defend our country we need a strong defense_____.

Because John had a problem with drugs, he enrolled in a rehabilitation_____.

Building the addition on our house was a big_____.

I can't wait to get back to school so I can work on my art
_____.

Our school does well in sports because we improved our athletic
_____.

His cancer was cured as a direct result of his treatment
_____.

In one class after another, and in workshop after workshop, the results were the same. As I read each statement aloud, the participants responded to each blank in near-perfect unison: project, program, project, program, program. . . When they were not given time for nuanced reflection or debate, each participant agreed on exactly how each statement should be completed. Everyone knew which endeavors were programs. The experiment seemed to reveal that they had clear internal expectations of what constitutes a program.

I then challenged each group to identify what was common about those endeavors that they had identified as programs. Their answers were familiar: "They were bigger; they took longer; they were more expensive; and they were more complicated, more difficult, or more strategic." But when each answer was given, we posed another question: *Why?* Why were the "programs" bigger or longer, more expensive, more complicated, more difficult, or more strategic? It was an easy exercise that drilled deeper into the question of what makes programs different, in an attempt to identify a single root cause. And time after time it led to this conclusion about what was common in programs: *A program's workstream requirements were uncertain.* One could not know with certainty what would need to be done to successfully deliver the intended program benefits.

Programs pursued goals via strategies that could not be promised to work; they depended on the delivery of outcomes that could not be guaranteed. It was often because program outcomes depended upon the responses or behaviors of people (participants, stakeholders, competitors, or customers, for example), and those behaviors could not be precisely predicted. At other times, it was because one couldn't predict or guarantee tangible outcomes that might be achieved (for example, the technical data obtained through research, or the results of medical treatments). Still other times it was because benefits were being pursued in unstable or uncertain environments (where regulations might change, or the availability of resources is uncertain, for example). Often, it seemed, it was for combinations of these reasons. In each case that we studied, uncertain outcomes were likely to result in new understanding and a consequent need to adapt the approach that should be used to deliver an endeavor's intended benefits. And in each case, the need to adapt might lead to complex issues that would best be resolved through adaptive leadership approaches.

These discussions might lead us to believe that the fundamental difference between projects and programs was that programs sought to deliver benefits via uncertain outcomes that might expected to spawn the emergence of complex challenges. *Programs needed to focus more specifically on managing outcome uncertainty and complexity.*

In contrast, projects focused on the delivery of benefits via more definable and predictable outputs. The principle challenges faced by projects were operational in nature. *Projects needed to focus more specifically on managing operational uncertainty and complexity.*

Programs required a learn-and-adapt management style, whereas projects more often required a command-and-control style.

The responses of students and workshop participants provided a basis for proposing a new definition of a program:

> A ***program*** is an endeavor that seeks to deliver benefits via activities that by their nature have uncertain outcomes. Programs need to be managed in a manner that enables adaptation of their strategies and plans in response to the outcomes that they produce.
>
> The outcomes required by programs are pursued via projects, subprograms, and other program-related activities.

It is perhaps an imperfect definition, ripe for improvement based on the contributions of others. But it was satisfactory (at least to this academic, his students, and clients) for a number of reasons.

- It begins with the more holistic identification of a program as an *endeavor*—and not as a sum of its component parts.

- It emphasizes a program's intended purpose early—*to deliver benefits*.

- But it simultaneously ensures that the distinguishing feature of programs is highlighted—*uncertain outcomes*.

The first sentence of this description seems to capture the essence of a program in a way that would be easy to understand by all, and a way that clearly distinguished programs from projects (see below).

The second sentence of the definition emphasizes a point that all stakeholders found to be critical—that the uncertain nature of programs requires that they be managed adaptively.

The final sentence provides a link between this new definition and the definitions of a program most often quoted in Standards and other publications. It acknowledges the fundamental structure of programs— that they are comprised of *projects, subprograms, and other program-related activities*—is not changed as a consequence of having established a new outcome-focused program definition.

It has been interesting to explore the reactions of stakeholders to the above redefinition of programs. Executives (in particular) commonly observed that most of the important initiatives their organizations were pursuing could be considered to fit the new program definition—even initiatives that had not previously been classified formally as programs. These might have included initiatives being overseen by a "special committee" or a "task force," or groups of activities that were being championed by executives without having been formally organized as programmatic endeavors. They included, for example, endeavors seeking to change business processes or streamline organizational infrastructure, or initiatives to improve the human resource policies, personnel development, or morale. From the point of view of this programmaticist, that was a very good outcome. It resulted in an expanded executive awareness of how program management principles and practices (and program managers and leaders) might contribute more broadly to the future success of their organizations. It heightened awareness of the broader importance of the programmatic sciences.

The discussions also stimulated stakeholders to ask additional questions about the definitions of "program management" and "program managers," and about whether a corresponding redefinition of projects and project management might be necessary.

REDEFINING PROGRAM MANAGEMENT

The third edition of Project Management Institute's *Standard for Program Management* has defined program management as "the application of knowledge, skills, tools, and techniques to a program to meet program requirements and to obtain benefits and control not available by managing projects individually." It explains that program management's role is to integrate and align a program's components (projects, subprograms, and other program activities) so as to support program goals.

Students and stakeholders observed that while the Standard's definition of program management was appropriate in its focus on the delivery of benefits through program goals, it was still clearly grounded in traditional component-based definitions of a program. They proposed that a new definition of program management, focused on the need for adaptive leadership, might be more appropriate and valuable. Their responses led to proposals of new definitions for program management and for program managers:

> ***Program management*** is a profession in the programmatic sciences that ensures the optimal delivery of program benefits by adaptively managing program strategies and plans. Program management involves the application of specialized knowledge, skills, tools, and techniques to ensure that programs are responsive to the outcomes they generate as they pursue their intended benefits.
>
> Program management is practiced by program managers who work collaboratively with project managers, subprogram managers, and other members of their program teams to ensure the completion of required program activities and the delivery of important program outcomes.

Stakeholders embraced this description for reasons related to the redefinition of programs. It was viewed as an improvement over current standard definitions because:

- It asserts that program management should be viewed as *a profession in the programmatic sciences*—and not merely as a role. Program managers agreed that the treatment of program management as a role diminished recognition of the specific knowledge and skills required for its effective practice.

- It confirms that program management should focus on *optimal delivery of program benefits by adaptively managing program strategies and plans* to make clear its unique focus and its distinct leadership mindset.

- It acknowledges program management's application of professional *knowledge, skills, tools, and techniques*, consistent with current Standard definitions.

- It emphasizes that *program management works collaboratively with project management*.

Stakeholders suggested that an appropriate new definition of program managers would be:

> ***Program managers*** are professionals who are responsible for managing a program's pursuit of its intended benefits. Program managers are responsible for ensuring that a program's strategy and plans are adapted appropriately in response to program outcomes, to ensure the most effective pursuit of targeted program benefits. Program managers are adaptive leaders who work closely with project managers, subprogram managers, and other members of their program teams to ensure completion of required program activities.

When considering an improved definition of a program manager, stakeholders sought to ensure that:

- The program manager was defined as a *professional* whose role was focused on *delivery of benefits*, so as to distinguish the role more explicitly from that of a project manager who might be more focused on the delivery of outputs (on time, on budget, and to specifications).

- The program manager's role in *ensuring that a program's strategy and plans are adapted in response to program outcomes* was emphasized so as to make certain the program manager's role in managing a program's response to *outcomes* was clear.

- The program manager's important relationship with project and subprogram managers was appropriately acknowledged.

Upon review, stakeholders agreed that the above definitions might still be imperfect. They were certainly different from those traditionally cited in Standards. It will take time to determine if they can rise to a standard level of acceptance. Indeed, some elements of the definitions might even be considered to be aspirational. (It could be argued, for example, that program management has not yet met the formal criteria of a "profession" because it does not require university-level qualifications, or have typical professional barriers to entry and practice.) But to most, that was alright. Most journeys into uncharted areas begin with an aspirational first step.

Stakeholders were generally pleased with these new definitions. They felt that they began to describe (in terms suitable to a professional standard) the subject matter, the discipline, and the roles and responsibilities of those outcome sage–programmaticists that they had previously identified as being so valuable to the management of complex projects and programs. Those who had participated in our extensive discussions about project and program management—whether they were discussions about Exasperados and the emergence of first- and second-generation programmatic systems, project management's identity crisis, the evolution (and limitations) of two-party project oversight systems, insights from complexity leadership theory, or the emerging literature and research on program(me) management—were unanimous in stating that these new definitions represented "another step in the right direction." It is my (and their) hope that their publication will stimulate additional discussions which may result in their further refinement and acceptance.

REDEFINING PROJECTS AND PROJECT MANAGEMENT

In my initial discussions with various stakeholders, most had expressed comfort with the common definitions of projects, project management, and project managers as defined in currently available project management standards. They observed that those definitions were principally based on traditional conceptions of projects and project managers, and that the conceptions of project management were not altered dramatically as a consequence of our newly proposed definitions of programs and program management. The value of existing project management standards (and by inference, of the definitions used within them) was not disputed.

The basic definitions provided in the Project Management Institute's *Guide to the Project Management Body of Knowledge*, 5th ed., for example, are as follows:[5]

A *project* is a temporary endeavor undertaken to create a unique product, service, or result.

Project management is the application of knowledge, skills, tools and techniques to project activities to meet the project requirements.

The *project manager* is the person assigned by the performing organization to lead the team that is responsible for achieving the project objectives.

---

[5]A Guide to the Project Management Body of Knowledge (PMBOK® Guide), 5th ed., Project Management Institute, Newtown Square, Pennsylvania, 2013.

After going through a process for redefining programs and program management, however, it seemed reasonable to question whether redefinition of project-related terms should also be considered. Students and workshop participants agreed that new project definitions might more clearly highlight the differences between projects and programs or project management and program management. They might reduce ambiguity about the roles of a project manager and improve understanding of the relationships between project and program managers within programmatic systems.

Students and workshop participants proposed that project-related definitions could be restructured in a way that is reminiscent of program-related definitions:

> A *project* is a temporary endeavor that seeks to deliver unique value and benefits via activities that deliver predefined outputs and/or targeted project outcomes. Projects are managed in a manner that seeks to ensure efficient completion of work and delivery of work products on time, on budget, and to specifications.
>
> *Project management* is a profession in the programmatic sciences that focuses on the design and completion of work plans to ensure the efficient delivery of work products on time, on budget, and to specifications. Project management is practiced by project managers who apply professional knowledge, skills, tools, and techniques to ensure the effective management of operational uncertainty and the resolution of operational complexity.
>
> *Project managers* are professionals who are responsible for managing a project's pursuit of its intended outputs and/or outcomes. Project managers are operational leaders who are responsible for ensuring that a project meets its operational goals for delivering work products with proscribed specifications—on time and on budget.

Stakeholders generally agreed that these new definitions support a better understanding of the roles of projects and project management under a programmatic system that seeks to distinguish an operational (output)-oriented role of project management from an adaptive (outcome and benefits)-oriented role of program management. They observed that these new definitions would enable project managers to more clearly define their roles and their responsibilities as they seek to serve as operational savant–programmaticists. Stakeholders were ready to explore how separation of the project and program management roles might work under a three-party system—how it might improve their organizations' management of complex endeavors. (We will discuss the adoption and function of three-party project oversight systems in the next chapter.)

However, before beginning those discussions, many stakeholders sought first to understand the potential significance of these new definitions to their own personal circumstances; before discussing how programs or projects might best be managed under reconceived (three-party) programmatic systems, they wanted to explore whether their own important endeavors should be considered programs or projects. The reason was obvious; the answer to this question could have profound implications to their own roles and responsibilities.

For many, distinguishing their endeavors as programs or projects was obvious and (therefore) easy. But for others it was not.

Is It a Program or Is It a Project?

Stakeholders began our interviews and discussions with specific examples of programs and projects in mind. They frequently referred to examples from their organizations or their past experiences. They would often use these as reference points during our discussions—as benchmarks of organizational programs or projects suitable for use in testing their beliefs.

Stakeholders had similar preconceptions about the roles and responsibilities of program or project managers. They often "benchmarked" these titles to programmaticists whom they believed filled each of those roles well (based on their own organizations' expectation of program or project manager roles and responsibilities). In group discussions with stakeholders from different organizations, quite a bit of time was spent comparing their individual benchmark experiences and trying to understand the similarities and differences in their preconceptions.

Unfortunately, preconceptions about organizational programs and projects, and program managers and project managers, could prove to be a bit of a problem. There was not the same degree of unanimity about "program" and "project" labels as we previously saw in our fill-in-the-blank exercise. There were significant disparities in how individual organizations had used these labels and titles. What was a program in one organization might be considered a project in another. What project managers did in one organization might be reserved for program managers in another. These inconsistencies made it more difficult to examine stakeholder views. They made it necessary to "translate" a stakeholder's message whenever he or she used the terms "project" or "program." It was more difficult to decipher a stakeholder's true views when the labels of projects and programs were applied in proprietary ways.

As we struggled in our discussions about whether a given initiative should be labeled as a program or project, it became apparent that there was yet another issue: Some stakeholders were resistant to changing their organizations' labeling conventions because re-assignment of those labels had personal implications. Stakeholders were vested in their organizations' current use of those titles; organizational titles were commonly used to define the reporting relationships of an individual or the priority that would be assigned to a specific initiative. Sometimes they were used to benchmark salaries. Initial conversations about changing program or project labels were sometimes tense.

As labeling conversations evolved, however, there was often a change in tone. The change, I believe, was based on stakeholder recognition that the differences between programs and projects (as they are proposed above) were more tangible and important than had previously been appreciated. There was a logical basis for distinguishing the two. More precisely using these terms led to a clearer understanding of the kinds of leadership that a programmaticist should be expected to provide and the leadership skills that would lead to professional success. Most stakeholders believed that clarifying leadership expectations for their endeavors would be a very important and valuable outcome—one which would (in the long term) facilitate their professional growth.

As our conversations progressed, stakeholders seemed to grow more comfortable with the perspective that program and project management were both important to the effective management of organizational endeavors. The choice between filling the operational savant or the outcome sage role became less of a choice about titles and positions, and more of a choice about knowledge and capabilities. With continuing conversations, most stakeholders agreed that the proposal of a new approach for defining programmaticist roles and responsibilities "made sense." That, I believe, was the most important test of their potential.

Still, some stakeholders expressed concern that the nature of their organizations' endeavors—whether they were programs or projects— might not be completely understood or agreed upon by either their governing committee members or the programmaticists responsible for them.

To those who had participated in our discussions to this point, it might seem that they shouldn't be confused; programs pursue value via strategies that rely on uncertain outcomes, and projects deliver value via activities that are expected to have predictable outputs and/or outcomes. To answer the question "Is it a program or project?" it seemed that one needs only to ask "What are the goals?" and "How will they be delivered?" The answers to those questions should enable one to determine whether an endeavor will be a project or program, right?

It was quite interesting to listen to executives and programmaticists as they tried to answer those questions; even when discussing the exact same initiative there were often disagreements on whether that initiative should be considered a program or project. It was fascinating to observe. And as we considered example after example, case study after case study, a pattern emerged: The disagreements were often related to different understandings or assumptions about which goals had been delegated to the program or project team and which goals remained the responsibility of its governance committee.

Consider, as an example, an endeavor that seeks to deliver benefits by launching a new product into a competitive market. The goals of such an initiative might be expressed in this way:

- To ensure that the product is manufactured efficiently, in sufficient quantities, to product specifications;

- To ensure the product is packaged effectively and readily available to ship to market;

- To design, produce, and distribute marketing materials for use in promoting the product; and

- To train salespeople about the attributes of the product.

These goals, one might argue, should be expected to satisfy the goal "to deliver benefits by launching a new product into a competitive market." And they would—if it was presumed that the product would be successful. These goals focused most on the word "launch."

The goals for the initiative might also be expressed in a different way, however. They might be:

- To launch a product that is differentiated from the competition;
- To ensure that the product achieves the market share targets that are required for success;

- To generate cash flow for the organization based on increasing product sales;

- To optimize the product's generation of profit; and

- To ensure that the organization realizes an acceptable return on its product investment.

These goals are also consistent with the overarching goal "to deliver benefits by launching a new product into a competitive market." This set of goals differs from the first set of goals in its more explicit description of outcomes, and in its inherent recognition that launch of the product cannot (by itself) be presumed to result in the delivery of benefits. These goals focused most on the word "benefits."

There are significant qualitative differences between the two sets of goals. The former group of goals can be satisfied (merely) by the generation of outputs (product, packaging, marketing, and training materials). The latter group of goals depends on the generation of outcomes (recognized differentiation, abilities to compete, maximization of sales, profit, and return) (see Figure 10.2).

By our new definitions, it might be expected that the former group of goals would be assumed by one or more project teams led by an output-focused project management professional(s). These goals can be achieved principally by using an operationally focused leadership style to manage the efficient completion of work.

In contrast, the latter group of goals might be more effectively managed by a program team led by an outcome-driven program management professional. These goals are likely to require that outcomes be realized and then used to refine strategies to improve

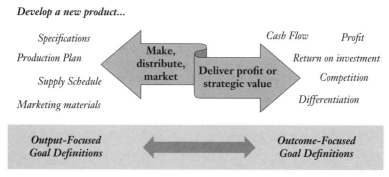

Figure 10.2   Defining the goals of an organizational initiative relating to the launch of a new product.

subsequent outcomes. They might be expected to result in the itera-tive assessment and refinement of any number of things: the product, its packaging, the marketing materials, salesperson training, customer feedback, or pricing, for example.

Different interpretations of an initial mandate ("to deliver benefits by launching a new product into a competitive market") can result in dif-ferent requirements for managing the initiative. Is the initiative a project or a program? Once again, the correct answer is: "It depends"—this time on the specific goals that are placed under the authority of the responsible programmaticist and his or her team.

It is also interesting to explore the above example from the perspec-tive of a governing committee. A committee that needs to achieve the second set of goals might be considered to have two choices.

One choice might be to pursue a program-based approach. By that approach, responsibility for achieving the desired benefits would be del-egated to a program team led by a program manager. The program team would be expected to initiate (or request the initiation of) projects to pursue the first set of goals (and any other goals that the team believes are important). These projects would produce outputs (for example, pack-aged product and marketing materials) which result in outcomes (for example, quarterly sales and profits). The program team would monitor those outcomes as they were realized, then initiate additional projects or programs that might become important to the realization of the second set of goals. It might, for example, initiate a market research project to assess the reasons that customers haven't selected their product, or a training program to improve sales force effectiveness. The program team would thereby assume an adaptive leadership role, changing the program strategy and plans as necessary to ensure that its goals were achieved.[6]

An alternative choice might be to pursue a project-based approach. By that approach, the governing committee would be expected to del-egate responsibilities for the generation of outputs (as listed in the first group of goals) to one or more project teams. If the second set of goals is not achieved as a consequence of pursuing the first set of goals, it would become the governance committee's responsibility to adapt the endeavor's strategy, and possibly to commission additional projects. In

---

[6]In this example, it should be noted that the program manager might also be called a "product manager." Product management, I would argue, should often be viewed as a specific application of program management.

Table 10.1   Examples of Output-Focused versus Outcome-Driven Goals for Various Kinds of Initiatives

Type of Initiative	Output-Focused Goals	Outcome-Driven Goals
Product development and launch	• Manufacture • Package • Establish supply chain capabilities • Produce and distribute marketing materials • Train salesforce	• Achieve market penetration • Generate cash flow • Generate profit • Differentiate product • Beat competition • Maximize return
Information technology systems	• Design system architecture • Meet user requirements • Purchase required hardware • Put software into production • Design and deliver training • Provide customer support	• Achieve performance targets • Ensure system stability • Ensure customer adoption • Achieve high customer satisfaction ratings • Increase user productivity • Demonstrate financial value and adequate return on investment
Research and development	• Secure resources/budget • Conduct experiment(s) • Complete data analysis • Generate research reports	• Interpret analytical results • Refine hypotheses • Refine experimental plan • Make discoveries that are patentable and valuable
Construction (road)	• Define routes • Create work plan • Construct to specifications • Open on time	• Improve traffic patterns • Reduce commute times • Improve quality of life • Support local politicians

Type of Initiative	Output-Focused Goals	Outcome-Driven Goals
Educational	• Schedule classes • Pay tuition • Do homework • Fulfill requirements • Earn a degree	• Enhance important competencies • Increase insight • Contribute more in workplace • Become smarter • Get high grades • Improve recognition • Receive pay increases • Earn a significant promotion

this example, the governing committee would have assumed the adaptive leadership role (in addition to its enabling leadership role).

The distribution of responsibilities under a project-based approach is consistent with the distribution of responsibilities previously described under the two-party fully governed project oversight model. There is a lesson in that: *using a project-based approach for pursuing outcome-based benefits often requires that a governance committee assume responsibility for the adaptive leadership function*. It requires that the governance committee assume responsibilities that would, under a program management approach, be assigned to the outcome sage–program manager. We spent quite a bit of time discussing the challenges of that approach in Chapter 7. Under many conditions—and especially in organizations that are big, in organizations that pursue a large number of programs and projects, or in organizations that pursue programs and projects that are uncertain and complex—that is not easy.

"Is my initiative a project or a program?" The answer, it seems, may be complicated. It depends on the nature of the goals being pursued. To answer the question requires asking another: "What are the initiative's goals?"

It can be observed, however, that asking the question of "project or program" when initiating endeavors is itself a very valuable exercise for most organizations. It stimulates them to more carefully examine the endeavor's goals and the potential impact of outcome uncertainty and complexity. It prompts them to be thoughtful in defining their true intent.

Asking the question "project of program?" is also valuable to us, because it leads to another important observation: *The decision to label an initiative as a project versus a program should be viewed as a choice about how its goals will be defined and how it will be managed by its assigned programmaticist(s)*. The decision should be recognized as *a choice* about which goals will be assigned to the program or project team(s) and which will be assumed by its governing committee(s).

How do organizations *actually* decide what choices they will make? Many times it is based on the considerations that we have highlighted. Application of the existing project and program management standards does point us in the right direction. Project management standards are clearly focused on excellence in the management of operational uncertainty and complexity, and the efficient delivery of project outputs and outcomes. Current program management standards and guides focus on principles and practices that are important to the management of outcome uncertainty and complexity, and to the effective delivery of benefits. (They focus, for example, on the need to accept that programs are usually cyclic—that they depend on work plans that produce outcomes, and outcomes that produce additional work plans.)

Unfortunately, however, these standards have not yet resulted in a consistent use of the "program" and "project" labels. I am hopeful that the definitions afforded in this chapter will help. However, while stakeholders generally agreed that new definitions would help, they noted that it might take time; some of them expected resistance to the introduction of new terms within their individual organizations. They observed that their organizations may be reluctant to accept that teams need to assume responsibility for managing with the adaptive approach we have described for "program management."

Why would such issues arise?

BARRIERS TO ACCEPTANCE

The choice of whether to manage an initiative as a project or program (as we have defined them) might be significantly influenced by the willingness of executives to accept and affirm the existence of outcome uncertainty. Stakeholders observed that some executives were unwilling to recognize that outputs (no matter how well-defined and pre-cisely delivered) may *not* have the value that was predicted and expected. They observed that the reluctance of executives to accept outcome uncertainty sometimes led to inappropriate treatment of programs as projects, and to expectations that operationally oriented management of these projects should always deliver the desired benefits. As explained by one programmaticist: "It is understandable that executives would want to think this way. Focusing on operational issues reinforces their illusions that success [in delivering benefits] depends on things we can control." My discussants agreed that in the presence of outcome uncertainty, success can be outside of a programmaticist's control. They believed that acceptance of the principles of program management requires certain stakeholders to also come to that realization.

In other discussions, my interviewees noted that the choice of whether to manage an initiative as a program or project might also be influenced by an organization's confidence in its program management capabilities. Organizations that were immature in program manage-ment (as we have defined it) were often reluctant to entrust their pro-grammaticists with the adaptive leadership role. They were unwilling to allow programmaticists to more autonomously manage outcome-based uncertainty and complexity.

My interviewees believed that the reluctance of these organiza-tions to support program-based approaches was based (in part) on their failure to have developed competent outcome sage–programmaticists. Their historical focus on traditional, operationally focused conceptions of project management had resulted in the exclusive development of operational savants. Interviewees believed that these organizations' prior successes had blinded them to their eventual needs for more tech-nically savvy outcome-oriented programmaticists. In the absence of such programmaticists, it became less likely that an organization would even consider the sanctioning of adaptively managed programmatic models. As explained by another programmaticist: "Program-based approaches require executives to delegate responsibilities that [under two-party systems] would otherwise be theirs. They are reluctant to do that when they believe that no one else can adequately replace them."

I often asked my interviewees whether their organizations would consider adopting more adaptive models of programmatic leadership. "What would it take for your organization to accept that two forms of programmatic leadership (operationally focused and outcome-driven) were required?" Stakeholders agreed that their organizations would need to more clearly understand the answers to three questions:

1. What would be the responsibilities of each key participant in such a system—the executive management, project management, and program management functions?

2. How should these three parties be expected to work together? (Or, stated differently, what relationships should exist between them?)

3. Why would such a system be expected to improve management of their (complex) projects and programs?

Let's explore these three questions in the next chapter, as we discuss our proposal for a third-generation (three-party) programmatic oversight system.

CHAPTER 11

Introducing Third-Generation Programmatics

THE COMPLEXITY-MANAGEMENT ROLES OF PROJECT AND PROGRAM MANAGEMENT

To those who are reading this book, the answer to the first question raised at the end of Chapter 10 (What would be the responsibilities of executive management, project management, and program management in a three-party programmatic oversight system?) might by now be evident.

We observed in Chapter 8 that three-party systems have already been tested by organizations that needed to effectively manage the large amounts of operational and outcome uncertainty that were commonly associated with complex projects and programs. Their experimentation with such systems was driven by a need for programmaticists who could act as both operational savants and outcome sages. We also observed in Chapter 8 that those roles could be satisfied by assigning two programmaticists to manage complex programmatic endeavors: one project manager to assume principle responsibilities for managing operations, and a second programmaticist (later identified as a program manager) to assume principle responsibilities for managing a program's responses to project outcomes. Organizations that tested three-party systems often used programmaticists who had different skills and competencies to fill each of these two roles. They expected the two to work collaboratively under the direction and authorization of a governing committee. Chapter 8 (Figure 8.1) provided a blueprint for the design of a three-party programmatic oversight system which is summarized in Table 11.1.

In Chapter 9 we discussed the theoretical basis for expecting that a three-party system would be most effective for managing complex programmatic endeavors. That chapter's discussions of the "science" of

Table 11.1   Primary Foci of Project and Program Management Professionals, and of Their Primary Governance Committees

Types of Uncertainty and Complexity to be Managed	Project Management (Operational Leadership)	Program Management (Adaptive Leadership)	Primary Governance (Enabling Leadership)
Operational	✓		
Outcome		✓	
Stakeholder	✓	✓	✓
Organizational	✓	✓	✓
Environmental			✓

leadership showed how the leadership requirements of complex projects and programs aligned well with our conceptions of operationally focused and outcome-focused programmaticist roles, each supported by enabling leadership (governing committees). The insights of that chapter enabled us to better understand the tensions that were associated with two-party (bureaucratic) project oversight systems, project management's identity crisis, and the emergence of Exasperados. They gave us reason to believe that unique benefits could be found in three-party systems. Chapter 9 suggested that organizations pursuing complex programmatic endeavors would benefit from a leadership system that fostered the independent development but collaborative application of enabling, operational, and adaptive leadership.

In Chapter 10 we explored the more formal assignment of the enabling, operational, and adaptive leadership roles to the governing committee, project management, and program management functions, respectively. We observed that to support these assignments, we should adapt our definitions of programs, projects, program management, and project management. Projects and project management should be principally focused on delivering project outputs and their associated project-level outcomes. They can be viewed as being responsible for operational leadership. Programs and program management should be principally focused on delivering benefits through program-level outcomes. They can be viewed as being responsible for adaptive leadership. We also observed that the newly proposed definitions of programs, projects, program management, and project management are already well-aligned with emerging research on the practice (and the science) of program management.

To accept these proposals requires that we consider changes to our "Standard" conceptions of the program and project management roles. It requires that we return (to some extent) to *first-generation programmatics'* operationally focused definitions of the project manager's role, which were discussed in Chapter 2. Doing so ensures that project management will remain focused on its traditional mission—to deliver project outputs on time, on budget, and to specification.

These proposals also encourage us to adopt an outcome-focused redefinition of the program manager's role. In doing so they enable us to look at the project management approaches taken in *second-generation programmatics* in a different way: They enable us to recognize that the second-generation programmatics approaches discussed in Chapter 3 actually describe circumstance-specific assignments of adaptive leadership responsibilities to a selected programmaticist (a uniquely empowered "project manager"). When viewed in this way, second-generation programmatic approaches might be thought of as prototypes of a third-generation approach.

DEFINING THIRD-GENERATION PROGRAMMATICS

The narratives told in each of the preceding chapters lead to the proposal of a new approach for managing complex programmatic endeavors: a *third-generation programmatic approach*. **Third-generation programmatics** may be defined as an approach for managing organizational programs that depends upon the collaborative contributions of two unique types of programmaticist-leaders: a project manager (or leader) responsible for providing operational leadership, and hence for delivering project outputs and their outcomes, and a program manager (or leader) responsible for embodying adaptive leadership, and hence for optimizing delivery of program-level outcomes. Third-generation programmatics employs a three-party framework for managing programs through leadership that is collectively provided by governing committees, project management professionals, and program management professionals.

According to the three-party program management framework, project and program management are responsible for stimulating, integrating, and (ultimately) embodying the operational and adaptive leadership roles critical for the function of complex adaptive systems. They are also responsible for oversight of project and program teams, respectively.

Governing committees are responsible for establishing organizational conditions that support project and program management; they serve in an enabling leadership role. Governing committees assume responsibility for ensuring that the strategy and goals being pursued by project and program management remain aligned with the needs and constraints of the organization and the environment in which it operates.

Under the three-party (third-generation) program oversight system, project managers, program managers, and governing committee members interact as a complex adaptive system responsible for assuming principle leadership roles in managing operational, outcome, and environmental uncertainties and complexities (respectively). The responsibilities of each also require them to interact dynamically with (a sometimes large number of) organizational stakeholders and committees. Each has the potential to contribute to or to help manage organizational and stakeholder complexity. To effectively oversee the pursuit of complex endeavors, all three parties must work together to manage organizational and stakeholder uncertainty, and to solve organizational and stakeholder complexity (see Figure 11.1). Thus, each has a specific role in fulfilling the new programmaticist credo: to manage the uncertain and solve the complex to deliver program value.

As I have explored potential applications of the three-party framework, I have found that its premise and its promise are intriguing to organizational executives, programmaticists, and students of program

Figure 11.1   The three-party framework for leadership and management of complex programmatic endeavors.

management alike. The narrative told to this point has resonated well with those who are responsible for (and sometimes struggling with) the management of very complex projects and programs. Most professional programmaticist interviewees find that studying the science of programmatics enables them to better understand their own roles and responsibilities, and those of their colleagues. They are especially grateful to be introduced to a "language" that enables them to more precisely compare their organizational experiences. (I have tried to introduce that language in this narrative by introducing and defining those terms that have been most valuable.) As my discussions with stakeholders progressed, it was especially interesting to discuss the three-party framework (depicted in Figure 11.1) with interviewees who believed that their organizations had already tried similar approaches. There were two types of responses; they both made me feel like a police sketch artist.

The reactions of some seemed to scream: "That is him; I would recognize him anywhere." These responses usually came from interviewees whose organizations had found success using prototype three-party systems to manage complex projects and programs. They would have had me write "Wanted" across the top of the page.

Only a few of my interviewees responded this way, however.

The remaining reviewers studied the picture and eventually said, "It isn't quite the same." They then went on to explain the differences: "For us, the program and project management functions were much more similar to each other; they overlapped much more." "The governing committee was further removed; it didn't overlap so much." "Environmental complexity was much more (or less) prominent." "For us, program management also had a role in managing environmental uncertainty." Their comments were varied, but their message was the same: "That is not *exactly* the system that we tested." This second group of stakeholders reported having had mixed success with their three-party models. Several observed that with the picture as a guide, their journey may have brought them to a different (better) place.

The comments made by this latter group of stakeholders usually led to comparisons of what was intended to happen within their three-party system (what it might be expected to look like, based on Figure 11.1) with what had actually happened in their organization's example (what it did look like). Their comments suggested that their organizations needed to better understand the precise definitions and purpose for each part of the system, and the relationships that should exist between them. Only then could their organizations distinguish whether their reportedly "mixed" success was because the system couldn't serve them well, or whether it was due to a failure to ensure its proper function. (Often, upon review, we could find evidence of the latter.)

Their comments highlighted our second question from above: How should each part of a third-generation three-party programmatic oversight system come together to work with the others?

ROLES AND RESPONSIBILITIES IN THE THREE-PARTY SYSTEM

Admittedly, it is difficult to discern the relationships that should exist *between* each component of the three-party system by looking at the framework presented in Figure 11.1. The overlaps between each of the parties are significant. As different as our descriptions of each leadership domain may be, they still have much in common.

When seeking to understand the relationships between each domain, it is better to imagine them as far less connected—to focus on the space *in between* each leadership function, and to thereby examine the relationships that are necessary to keep them appropriately connected and separated. Expanding our view of the three-party framework enables us to more easily explore how the system should work. An expanded view of the three-party framework is shown in Figure 11.2. We will discuss the nuances of this figure in the next few sections of this chapter.

In the three-party programmatic oversight system, the roles of the *governing committees* (serving in their enabling leadership role) are similar to those discussed under the two-party systems common to first- and second-generation programmatics: Governing committees are expected to assume responsibility for defining the overarching strategy of the organization that they govern. They define a high-level plan for how that strategy might best be pursued, and they install and support the organizational infrastructure required to pursue the organization's goals and objectives. Governing committees would, for example, sponsor the development of (or access to) the operational (line function) capabilities that their organizations require. Most times, they do this via bureaucratically organized hierarchical management structures that have been common since the Industrial Age. (Though in modern times, line function capabilities are increasingly being obtained through outsourcing or partnering.)

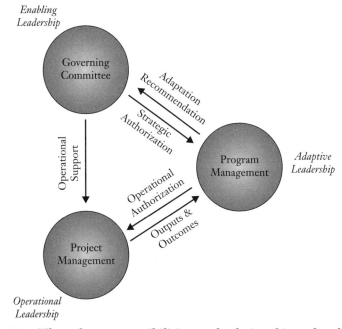

Figure 11.2   The roles, responsibilities, and relationships of each leadership function in the three-party programmatic oversight system.

Governing committees also assume responsibility for defining their organizations' strategic direction and for launching new initiatives to bring about organizational growth or change. Such initiatives can be diverse in nature. They might include (for example) initiatives to design and deliver new products or services, to introduce more efficient practices or processes, or to build new infrastructure, competencies, or capabilities. Initiatives such as these are different from the everyday activities that constitute organizational operations. They are most effectively pursued via temporary initiatives to achieve the targeted goals. They are best pursued via projects or programs.

In fulfilling each of the responsibilities listed above, a governing committee in a three-party programmatic management system might appear to be functioning much the same as governing committees in more traditional two-party project oversight systems. When using a three-function program oversight system, however, the designation of an initiative as a project versus program becomes quite significant. It defines the relationships that should exist between the governing committee and the endeavor that is about to be launched.

Projects (as we have defined them in the previous chapter) are initiatives that can be expected to deliver predefined outputs. The pursuit of project outputs results in the generation of outcomes that may or may not be predictable. However, the focus of projects is on the delivery of outputs to precisely prescribed specifications, on time, and on budget. Under the three-party system, governing committees should expect that projects will be managed in a way that maximizes efficiency and control. Projects deliver value by precisely delivering work products.

Programs are initiatives that usually rely on projects to get their work done. Programs, however, are different from projects because they rely on project outcomes that cannot be controlled; programs (like it or not) deliver their value via outcomes that are inherently uncertain. Programs must be adaptively managed so as to ensure that the knowledge gained as a consequence of project outcomes is used to refine program strategies and plans. Under the three-party system, governing committees need to manage programs in a way that encourages adaptation of program strategies in response to outcomes.

To understand the differences between outputs and outcomes, and how a project might be expected to generate each, it is helpful to recall our Chapter 2 example of a project to study a drug's effectiveness and safety. The *output* of the project—a high-quality report of results, produced to exacting specifications—is clearly different from the *outcome* of the study—the conclusions about the drug's effectiveness and safety as described within that report. A project team seeking to support drug development would focus on conducting a clinical study to exacting specifications, and on delivering a study report (an output) that described the results of that study (its outcomes). The program team seeking to develop that drug for market would focus on determining whether the clinical study *outcomes* had satisfied the program-level goals—whether they demonstrated the safety and effectiveness of the drug. Fully satisfying the program team's drug development goals might require the collection and analysis of outcomes from several clinical studies (projects), each documented in the outputs of their respective project teams and each influenced by the results of prior studies.

As a consequence of the differences between projects and programs, they have different leadership needs. *Under a three-party programmatic oversight system the leadership needs of projects and programs are addressed using different approaches for their oversight and management.*

Projects Sponsored by Governing Committees

Under the three-party oversight system, *projects sponsored by governing committees* are generally managed using first-generation programmatic approaches that we have previously described as being effective for project oversight: Projects are assigned to managers and teams who define the project's operational plans for producing the desired project outputs. Governing committees approve and resource these plans, and they authorize the project manager (and his or her team) to pursue them. Project teams seek to efficiently deliver the defined project outputs—on time, on budget, and to specifications. In exchange for their agreement to deliver results "as contracted," project managers (and their teams) are empowered to work with a degree of autonomy and independence. To ensure that a project is pursued according to plan, its governance committee will expect to review and approve any changes to the project's goals, strategy, and plans before they are implemented.

Thus, organizational endeavors that do not have significant outcome uncertainty can be managed via traditional two-party project management approaches—even in organizations that have a three-party programmatic oversight system. This two-party project management system is embedded within the three-party framework, as shown in the shaded portion of Figure 11.3.

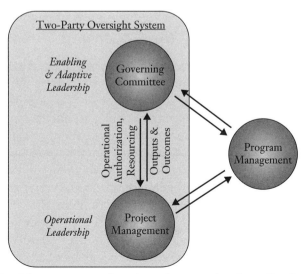

Figure 11.3 Management of projects in organizations that have a three-party programmatic oversight system, using two-party approaches.

Under the uncertainty- and complexity-based definition that we have proposed for a project, the designation of an organizational initiative as a "project" should result in a clear understanding that it will be managed so as to deliver designated *outputs* precisely as promised—on time, on budget, and to specifications. It establishes clear expectations that operational change will be monitored and controlled to ensure efficient delivery of output-focused goals.

The primary focus of projects is managing operational uncertainty and complexity. Thus, operationally focused project managers should assume responsibility for controlling and managing the operational activities of governance-sponsored projects. In turn, governance committees would assume responsibility for managing a project's environmental uncertainty and complexity. In the event that the pursuit of project-related outputs results in the generation of unexpected outcomes that are significant to the project's ultimate value, it would generally be expected (as it had been under two-party project oversight systems) that the governing committee would assume responsibility for managing outcome uncertainty and complexity.

Note that under the proposed complexity-based management system, managing organizational and stakeholder uncertainty and resolving organizational and stakeholder complexity are the joint (overlapping) responsibilities of both the project manager and his or her governing committee members (see Figure 11.1).

Programs Sponsored by the Governing Committee

Programs sponsored by governing committees are managed in a different way under the three-party programmatic oversight system. They are managed via the entire programmatic oversight system depicted in Figure 11.2: Programs are assigned to program managers and teams who assume responsibility for defining program strategies. Such strategies typically support delivery of the intended program benefits while simultaneously generating knowledge that may lead to refinement of the program's strategies and goals. (Based on the inherent uncertainty of programs, it is common that early strategies will need to be refined.) Program strategies are usually presented to governing committees for review and endorsement before program managers are authorized to begin their pursuit, inasmuch as programs must be supported (enabled) by the governing committees who sponsor them.

In the most common of circumstances, authorized program strategies are pursued via the initiation of projects (whose complexity-based definitions, roles, and responsibilities should by now be familiar). Projects sponsored by program teams (the "daughter projects" we referred to in Chapter 7) differ from projects sponsored by governance committees in one important way, however; they are primarily accountable to the program team instead of the governing committee. Under most circumstances, the plans of these projects will be reviewed and endorsed by their sponsoring program team, which then takes responsibility for securing resources for their execution. (Sometimes programs are given independent resourcing authority; at other times they secure resources via an appeal to the program's primary governing committee.) The project teams retain responsibilities for efficiently pursuing project plans and for delivering the expected project outputs and resultant project outcomes. Project outputs and outcomes are monitored by the program team. When outcomes continue to support the program's strategy for delivering benefits, programs can continue to support the initiation and conduct of projects according to their initial (governance-supported) plans. When outcomes indicate that a change in strategy or plans is appropriate, however, programs define those changes and make the required adaptation recommendations to their primary governing committees. The flow of this process was captured holistically in Figure 11.2.

A close examination of the three-party program oversight system reveals that by its sponsorship of projects, the program management function actually assumes two leadership roles. It assumes the adaptive leadership role within the three-party context of the program and its governing committee (as originally depicted in Figure 11.2). It also assumes an enabling leadership/oversight role with respect to a two-party relationship that it has with its projects. The two-party managing relationship that programs have with their projects is embedded within the three-party framework, as shown in the shaded portion of Figure 11.4.

As I have reviewed the three-party programmatic oversight model with various organizations, executives, programmaticists, and stakeholders, many find it valuable to examine the dynamics of the model (and the types of leadership required by it) using the narrative approach captured in the next few paragraphs. I invite readers to follow the dynamic interactions of each of the narrative's three parties using Figure 11.4. The story begins in the "definition phase" of a program when a governing committee decides that it wants to pursue a program that depends on outcomes that are uncertain.

- The governing committee identifies stakeholders who will be assigned to a program team that will become responsible for

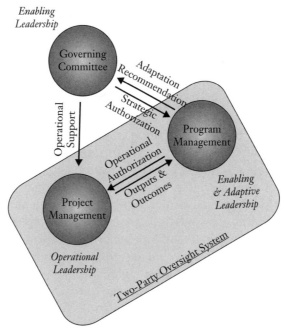

Figure 11.4   Oversight of projects by programs, using a two-party project oversight system within a three-party programmatic oversight system.

pursuing the organization's goals; the governing committee secures the stakeholders' involvement for the effort ahead (enabling leadership).

- The governing committee communicates the organization's strategic goals to the program team, along with any initial constraints under which they are expected to work (enabling leadership).

- The program team considers various options for pursuing program goals; it profiles the uncertainty associated with each option and adapts its strategies to maximize the likelihood of success (adaptive leadership).

- The program team begins to define the projects and project teams that would be required to pursue the efforts being contemplated; it communicates strategic goals and options to project team members to determine which approaches are most operationally feasible (enabling and adaptive leadership).

- Working collaboratively, members of project and program teams define the operational requirements of each option; they adapt their proposed strategies to increase the likelihood of program success; together, they identify options that are most attractive for pursuit (adaptive and operational leadership).

- The program team (with project team support) recommends the preferred program strategy to the governing committee; together, representatives of the program and project teams work with the governance committee to identify the preferred approach for pursuing the program; they may further adapt the program's strategies and plans (for example, in response to environmental issues or considerations) (enabling, adaptive, and operational leadership).

- Throughout this process, the governing committee, program team, and project teams interact with individual stakeholders and secondary governance committees to marshal support and to manage stakeholder and organizational uncertainties that might otherwise impede the endorsement of the program's strategies and plans (enabling, adaptive, and operational leadership).

- The governing committee authorizes a program strategy and enables pursuit of the program by allocating resources to projects as appropriate (enabling leadership).

- The governing committee delegates primary managerial responsibility to the program manager (enabling leadership).

- The program manager and team more formally define goals to be pursued by each of the program's projects (adaptive and operational leadership).

- The project teams pursue those goals within their organization's and/or program's operational constraints (operational leadership).

The story continues in the "benefits delivery" phase of a program, as the program pursues its goals in its effort to deliver its targeted benefits.

- The projects that have been initiated (under the authority of the program) generate their outputs according to plan; the delivery of outputs sometimes results in the generation of outcomes; the project teams deliver the outputs and outcomes to their sponsoring program team (operational leadership).

- The program team reviews the outcomes generated by its project teams, assessing their potential impact on the program's strategy and plans; the program team determines whether program

strategies or plans should be adapted in response to the outcomes received; the program team works collaboratively with
its project teams to identify and optimize any changes to plans
and strategies that may be required (adaptive and operational
leadership).

- The program team makes recommendations for the adaptation
of program strategy and plans to its governing committee (adaptive and operational leadership).

- The governing committee reviews team recommendations and
discusses any need or desire for further changes (based, for example, on environmental issues that might need to be addressed);
the committee authorizes changes to the program's strategy and
plans as necessary and appropriate (enabling, adaptive, and operational leadership).

- The program team communicates new authorizations to the
project teams, enabling the initiation of new workstream activities, so as to generate additional outcomes and outputs (enabling,
adaptive, and operational leadership).

- The governing committee provides new resources and support
as necessary to support the changes it has authorized (enabling
leadership).

- The project teams pursue those goals within their respective
operational constraints (operational leadership).

Based on the ricocheting contributions and involvement of each of
the participating groups, we can conclude that the governing committee,
program management, and project management functions defined within
the three-party programmatic oversight system all make specific and significant leadership contributions at various times in a program's lifecycle.
Each of these parties' contributions are critically important; no single leadership type (enabling, adaptive, or operational) would be effective without
the others. Removal of any one party from the model would result in the
need for another party to assume its role, inasmuch as each role is critically
important to the effectiveness of a complex adaptive system.

When reviewing the dynamics of the three-party system, the
phases of a program are rarely as simple or as linear as the narrative above might suggest. The benefits delivery workflow, for example,
becomes more complicated as programs sponsor greater numbers of
projects, each with its own timeline, and outcomes are realized in an

asynchronous fashion. The unsynchronized pursuit of projects within programs leads to unsynchronized demands for enabling, adaptive, and operational leadership. As a consequence, managing programs often requires more continuous participation of leadership functions than might be implied by the workflow described above.

Because we are focusing on the management of active programs, it is not necessary to discuss a workflow associated with closing a program. (A program is closed when its governing committee or program team determines that no further work will be performed in pursuit of new program goals.) Closing a program under most programmatic systems is recognized as a fairly linear process that is well described in program Standards. It might be interesting to note, however, that "closing a program" can be viewed as something more than an operational endeavor; it can be viewed as an expression of enabling leadership. The decision to close a program enables those who were involved in it to reallocate their time and energy to another endeavor. It enables the staffing of other programs and/or projects.

The narrative above provides a general outline of how the three-party program oversight system can be used to manage projects and programs. Under this system, the fundamental roles and responsibilities established for "projects sponsored by governing committees" and for "projects sponsored by programs" are similar. In both cases, projects are expected to dedicate themselves to the delivery of outputs (and any associated project-level outcomes) within the project's defined time, budget, and specification constraints. Such projects are best led by a project manager who most intently focuses on the management of operational uncertainty and the resolution of operational complexity. The three-party model employs a consistently operational definition of the roles and responsibilities of the project management function. It might therefore lead to a clearer recognition and understanding of project management's focus, and perhaps the eventual resolution of its identity crisis.

Subprograms Sponsored by Programs

We noted earlier in this chapter that programs may also sponsor subprograms. During interviews and discussions, stakeholders agreed that managing subprograms sponsored by programs (or "daughter programs," as we referred to them in Chapter 7) presents different challenges than managing projects.

Subprograms might be initiated when the specific workstreams required by a program are themselves expected to deliver outcomes or benefits that are uncertain. Consider, for example, a program that seeks to deliver benefits (perhaps profits) by producing an innovative product (let's say a long-range electric car) that relies on the development of new technologies (higher-capacity batteries, more efficient electric motors, faster battery chargers). Such a program might be expected to initiate projects to oversee workstreams with definable outputs (automobile parts, manufacturing facilities, showrooms, marketing materials) or to generate outcomes (favorable reviews, high vehicle reliability, good resale value, high sales volume). However, it might also require the initiation of programmatic endeavors to oversee workstreams pursuing uncertain outcomes or benefits (for example, research programs related to the development of new technologies). These endeavors should be managed as subprograms.

Subprograms differ from the projects sponsored by the program because they need to *adaptively* pursue outcomes that are required by the primary (parent) program. (In our example, subprograms might be initiated to develop the higher-capacity batteries, more efficient electric motors, and faster battery chargers.) Managing subprograms adaptively would improve their abilities to respond to outcomes generated either as a result of their own project activities or as a result of outcomes generated by other subprograms or projects. (The results of battery research might influence strategies for pursuing new motor and charging station technologies, for example.)

A subprogram's need to be managed adaptively suggests that it should also be managed via a three-party programmatic oversight system. In sponsoring subprograms, the primary program team should assume an enabling leadership role, much as it does when sponsoring projects. It would thereby become responsible for activities that would otherwise be expected of a governing committee: It would sanction the initiation of subprograms, review and approve their strategies, ensure that they were appropriately resourced, oversee their progress, and review and approve significant changes to their strategies and plans.

In turn, a program manager would need to assume the subprogram's adaptive leadership role. He or she (and the team) would define their subprogram's strategy and its operational plan, authorize the endeavors required to produce outputs and outcomes, and ensure that the subprogram's strategy and plans are adaptively aligned with knowledge gained in the pursuit of its goals. Subprogram managers would need to collaborate with the project managers responsible for the subprogram's projects. Those project managers (in turn) would ensure that the subprogram's operational needs are pursued. Subprograms thereby become a complex adaptive system functioning under the sponsorship of the program—a complex adaptive system that is, at its essence, an extension of another complex adaptive system (see shaded area in Figure 11.5).

When viewed in this way, a program manager needs to possess advanced competency and credibility as an organizational leader. To be effective in serving the program manager role, the programmaticist needs to possess knowledge, skills, and experience that enable him or her to comfortably switch between an adaptive leadership and an enabling leadership role. He or she needs a leadership personality that enables him to be adaptive.

A review of the literature from program management research and a survey of my stakeholder-interviewees confirmed that it is not unreasonable to expect that a program manager would be able to assume these two roles. Unlike the relationship between program and project management (where learn-and-adapt and command-and-control

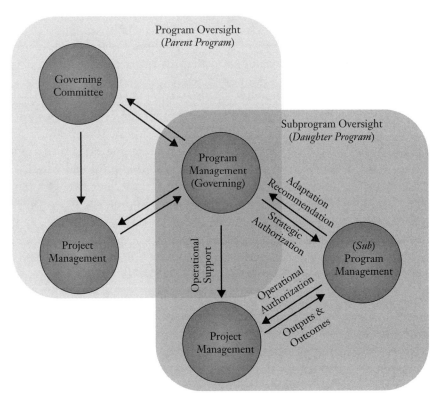

Figure 11.5   Oversight of a subprogram by a program.

management styles might be expected to sometimes lead to conflict), we could identify no overt reason to expect that the enabling and adaptive leadership styles couldn't comfortably co-exist within program manager-leaders as complementary skill sets. It should not be surprising: The two-party programmatic oversight systems that have been prevalent since the Industrial Age have generally relied on executive management to serve in both the enabling and adaptive leadership roles. We will explore the nature of programmatic leadership and current research on competencies required for program management success in much more detail in Chapter 13.

In my interviews with organizational stakeholders, discussions about programs-within-programs led to an additional observation: Many stakeholders observed that understanding the three-party framework provided them with a different perspective on their organizations. It enabled them to view their organizations as a series of endeavors nested within other endeavors. They frequently observed that the highest-level goals of their organizations were, in essence, organization-wide programs. These in turn were supported by programs or projects, which in turn were supported by others, and so on. Thus, stakeholders observed that their organizations could be viewed as sequentially nested programs within programs, with projects to support them. It is an interesting observation, inasmuch as it suggests that an organization's leadership structure could actually be redefined using programmatic breakdown structures that focus on the complexity management and complexity leadership responsibilities of various stakeholders and committees, each in the context of their program affiliation(s). Many stakeholders felt that program-based descriptions of their organizational structure might provide a refreshing alternative to the bureaucratic functionally focused organizational charts that most organizations find familiar. We have begun to explore more advanced methods for mapping such things; it is a subject for the future.

Other Activities Sponsored by Programs

We noted earlier in this chapter that programs may also pursue "other program-related activities." During interviews and discussions, stakeholders generally believed that the management of other program-related activities was relatively straightforward. These activities were viewed (in the words of one interviewee) as "the operations side of program management." Other program-related activities were most commonly the responsibility of program support staff who reported bureaucratically to project or program management departments or (in some instances) to a program or project management office (PMO) that supported their organization's programmatic endeavors. These activities might include, for example, tasks that provide logistical support to program teams, or that generate program-specific reports or communications. Stakeholders agreed that the management of these activities would not be expected to change significantly with the introduction of the three-party systems that support third-generation programmatics.

Having discussed key components of the three-party programmatic oversight system, and the relationships and leadership that are necessary for it to function effectively, many stakeholders pondered the third of our key questions from the end of Chapter 10: What benefits would be expected from a third-generation programmatics three-party programmatic oversight system?

BENEFITS EXPECTED FROM THE THIRD-GENERATION PROGRAMMATICS APPROACH

To understand what benefits might be realized from a three-party program oversight system, it is best that we examine the fundamental tenets upon which it is built. They may be summarized in this way:

- Programs and projects are fundamentally different from each other.

- Being an effective program versus project manager often requires different knowledge and skills, and different leadership mindsets.

- Program benefits and goals could be most effectively pursued via a collaboration that leverages the knowledge and leadership perspectives of three parties within the organizational environment: program managers, project managers, and their governing committees.

These tenets provide a helpful framework for examining the system's potential benefits and value. We have mentioned some of the benefits previously, inasmuch as our design and "discovery" of the three-party system was itself guided by the valuable experiences of a diverse pool of programmaticists and executive stakeholders. Nonetheless, it will be valuable to review these benefits collectively.

Benefits of Distinguishing Projects from Programs

The first set of benefits that an organization might realize is based on the importance of recognizing the fundamental differences between projects and programs. Projects, we observed, should be accountable principally for delivering outputs. Their singular focus on doing that efficiently (and as planned) ensures that they will enhance an organization's operational efficiency. Project outputs may result in outcomes that are uncertain, and therefore not controllable in the same way as the efficient completion of the project. It is the project's responsibility to ensure that such outcomes are delivered efficiently, in spite of its lack of control over them.

Programs, in contrast, should be accountable for delivering benefits— benefits that rely on the uncertain outcomes of projects. Programs focus on how best to pursue those outcomes that will ultimately result in benefit realization. The "work" of programs lies in assessing project outcomes, assimilating the knowledge and understanding that they provide, and identifying how program strategies and plans should be adapted to ensure that the desired program benefits are (eventually) realized. It is the program's responsibility to ensure that benefits are delivered efficiently, in spite of the imprecise delivery of project outcomes.

Understanding (and accepting) the differences between projects and programs is vitally important to organizations that pursue complex initiatives because it leads to a better understanding of what should be expected from programmatic endeavors. It leads to a more realistic assessment of what can and cannot be promised, and a more insightful examination of the uncertainties and complexities that a programmatic endeavor faces. That, in turn, results in a better understanding of approaches for managing those uncertainties and resolving those complexities. Perhaps most importantly, understanding the differences between projects and programs leads to a better perspective on how one should define the success of a project or a program. It seems reasonable to expect that it will ultimately lead to an increased likelihood of achieving that success.

To understand how it might help, it is perhaps worthwhile to consider a case study in the measurement of success. Like so many studies of project success, it began with a study of the reasons for failure.

I was working with an organization seeking to improve their "project management" performance. Executive managers feared that performance had slipped substantially; they observed that their projects were more routinely delayed, and that they could no longer trust their schedules or budgets. Despite years of seeking better control over projects, it seemed that their slippage had grown only worse.

Our investigation began with a study of the root causes of slippage, and initial results confirmed the executives' fears. Over the previous twelve months only 30 percent of the organization's projects had kept to their plans. Project management professionals were shocked at the result; some were angry that they had supported the study in the first place. They feared that the numbers might be used against them.

They might have, had that been the end of the story.

However, as part of our study, we had done something else. We also asked programmaticists, their teams, and their executives to provide explanations for slippage of projects. We interviewed stakeholders to determine "consensus views" of the reasons for each incident of slippage, and then we examined the type of uncertainty that each of these causes reflected. The results of the interviews are approximated in Table 11.2

We observed that the causes of slippage were closely related to the uncertainty and complexity that we previously described for our complexity-management model (see Figures 4.2 and 11.1). The predominant cause of slippage was the realization of *outcomes* by the projects. The outcomes delivered by projects were subtly different than had been presumed in the projects' strategies and plans, and those differences had often led to changes in what would be required in the projects' next-step activities. This outcome-related slippage resulted in long delays in the timelines to the next major project milestone. The incidence and the magnitude of outcome-related slippage made

Table 11.2 Analysis of Slippage in a Portfolio of Projects

Reason for Slippage in Timeline to the Next Major Milestone	Incidence	Average Magnitude	Related Uncertainty
Task Execution	15%	2 months	Operational
Results of Activities	80%	11 months	Outcome
Organizational Indecision about Next Steps	40%	3 months	Stakeholder or Organizational
Regulatory Edicts	5%	12 months	Environmental

Note: The incidence of slippage adds up to greater than 100 percent because slippages due to task execution, results, and regulatory edicts were sometimes also associated with indecision about the appropriate organizational responses. In these instances the magnitude of slippage was apportioned to each of the causes, as estimated by interviewees. (Incidence numbers were rounded to the nearest 5 percent.)

it (by far) the most significant source of strategic and operational complexity.

In contrast, task execution, an *operational* cause of slippage, happened infrequently and was of far smaller magnitude.

The results of the study were clear. The organization was actually not so bad at *project* management (as we have defined it). The slippage associated with the delivery of outputs (2 months) and the frequency with which it was encountered (15 percent) were relatively small. The organization ran projects well. Its issues were related to their pursuit of *programs*. The program-level slippage that resulted from the realization of unexpected outcomes was large (11 months), as was the relative frequency with which it was encountered (80 percent). This organization had not previously recognized the difference between projects and programs.

A retrospective analysis of the organization's portfolio revealed that the increased frequency of slippage was most likely due to the organization's recent pursuit of programs whose outcomes were increasingly uncertain, and whose outcome-related issues were now more complex. (It may also have been exacerbated by the organization's intentional focus on obtaining better operational control; stakeholders speculated that the organization's obsession about operational rigor and control made it less likely that the potential impact of outcome-related uncertainty would be acknowledged in its plans.)

The retrospective analysis also revealed that slippage due to organizational indecision had doubled in duration during this same time period; outcome uncertainty had apparently resulted in an increase in stakeholder and organizational complexity. It resulted in an increase in the time it took to reach organizational consensus about changes to be implemented in response to program outcomes. Primary and secondary committee meetings had become much messier.

The increase in programmatic slippage could be traced back to a company announcement that it would focus its efforts on new and innovative programs (and correspondingly devote less effort to its more predictable lifecycle management projects). The increase in slippage had resulted from a strategic decision to pursue programs that were inherently more uncertain and thus unavoidably more complex. It could be traced to a move away from the conduct of projects and towards the conduct of programs.

The organization's newfound recognition of the differences between programs and projects stimulated them to develop new methods for budgeting and planning. Members of the organization studied benchmarking information on the probabilities of outcome success, and introduced more precise methods for risk-adjusting their operational projections. They began setting goals using probabilistically adjusted measures that took outcome uncertainty more formally into account. They modified their approaches to portfolio selection and portfolio management to ensure that they were not assuming too much outcome-related risk. And they changed the criteria by which they measured success: Projects were measured by their production of outputs and project-level outcomes; programs were measured by their delivery of benefits and program-level outcomes. Recognizing the qualitative differences between projects and programs enabled the organization to more effectively choose its portfolio, manage expectations, and plan its path forward. It enabled the organization to better understand its business model and strategy.

It also led to questions about its approaches for managing its projects and programs—and about the different skill sets required for project and program management.

Benefits of Distinguishing Project Management from Program Management

The second set of benefits that an organization might realize is based on the importance of recognizing the fundamental differences between project and program management, and the leadership skills required for each of them. Project management, we observed, is a profession that is responsible for designing and completing work plans and for ensuring the efficient delivery of work products. It is practiced by project managers who serve in an operational leadership role, often employing a command-and-control style of leadership to ensure that work is completed according to its prescribed plan. Its focus is on ensuring that work is completed quickly, efficiently, and collaboratively.

Program management, in contrast, is a profession that optimizes the delivery of program benefits. Program management focuses on adaptively managing program strategies and plans as they are pursued via projects and subprograms—on assessing project or subprogram outcomes, learning from them, and then adapting program strategies to ensure the efficient delivery of intended program benefits. Program management is practiced by managers who serve in an adaptive leadership role, most often employing a learn-and-adapt style of leadership. Program management ensures that the work being performed will deliver its intended benefits and value.

Recognizing the differences between project and program management is vitally important to organizations that pursue complex initiatives, because it enables them to identify and develop individuals who have the operational- and outcome-focused leadership styles required to successfully pursue complex programmatic endeavors.

Ensuring that project management focuses on operational matters enables organizations to develop highly capable and focused operational savant–leaders, schooled in the tools, techniques, practices, and processes that have been developed and refined by professional project managers for more than half a century. It enables those leaders to develop operational leadership skills unencumbered by the need to assume the sometimes conflicting adaptive leadership role of a program manager, and unfettered by the requirements for advanced program-specific technical knowledge and experience that are often required of an outcome-focused programmaticist leader.

Ensuring that program management focuses on adaptive leadership competencies and responsibilities enables organizations to develop equally capable and dedicated outcome sage–leaders, deeply schooled in analysis of the technical or behavioral outcomes that are required for program success. It enables the recruitment and advancement of professional programmaticists who are individually focused on the development of innovative strategies for solving complex problems. These are leaders who are personally recognized for their abilities to adapt to unexpected outcomes, and who are exceptionally skilled in stimulating the dynamic exchange of ideas and information as they work in the context of complex adaptive systems (described in Chapter 9). Program managers can achieve higher levels of adaptive performance when they are unencumbered by the need to assume the sometimes conflicting operational leadership role of the traditional project manager.

The ability to distinguish between project and program management (and the skills desired of project and program managers) enables organizations to advance their own competencies in the two types of leadership that are required for programmatic success. It enables them to focus separately and specifically on educating project managers in first-generation programmatic approaches that facilitate the management of operational uncertainty and complexity, and program managers in adaptive leadership and the management of outcome uncertainty. And it enables organizations to more clearly define how they will bring these skills together in ways that would otherwise not be possible.

Distinguishing between project and program management enables organizations, through collaboration at the team level, to build centaurs of programmatic excellence that might be difficult to find otherwise. And it does so in a way that enables a precise pairing of individuals who have the specific skills required by a given program team.

The benefits of such a pairing can be profound.

We have previously noted that under second-generation programmatic systems, secondary governance and review committees are most often chartered or sponsored by senior executives who are members of a program's primary governance committee(s). Those secondary committees usually come into existence to support committee members in their bureaucratic leadership roles. They are usually effective in ensuring that primary governance committee members are well prepared to provide enabling leadership.

As we discussed in Chapter 7, however, in organizations that are large, pursue a large number of initiatives, or pursue initiatives that are highly complex, there may be many secondary governance committees. These committees represent "organizational silos." They make it difficult for governance committees to provide cross-functional operational or adaptive leadership.

Distinguishing between project and program management, and assigning project and program managers who are individually accountable for integrating the operational and adaptive leadership perspectives of secondary governance and review committees addresses this problem. Establishing the operational savant project management and outcome sage program management roles within a three-party system provides program teams and their organizations with a role-based mechanism for ensuring that the operational and adaptive leadership perspectives of secondary governance committees are fully integrated when managing programmatic complexity (see Figure 11.6). Making *individuals* responsible for the holistic management of operational and outcome uncertainty seems to reduce organizational dependence on background documents. Moreover, it ensures that the views of secondary governance and review committees are well-represented when programmatic decisions need to be made. It thereby positions governing committees, project managers, and program managers to jointly, collaboratively, and more effectively address organizational and stakeholder complexity.

To understand the practical value of these capabilities, it is helpful to examine the steps that were taken in the organization described in

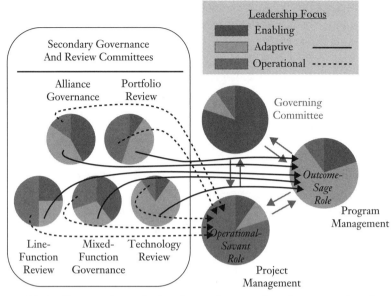

Figure 11.6   Integration of adaptive and operational perspectives by program and project managers who serve in the operational savant and outcome sage roles.

our project slippage case study discussed earlier in the chapter. We previously observed that recognizing the difference between programs and projects had stimulated the organization to introduce new methods for budgeting and planning, goal-setting and risk assessment, and measuring portfolio, program, and project performance. It also had another effect. It stimulated the organization to introduce new approaches for leading and managing programs and projects.

Having recognized that their organization needed to improve its management of outcome complexity stakeholders committed themselves to the development of a group of professional program managers. They recruited savvy professionals who had demonstrated unique talents for leading technically oriented teams—individuals who understood outcome complexity and who were recognized to be effective in facilitating discussions about it. They then educated those professionals in the art and the science of adaptive leadership and program management. They taught them how to work collaboratively with organizational project managers in an environment that emphasized "shared leadership" responsibilities—an environment best described as a "complex adaptive system." And in doing so, they developed outcome sage–programmaticists.

The results were well received. Stakeholders within that organization reported that their outcome sage–program leaders were highly effective in leading their teams in the analysis of outcomes and in identifying strategies for pursuing program goals. They were valued for their ability to stimulate strategic discussions among stakeholders who were dispersed among the organization's secondary review and governance committees. They were effective in integrating those stakeholder perspectives, and in identifying options for resolving complex outcome-related issues. Stakeholders confirmed these program managers provided their organization with a previously unavailable centralized source of information and analysis about the resolution of outcome-related complexity. They observed that the development of program managers helped them to more holistically and realistically define the expectations they should have of their programs, and to more quickly and incisively respond to outcome uncertainty and complexity.

It would be difficult to determine whether the introduction of program managers reduced outcome-related slippage that had spawned the changes in that organization; in the years that followed, the organization pursued even more uncertain and complex programs. It is impossible to determine what would have happened had they not introduced a professional program management function. However, the confidence that the organization showed in pursuing more complex programs seems to support the belief in its program managers' effectiveness. And there was at least one other measure that supported this conclusion: The introduction of program managers was associated with a halving of slippage due to outcome-related organizational indecision.

In this case study (and in others that were similar), recognizing the differences between project and program management and introducing formal program management capabilities had another benefit: It stimulated recognition that program management could be more than "just a role"; it triggered programmaticists to pursue program management as a long-term professional career. It made it easier to recruit leaders with relevant technical experience, and stimulated their professional interest in the science of program management. It eventually led to the development of a "pipeline" of program leaders ready to assume an adaptive leader's responsibilities for managing some of the organization's most important strategic initiatives.

The more formal definition of the *project* manager's role similarly led to broader recognition of its organization-wide importance. Project management's operational (versus outcome) focus was no longer misunderstood. Stakeholders became more aware of the significance of the profession and of how it was expected to contribute to the success of their organizations. This change resulted in a greater appreciation of the irrefutable value of more traditional applications of project management principles and practices. It led to a greater appreciation for the meaning and value of project management certifications and training, while (perhaps most importantly) erasing perceptions that project management was a less mature or less important version of program management.

Recognizing the differences between program and project management resulted in a clearer understanding of the levels of competency important to the practice of each. For example, this recognition resulted in the more complete separation and expansion of project and program management career ladders, and in the dispelling of notions that advancing one's career in project management *required* the assumption of program management responsibilities. This was a critical development.

In several organizations with which I have worked, a project manager's career growth required his or her progression to a program manager role. It required, in essence, that their most capable and experienced project managers denounce their focus on operational execution to assume the adaptive responsibilities of an outcome-focused program manager. This often had unintended negative consequences. It deprived organizations of some of their best project managers, and many project managers found that this transition was difficult. Recognizing this, many organizations were hesitant to routinely give program management roles to their project managers. Too often, the result was a decrease in the morale and performance of an organization's best project managers.

Many organizations that have implemented three-party systems have found it far more beneficial to ensure that their elite project managers have opportunities for advancement and increased recognition in project management. The clearer recognition of a project manager's importance as an essential contributor to the three-party programmatic system often makes this a more acceptable option.

In the case study above, establishing a clear separation between the skills and the competencies expected of project and program managers enabled each to grow in a manner that was more consistent with their leadership strengths. In my experience working with organizations like these, I have found this observation to be generally true: Distinguishing the roles of project and program managers (when approached in the right way—as a change management program) eventually results in fewer organizational programmaticists identifying themselves as programmaticist-Exasperados.

That, by itself, is a very good thing.

Benefits of Implementing the Three-Party System

The third set of benefits that an organization might realize comes from implementation of the three-party system—a system that seeks to produce leadership synergies by stimulating interaction and collaboration between its three different leadership groups.

The three-party system employed by third-generation programmatics first seeks to deliver benefits by satisfying the *leadership needs* of complex programs and organizations. The system is expected to produce leadership synergies by providing programmatic endeavors with ready access to the enabling, adaptive, and operational leadership behaviors that are critical to the function of complex adaptive systems. The goal is to stimulate the productivity of program and project teams by ensuring that the relationships that need to exist between each leadership "party" are clearly understood and fulfilled. In doing so, the three-party system ensures that the innovative and creative capabilities of "complex adaptive teams" will be effectively exploited.

The three-party system next seeks to deliver benefits by ensuring that the *complexity management needs* of the organization and its teams are well understood and satisfied. The system is expected to improve the management of complexity by bringing together the primary governing committees that are usually responsible for managing environmental complexity, program teams that are responsible for managing outcome complexity, and project teams that are responsible for managing operational complexity. The three-party system further improves the management of stakeholder and organizational complexities by ensuring that governing committees, program managers, and project managers all fully understand the relationships that should exist between them, their secondary governance and review committees, and other stakeholders. It seeks to ensure that each of the three parties recognize that they are collectively responsible for managing organizational and stakeholder complexities. Clearer assignment of complexity management responsibilities to each of the parties in the third-generation programmatic system usually leads to more effective management of programmatic complexity—and ultimately to greater programmatic success.

The benefits expected from implementing a third-generation (three-party) programmatic oversight system appeared to have been realized in the case study we described earlier in this chapter. That organization eventually chose to align its organizational structure according to the tenets of third-generation programmatics:

- It established distinct program and project management groups, and organized them under the direction of a single department. In doing so, it maximized communication, coordination, and collaboration between them, and it ensured that the relationships intended to exist between program and project managers were appropriately cultivated.

- It established regular (informal) meetings between program and project management professionals and the governing committee members that sponsored their initiatives. In this way, it sought to ensure a more routine exchange of enabling, adaptive, and operational leadership perspectives, and it increased the opportunities for new ideas to emerge as a consequence of those leadership contributions.

- And it was diligent in ensuring the consistent engagement of all three of its leadership parties in any meetings intended to generate "complex adaptive results." It became rare, for example, that an initiative's program manager would attend an important meeting without the concurrent participation of his or her project management counterpart(s).

After implementing its third-generation programmatic approach, the case study organization reported that it realized dramatic improvements in its management of complex programmatic endeavors. The results that were achieved seemed to affirm the expected value of the approach. Executives and programmaticists from other organizations increasingly sought to determine whether that organization's approach might be effectively adopted in their own organizations. The answer, of course, is: "It depends."

We will further discuss key considerations in the implementation of third-generation programmatics in the next chapter.

CHAPTER **12**

The Decision to Implement Third-Generation Programmatics

During the course of my interviews and discussions with executives, programmaticists, and other organizational stakeholders, there were many occasions for us to discuss changes that they might have proposed for their own organizations' programmatic oversight systems. The nature of these discussions changed over time, as we discussed the managerial strengths and weaknesses of two- versus three-party programmatic oversight systems. Stakeholders from large organizations or from organizations with large portfolios or highly complex projects and programs usually expressed interest in exploring the potential benefits of three-party systems. As they pondered the possibilities, however, they also expressed concern about their organizations' willingness to adopt a new programmatic model. In the words of one, "We have problems getting people to behave appropriately with our two-party model; how would we be able to get them to rally around a three-party model?" These discussions usually resulted in a verbal dissection of the issues that their organizations were experiencing with their current model for managing projects and programs, and a point-by-point discussion of how or whether moving to a three-party system might help. For those stakeholders who eventually concluded that it would be beneficial to switch to a three-party system, we ended with long conversations about how that could best be achieved. The challenges of introducing a new system could be complex, but after discussion they seemed a little less so.

Any decision to change an organization's programmatic oversight system (to change its approach for managing strategic endeavors) must be approached thoughtfully. I have found that organizational stakeholders usually make the choice to introduce a new system for one of two reasons: (1) The system that they are using is clearly failing them—they are on a burning platform, and they need to leap away from it for their very survival; or (2) they become convinced that the benefits to be realized from change are too attractive to ignore—they just "make too much sense."

I enjoy working with those on the "burning platform" because of their willingness to consider new thinking and approaches. The urgency of their circumstances ensures their conviction, and they are ready to make a big jump. The challenge for this group is to understand in which direction to jump before their current platform either consumes them or collapses. Staying put is no longer an option. This first group urgently seeks to become part of the second—to find a direction that gives them confidence because it makes so much sense.

Indeed, the best reason to pursue a new programmatic approach (whether or not one's platform is burning) is because it does make so much sense—because the benefits it promises are too valuable to resist. The challenge that many organizations face is deciding when that is true. (The diversity of stakeholder opinions and the personal agendas that drive them make complete consensus rare.) The sections below discuss things to consider when deciding whether to make the leap—the factors that are important, the issues to be faced, and the keys to eventual success.

CHOOSING BETWEEN TWO-PARTY AND THREE-PARTY SYSTEMS

In considering the choice between programmatic systems, it is important to acknowledge that the two-party programmatic oversight system provides a sound (and familiar) platform for managing the pursuit of many programmatic endeavors. Two-party fully governed programmatic oversight systems can be highly effective; most organizations have a long history of using them to pursue a variety of operational and strategic endeavors, and the ability of two-party systems to ensure delivery of outputs (on time, on budget, and to expectations) is undisputed. Two-party systems have a distinct advantage: The roles and responsibilities of each of the system's key participants (governing committees and their project managers) are well understood and appreciated within many organizations.

We have observed in our discussions that within most two-party systems the project teams assume primary responsibility for managing operational issues, while the governing committees assume responsibility for managing environmental issues. Both parties will contribute to the management of issues that emerge from stakeholders and other (secondary) committees.

The two-party systems of various organizations may differ in one important way, however. They may differ in how they assign responsibilities for managing outcome-related uncertainty and complexity. In some organizations it is expected that outcome-related uncertainty will be managed by the governing committees. In others, it is expected that project teams will take the lead in managing outcome uncertainty. These organizations don't assign individuals to an adaptive leadership role; they hope (and expect) that adaptive leadership will emerge as a consequence of the interactions that occur in the project and subcommittee environments. A third group of organizations holds less specific expectations. They seem to expect that project teams will consider outcome-related issues and propose solutions to their resolution. However, they also expect that the governing committee will retain primary accountability for examining adaptive responses and deciding which solution their endeavors should pursue.

Many of my interviewees reported that their organizations fell into this last group. Their governing committees hoped that adaptive leadership would emerge from their project teams, but they recognized that they might need to step in if it didn't.

It could be observed that many organizations do well with one of these two-party approaches. They are able to manage projects (and also some programs) reasonably well using oversight systems based on governing committees and the project managers (or leaders) whom they appointed. Their teams were able to find adaptive solutions to outcome-based issues within the context of their two-party systems. In those cases, it might be argued that there would not be enough value realized to warrant a move away from their two-party systems. The introduction of a three-party project oversight system might actually be perceived to paradoxically *increase* organizational or stakeholder complexity (by virtue of its seemingly unnecessary introduction of a second programmaticist, the professional program manager).

The successful use of two-party systems seems to support their continued use when outcome-related uncertainty and complexity can be efficiently and effectively managed by governing committee members and/or the project managers (and the teams) that they have assigned. As we have previously discussed, this is most often the case in organizations that are smaller, that have small portfolios, or that pursue endeavors that are not overly large or complex. Our observations support the continued use of two-party systems for oversight of projects and programs (or subprograms) when the governing committee and project team are efficient and effective in managing outcome uncertainty and complexity.

It should be noted, however, that the choice to manage a program via a two-party system does not change the nature of a program. A program's fundamental dependence on uncertain outcomes and its consequent need to be managed adaptively is not changed as a result of its oversight via a two-party oversight system. When managing a program using a two-party system, it is important to acknowledge the program's need for adaptive leadership, and to explicitly recognize from whence it is expected to emerge.

In other discussions, many organizational stakeholders reported that two-party programmatic oversight systems were no longer satisfying their needs. Their two-party platforms were burning, unstable, or perhaps undersized. These included several groups of stakeholders:

- Some noted that their initiatives required program management capabilities because they required the delivery of outcomes that were highly uncertain and profoundly complex; their initiatives depended critically on the day-to-day leadership of a program management professional who stimulated the adaptive capabilities of their programs, subprograms, and project teams.

- Others believed they needed program management capabilities because their initiatives required the leadership of a programmaticist with specialized technical skills that were absent in their governing committees or project teams; they needed to ensure that their programs could be managed by "experts" with specific knowledge or expertise about the outcomes they were pursuing.

- Still others believed that they needed program management capabilities because their organizational governance committees were now stretched to their "breaking points"; the demands of their line function organizations or the size of their portfolios had grown so large that their governing committee members were having trouble remaining acceptably engaged in the oversight programs (and their outcomes).

And many stakeholders cited combinations of these reasons as driving their need for a dedicated program management function.

Each of these stakeholder groups shared a common belief: Their organizations would derive substantial benefits from the contributions of outcome sage–programmaticists who understood and integrated organizational stakeholders' insights about outcomes, who stimulated the identification of adaptive responses to those outcomes, and who were highly effective in implementing adaptive changes as they became appropriate. Their organizations would benefit from having programmaticists who are specifically charged with managing outcome complexity.

Our observations on the limitations of two-party programmatic oversight systems, and on the benefits of introducing program management capabilities (as we have defined them), suggest that three-party programmatic oversight systems should be used when an organization would benefit from having its programs led by professionals with high-level competency in the management of outcome-related uncertainty and complexity (and the stakeholder and organizational complexities that are associated with them).

Third-generation (three-party) programmatic systems are especially valuable for the management and oversight of large and complex programs and programs that are sponsored by large and complex organizations. They should be implemented whenever an organization would benefit from having an outcome sage–programmaticist involved in the day-to-day management of its programs.

CHALLENGES FACED WHEN IMPLEMENTING THIRD-GENERATION PROGRAMMATICS

The decision to pursue third-generation programmatic approaches using the three-party programmatic oversight system is not without its challenges. During the course of my discussions—whether with stakeholders whose organizations had pursued three-party systems, with students who have championed the use of three-party systems in their own organizations, or with executives who have sought advice on improving their programmatic models—a number of issues were commonly cited as difficult.

The first set of issues relates to organizational (im)maturity in the science of managing programs.

Organizational Maturity in the Programmatic Sciences

Many modern organizations currently use programmatic oversight systems that have evolved significantly over time. The evolution of their two-party systems (via sequential, rational decisions made in response to various organizational pressures) has resulted in the development of multi-party programmatic oversight systems that have become remarkably complex (the "mess" that was depicted in Figure 7.10). Unfortunately, however, the stepwise evolution of their two-party systems was somewhat Darwinian in nature; it proceeded in the absence of a "master plan." That approach can be troublesome; Darwinian change enables survival of the fittest, but also extinction of the unfit. The first set of issues faced by organizations that seek to implement a three-party system relates to their existing culture of responding to pressures with incremental adjustments, and their lack of a longer-term blueprint for programmatic success. To ensure success, organizations need to move away from Darwinian approaches to programmatic science and move toward approaches that are based on "intelligent design."

The successful introduction of a three-party programmatic oversight system requires that its sponsors have a clear understanding of the science of programmatics. It requires that an organization's stakeholders understand the differences between outcomes and outputs, programs and projects, and program and project management. It necessitates that they be introduced to the five kinds of uncertainty and complexity that are faced by programs and projects, and that they come to recognize the specific roles of governance committee members, program managers, and project managers in managing each. It calls for executives and programmaticists to recognize that they must collectively and collaboratively contribute to the management and leadership of programmatic endeavors. It obliges them to participate appropriately. And it requires that everyone understand how organizations depend on the sometimes intense interactions of individuals (working in complex adaptive systems) to produce innovative and creative results. In short, it requires a more mature view of programmatic systems, how they are intended to operate, and how changing them may produce both intentional and unintended effects.

It is fortunate, stakeholders report, that this challenge is easily solved in organizations that are motivated to change (either because their platforms are burning, or because they believe change will bring benefits too valuable to ignore). The tenets of programmatic science can be taught—through seminars, workshops, academic courses, and written materials (like this one, I would hope).

Defining Programmaticist Authority and Autonomy

A second set of issues faced by organizations introducing third-generation programmatic approaches is the need to establish clear organizational agreements and understanding about the authority and autonomy that should be afforded to programmaticists. We noted in Chapter 5 that stakeholders have diverse opinions about the "ideal" amount of autonomy and authority that should be granted to them; the conceptions of a programmaticist's ideal role in modern organizations could be characterized as Traditionalist, Operationalist, or Inclusivist.

Traditionalist stakeholders believe that programmaticists should be responsible for efficiently and effectively managing the completion of work according to an endeavor's preapproved plans—on time, on budget, and to specifications. They believe that governing committee approval should be required before any significant changes are made to a project's plan or its strategy. *Traditionalist stakeholders have a first-generation programmatics perspective that reflects an Industrial Age view about the ideal roles and responsibilities of a project manager.* Their perspectives are usually aligned with the use of *two-party fully governed* programmatic oversight systems, where "fully governed" denotes that programmaticists are required to obtain approval(s) before a project's strategy or plans can be significantly changed.

Operationalist stakeholders believe that a programmaticist should be given a broader mandate for defining and refining operational plans, and for more independently managing operational uncertainty and complexity. They still expect that a programmaticist will ensure the delivery of outputs on time, on budget, and to specifications. However, they believe that project management professionals should be allowed to act more autonomously in managing how that is achieved. They expect professional project managers to manage the operational uncertainty and solve the operational complexity that their endeavors face. *Operationalist stakeholders have a third-generation programmatics perspective on the professional project manager's role.* They expect that programmaticists will function as the operational savants.

Inclusivist stakeholders believe that programmaticists should be personally responsible for managing (or ensuring the management of) their teams' responses to both operational and outcome-based uncertainty. They believe that programmaticists should be empowered to independently and autonomously manage both the strategic and operational approaches that their endeavors employ. *Inclusivist stakeholders have a third-generation programmatics perspective that describes the professional program manager's role.* Inclusivists expect that programmaticists will function as the outcome sages whom we've previously described, and—because projects sponsored by programs are accountable to program teams and the program management function (as depicted in

Figure 11.4)—that programmaticists will also have some responsibility for ensuring that a program's operational uncertainty and complexity are appropriately managed by Operationalist project managers.

As it turns out, the three common perspectives on a programmaticist's ideal role are precisely the roles that organizations need to fill in third-generation programmatic systems.

The full adoption of third-generation programmatic perspectives for the oversight and management of programmatic endeavors requires that the authority and autonomy of an Operationalist be assigned to high-ranking *project* managers. It requires that organizations accept a less-governed approach to project oversight—that major projects be governed via a ***two-party operationally empowered project oversight model***.

The adoption of third-generation programmatics requires that an Inclusivist's authority and autonomy be assigned to *program* managers. It requires that organizations embrace a more fully empowered approach to program and project oversight—that programs be governed via a ***three-party fully empowered programmatic oversight model***.

Finally, the adoption of third-generation programmatic perspectives requires that some project managers also operate under Traditionalist definitions of a project manager's authority and autonomy. Projects that are large and that contain complicated work plans are often managed by breaking them into individual workstreams that might be managed by other (perhaps less experienced) project managers. (Some people prefer to think of these workstreams as subprojects.) Such workstreams must often be rigidly monitored and controlled to ensure their work products are delivered precisely as expected, so that they can be effectively integrated with other outputs generated as part of the project. Such *workstreams may be best managed under Traditionalist definitions of a project manager's authority and autonomy, according to a two-party fully governed project oversight model*. By this approach, Traditionalist project managers would be accountable to the Operationalist project managers who are individually accountable for the primary project's goals.

The first step in resolving issues about how much authority and autonomy should be granted to a programmaticist is not to decide which *one* role will form the foundation of the programmatic systems; it is to recognize that all three roles may need to be present. To effectively manage large and complex programs often requires programmaticists who can fill each of these three roles within the third-generation programmatics framework.

The second step in resolving issues about authority and autonomy is to explicitly define the roles and responsibilities that need to be filled within each of an organization's programmatic endeavors. By clearly defining how goals will be pursued via programs, subprograms, projects, or subproject workstreams, an endeavor's requirements for programmatic leadership reveal themselves.

The third step involves the assignment of programmaticists and the explicit definition of their intended roles. For the proper function of third-generation programmatic systems, it is important that programmaticists and their organization's stakeholders clearly understand the authority and autonomy that is conferred on the leader or manager of each program, project, and workstream.

Many organizations that want to be clear in defining programmaticist responsibilities find it helpful to distinguish their programmaticists' roles by adopting a system that more closely links a programmaticist's expected responsibilities to his or her job title. One example of such a system is shown in Table 12.1. Organizations that use such a system typically develop competency models that contain explicit descriptions of the roles and responsibilities, authority and autonomy, and (perhaps most importantly) the behaviors expected of programmaticists who serve in each role.

The final (and sometimes most difficult) step in ensuring that programmaticists are afforded their expected authority and autonomy is

Table 12.1   An Example of How Programmatic Titles May be Used to Distinguish the Expected Roles and Responsibilities, Authority and Autonomy of Organizational Programmaticists

Prefixes to Designate Level of Competency or Experience	Principle Professional Title	Approach to Role	Usual Oversight Responsibility
Assistant, Associate, Senior	Project Manager	Traditionalist	Project Workstreams
Associate, Senior, Executive	Project Director	Operationalist	Primary Projects
Associate, Senior, Executive	Program Manager	Inclusivist	Subprograms
Senior, Executive	Program Director	Inclusivist	Primary Programs

to ensure that organizational stakeholders (executives, middle managers, programmaticists, and their team members) all come to know, to accept, and to respect the organization's assignment of programmatic responsibilities. Stakeholders can learn of the organization's "official" intent by educational means—from workshops, seminars, or other organizational communications. However, ensuring that organizational stakeholders will accept and respect their organization's (re-)assignment of management responsibilities can sometimes be difficult. Stakeholder acceptance and respect are uncertain outcomes of stakeholder interactions, and the issues that arise when stakeholders disapprove of or disrespect programmaticist assignments may be complex. It is important that senior executives reinforce and support their organization's decisions about the assignment of a programmaticist's role. Some organizations initiate a behavioral change program to ensure the expectations of the organization's stakeholders are communicated well and to facilitate their broad acceptance.

We have previously mentioned reasons that stakeholders might resist their organizations' delegation of more authority or autonomy to programmaticists; transferring adaptive leadership responsibilities to program manager-leaders, or assigning operational leadership responsibilities to project manager-leaders (as required under a third-generation programmatic oversight system), often requires that governing committee members cede authority that belonged to them under first- and second-generation systems. Executive committee members are sometimes unwilling to delegate that authority.

In discussions with executives and programmaticists as to why this might be, several reasons are commonly offered. The first is based on benevolence: Stakeholders observe (and executives admit) that executives commonly want to retain control over the strategies and operations of their organizations' programs and projects because they want to see them succeed. They exhibit a somewhat parental desire to guide and assist each of their "offspring" endeavors. Like most parents, they like being involved in the lives of their offspring. They take pride in their successes and want to be present in times of need. It is perhaps understandable that they would find it difficult to "let go," even when they know that they should.

But governing committee members may also want to review the proposed actions their offspring programs and projects for another reason. That reason is based on control. Governing committee members often observe that their offspring programs and projects may have significant effects on them as parents. As offspring become independent and make their own decisions, they may take actions that the parent doesn't like or appreciate. To delegate authority for cross-functional endeavors means that parents will lose an element of control over those actions and their effects. In the words of one executive: "How can I be sure they will do what I want them to do?" As programs and projects grow more independent, the truth is that sometimes executives can't.

Questions such as this one, raised by executives, reveal a third reason that stakeholders resist the delegation of authority and autonomy to programmaticists. This reason relates to trust. Executive stakeholders often express doubt that their organizations' programmaticists are ready to fill the leadership roles required by third-generation programmatic oversight systems. In discussions and interviews, executive stakeholders commonly opined that many of their programmaticists weren't capable of filling the outcome sage or operational savant programmaticist roles, as we have defined them. For example, they observed that the skills of their organizations' programmaticists in managing outcome-related uncertainty and complexity were inconsistent, perhaps because of the diverse backgrounds and experience of their organizations' "portfolio" of programmaticists. Most stakeholders cautiously agreed that programmaticist education and training programs might ease their concerns, but they continued to express doubts about the capabilities of certain individual programmaticists.

We will discuss the development of program management competency in the next chapter. However, this last reason for resisting the delegation of authority and autonomy to programmaticists reveals yet another challenge associated with the introduction of third-generation programmatic systems—the challenge of identifying appropriately skilled programmaticists to serve as project and program managers.

(Re-)Assigning Current Project and Program Managers

We have observed in our discussions that under three-party third-generation programmatic systems, the management styles, leadership skills, and technical knowledge required of project versus program managers are quite different. Project managers need operational leadership skills that are based on traditional project management principles and practices, whereas program managers need adaptive leadership skills focused more specifically on the assessment and realization of technical outcomes.

Stakeholders reported that under their legacy two-party programmatic oversight systems, their organizations had been inconsistent in their approaches for assigning programmaticists. It was common that some operationally focused *project* managers had assumed responsibilities for performing in outcome-focused *program* manager roles as the next step in their career development. Over the years, these *project* management professionals may have been asked to pursue training and education that would prepare them to manage outcomes, so that they could function as *program* managers. However, they were often only partially successful in acquiring the skills required of a program manager in a third-generation programmatic system.

Other stakeholders observed that their organizations had sought to convince technically oriented individuals who might be good at *program* management to study and learn the science of *project* management. These stakeholders also reported only partial success; many technically oriented programmaticists never completely learned the principles, practices, tools, and techniques of traditional project management professionals. Few earned project management certification.

Both of these groups had invested in the development of centaur-programmaticists in their efforts to adapt two-party programmatic oversight systems to the challenges of complex modern endeavors. They had sought to develop programmaticists who were invested in both roles, and in so doing had developed programmaticists who might resist or resent being reassigned to only one—particularly if they saw it as a diminution of their professional responsibilities.

When launching three-party third-generation programmatic systems, defining the appropriate assignment for these programmaticists could become a challenge. For the few programmaticists who were truly comfortable and effective in the centaur-like role of a combined program/project manager, division of their responsibilities seemed inappropriate and unnecessary. (Centaurs are rare; they should be nurtured whenever they are found.)

However, most other programmaticists were less successful as centaurs. Stakeholders reported (as we have previously discussed) that the majority of programmaticists who served in a combination program/project management role were better at one role than the other. The "roots" of their training or their management focus and style made them "a natural" in one role or the other. It could be challenging to determine in what role these programmaticists should be placed. Issues arose when they were told that they should no longer aspire to be centaurs.

Executives, programmaticists, and their colleagues sometimes disagreed on the most appropriate assignment(s) of any given professional programmaticist to a project versus program management role. Their differences of opinion were often based on how they valued or "weighted" the importance of several factors: a programmaticist's experience, prior performance, technical training related to outcomes, formal training in the programmatic sciences, and leadership style. Very often, stakeholder opinions were heavily influenced by a programmaticist's familiarity with a specific project or program. It was common for them to "default" to a programmaticist assignment that would cause the least disruption to their ongoing endeavors.

While working with colleagues there seemed to be no "magic formula" for assigning project and program managers. Most organizations I have worked with conclude that the best approach is to have honest discussions with programmaticists about how their individual skills might be most appropriately leveraged and their careers best directed in newly introduced three-party systems. For the sake of their programmaticists, their programs, and their organizations, most organizations recognize that the transition to a three-party system (as an organizational change program) can be achieved over time using an appropriate transition period.

Our analysis of the skills and the focus of project versus program managers indicates that the assignment of programmaticists to the project or program management role should be based on a balanced assessment of each individual's educational training, professional background, experience (and success) in managing uncertainty and complexity, and effectiveness in using command-and-control versus learn-and-adapt styles of leadership. Programmaticists with stronger backgrounds, experience, training, and success in the command-and-control management of operational uncertainty and complexity more clearly belong in project management roles. Those with stronger backgrounds, experience, training, and success in the learn-and-adapt management of outcome uncertainty more clearly belong in program management roles.

Assessing the skills and defining the assignments of programmaticists can sometimes be challenging, however. In my experience, when assigning one role or another to an organization's current programmaticists (as part of the implementation of third-generation programmatic approaches) it is critical to ensure that all stakeholders recognize that project and program management are both highly important to the success of the organization and its endeavors under third-generation programmatic systems. It is important that professionals in each role have opportunities for professional recognition, satisfaction, and advancement.

In our discussions to this point we have focused on the challenges faced by organizations as they assign their current programmaticists to the program and project manager roles required to support third-generation programmatic oversight systems. It should be noted, however, that the creation of third-generation systems often results in a need for additional program and project managers, as a consequence of assigning two programmaticists to complex endeavors that might previously have had only one.

Identifying and Assigning New Project and Program Managers

In my experience, organizations are reasonably adept at filling their needs for additional project managers. They usually have access to internal or external pools of project managers who are highly trained in the principles and practices of traditional project management. Many of them have long histories of investment in the development of project management competency. And, because competency in project management (as we have defined it) is not overly project-specific, they find it easy to identify project managers to support their third-generation programmatic systems. Stakeholders have reported that many of their organizations are successful in quickly identifying programmaticists who would be effective in the outcome savant role.

Stakeholders also report that filling outcome sage program management roles can be difficult.

The pool of individuals who are willing and able to fill the program manager role is often much more limited. Delivering outcomes and benefits from a program often requires a unique technical skill set. It may require the guidance of a program manager with knowledge, training, and experience related to the specific outcomes being pursued—a programmaticist with unique expertise or insight. But it may also require that the program manager rigorously investigate highly technical outcomes that are only tangentially related to his or her primary area of experience or training—a programmaticists who can *develop* expertise and insight. Stakeholders commonly report that these requirements limit the pool of prospective program managers. And, they observed, these are not the only qualifications.

Delivering outcomes and benefits from a program also requires that a prospective program manager possess the facilitation skills of an adaptive leader; it requires that he or she be uniquely capable of catalyzing the dynamic exchange of ideas to stimulate creativity and innovation in the program team environment. These skills may be difficult to teach (and to learn). Stakeholders report that finding them in individuals who are personally interested in assuming the outcome sage program manager role can be difficult.

Imagine yourself in a technical line function role where your abilities to contribute to the advancement of your discipline have become well recognized and appreciated. You have worked long and hard to obtain the technical training and experience required for success in your field. Imagine that, as an adaptive thinker, you have assumed an important role in stimulating innovation and creativity within your line function's area of expertise. And imagine that you are ambitious—you are hopeful that your skills will lead to line function advancement opportunities.

Now imagine that you are offered a program management role in the emerging field of "programmatic science." You might be intrigued at the thought of being responsible for an initiative deemed critically important to your organization's strategy. You might relish the thought of expanding your influence to include the broader work of a cross-functional team. You might like the thought of being in a program manager-leader role that provides you with exposure and access to the executives who manage your governing committee(s). And you might be grateful for having been recognized as having the unique skills required of a program manager. It is reasonable to expect that you would be complimented by the invitation to become one of your organization's program managers. However, it is easy to see that you might also feel conflicted. You would likely have many questions:

What impact might it have on me professionally to leave a seemingly stable line function role and assume responsibility for a programmatic initiative that (by definition) is temporary? Would I prefer to be a program manager (responsible for many technical outcomes) or to remain working in my chosen technical field? Would I be able to go back to my technical position when my program ends, or if I find that I am not happy in the program manager role? (Would my previous position still be available?) What opportunities exist for professional advancement, relative to the technical position I now hold? Do I want to spend the next part of my professional career joined-at-the-hip with the project managers? Will my new role and position be clearly understood, or will I be confused for a project manager? Is the third-generation three-party approach just another management fad? If it is, what will happen to me?

The answers to each of these questions would be important to any professional offered a program manager position in his or her organization. To a large extent, the answers determine how difficult it will be to fill program manager positions with candidates who are most capable and most likely to succeed.

How should such questions be answered? The answer (of course) is: "*It depends*"—on the circumstances, the commitment, and the challenges being faced by the sponsoring organization, and on the strategy of the organizational change program being used to introduce a three-party system. Questions about programmaticist preferences (Would I be happy?) are best answered through counsel and discussions between executives and their candidates. Questions about professional identity (Would people perceive that I've become a project manager?) can be answered with educational communications and workshops. Questions about the future (What happens when my project ends, and is this just a management fad?) should be answered with a long-term strategic plan.

Experience suggests that each of these questions is critical to internal candidates who might consider accepting a position as a program manager. As they are discussed, however, another question emerges about the implementation of third-generation programmatic oversight systems—one that rises to such a level of significance that it warrants its own deeper discussion.

To whom should program managers report?

Defining Reporting Relationships for Program and Project Managers

Recruiting program managers from an organization's line function disciplines can be a tricky business. Candidates who are recruited from internal departments are often intrigued by the prospects of their new roles and positions, but also concerned about what they must leave behind. Many express worry that they might become disconnected from the technical disciplines that had been the cornerstones of their professional careers, or from line function mentors who had contributed to their success. Some question whether they could return to their line function roles if they are not happy in their new roles as program managers. Still others ask whether they could try program management on a trial or part-time basis while reporting to their original departments.

The notion that a program management role could be assumed on a trial or part-time basis runs counter to the portrait that we have painted for the professional program manager in a third-generation program-matic oversight system. The importance of education and training in the programmatic sciences argues strongly for establishing program man-agement as a distinct and dedicated role—a profession.

Many stakeholders point out, however, that there are some advan-tages to having even full-time wholly dedicated program managers con-tinue to report to (or through) their original line function departments. It partially assuages program managers' fears about losing departmental "equity" when they first assume their new roles; it gives them comfort that they need not lose touch with their technical fields or the colleagues who had contributed to their prior success; it enables them to main-tain an identity that is clearly different from that of project manage-ment; and it calms fears that they would find themselves without a job if their program (or their organization's use of a three-party approach) is discontinued. Stakeholders observed that for all of these reasons, inter-nally recruited program managers were more likely to accept their newly offered program management positions when they were allowed to con-tinue reporting to their line function departments.

Stakeholders also observed that line function executives were more likely to support the introduction of a three-party project oversight sys-tem when its program managers continued to report through them. The introduction of a three-party system requires that governing committee executives delegate adaptive leadership responsibilities to the authority and control of the program manager. Stakeholders observed that govern-ing committee members objected less strongly to the delegation of that authority to someone who reported to or through them. They opined that executive stakeholders were more comfortable with that arrange-ment because it enabled them to feel that they were, in essence, retaining the authority by proxy.

Having now worked with a number of organizations as they imple-mented three-party systems, I can report that for all the reasons stated above, many of them do choose to pursue program management mod-els in which program managers (as we have defined them) continue to report to their original line function departments. I can also report, how-ever, that there are downsides to this decision. It results in other issues that need to be addressed to ensure the success of third-generation pro-grammatic systems.

The first kinds of issues that sometimes arise might be character-ized as "bureaucratically driven issues." These issues relate to the some-times inappropriate influence that a line function executive can have on the focus, the actions, and the behaviors of program managers who report to them. I have observed (and stakeholders have confirmed) that program managers who report to or through technical line function departments are often more responsive to the views and opinions of line function executives in their departments—and especially to the executives who are responsible for assessing their performance. As a result, program managers who report to technical line functions focus more intently on the resolution of uncertainty and complexity related to their "home" line function's responsibilities—sometimes at the expense of managing other sources of complexity. In programs that face an inordinate amount of uncertainty that is the program manager's home department's responsibility, this may be an acceptable or even desirable circumstance. However, in programs that require a more broadly or impartially focused program leader, this focus can become detrimental. In the words of one executive who faced such an issue: "The program manager needs to focus more on understanding and resolving the problems of other departments, if we are to stand a chance of achieving our goals."

Organizations that choose to have program managers report to technical line functions need to take steps to ensure that those managers lead their teams in a departmentally impartial way. In my experience, for example, it is helpful if program manager incentives and rewards are clearly based on their performance in delivering their targeted program (and not departmental) benefits. To improve a program manager's focus on his or her program's broader needs, it is also helpful if organizations affirm that the program manager-leader role is a full-time professional responsibility. Indeed, most program managers would agree that effectively managing a complex program is *at least* one full-time job.

The second kind of issue that commonly arises might be categorized as a "professional issue." These relate to the need to ensure that program managers acquire adequate knowledge and understanding of "programmatic science"—that they have (or develop) the knowledge, skills, and leadership competencies that are required for program management success.

We observed in our earlier discussions that important program and project management positions are too often assigned to individuals who are not educated or trained as programmaticists. Unfortunately, the routine assignment of program managers from line function departments further reinforces belief that serving in a program management role does not require unique knowledge and professional expertise. Allowing program managers to report to line function supervisors who are themselves untrained in programmatics has the same effect. However, to be effective in their roles in third-generation programmatic oversight systems, it is important that program managers, project managers, and their governing committees all clearly understand their responsibilities. They should, for example, be acutely aware of their responsibilities for collectively providing the adaptive, operational, and enabling forms of leadership that are critically important to program teams. And they should clearly understand their individual responsibilities for managing each of the five types of program uncertainty and complexity.

Stakeholders reported that the cultivation of such knowledge could be more challenging when program managers reported to leaders or managers in technical line functions. Program managers who reported to technical departments were less likely to undertake a systematic study of the standards of program management or the leadership requirements of their roles. Without education in the science of program management, program managers were left to "figure it out" by conducting what amounted to a series of managerial experiments to learn lessons that they might otherwise be taught. The combined experience of many organizations reveals that some of these program managers are eventually successful in their roles, but a good number of others (unfortunately) are not. And inconsistent success also has consequences.

The inconsistent performance of program managers in their roles reflects poorly, not only on the effectiveness of the individual program managers, but also on the organization's management systems. In interviews and discussions with a variety of stakeholders, inconsistent success was often reported to cause a loss of trust in the profession of program management and in the organization's programmatic oversight system. It caused many organizations to alternately conclude that problems they were facing were due to the inadequacy of a program manager or to a failure of their programmatic oversight system. Was it one, the other, or both? Without knowledge of the programmatic sciences, it can be difficult to tell.

When asked to provide suggestions for how success might be better ensured, stakeholders commonly proposed two possible approaches. Their first approach sought to remediate the problems with education: They proposed that program managers who reported to line function organizations should be more formally educated in the nature and practice of program management as we have described it—in the practice of programmatic science. Stakeholders who had successfully employed three-party programmatic oversight systems were unanimous in noting the importance of education. They recommended that basic education in the roles and responsibilities of stakeholders should be provided to each of the major contributors to the three-party system (program managers, project managers, and governing committee members) and also to those who work closely with them (line function managers, secondary committee members, and team members). They further recommended that program managers receive advanced training in the science of program management (for example, in the principles of managing programmatic complexity and of adaptive leadership). As a group, stakeholders reported that the performance of their program managers and of their entire three-party programmatic oversight systems was markedly better after program managers had been provided such education.

The second approach for improving the performance of their program managers and their three-party programmatic oversight systems involved more radical changes to an organization's bureaucratic structures. Several stakeholders observed that in their experience, *the development of program management competencies could best be ensured by establishing a separate line function department dedicated to the practice and advancement of program management* (as we have defined it for third-generation programmatic systems). This is a much more significant step because it requires a much bigger commitment to the implementation of a three-party programmatic oversight system. But, based on the experiences recounted by stakeholders who have pursued it, and on my own experience advising organizations, it is a step that is clearly worth considering.

ESTABLISHING DEPARTMENTS OF PROGRAM MANAGEMENT AND OF PROGRAMMATIC SCIENCE

The reasons for considering a program management department might be obvious by now. Establishing such a department can enable an organization to develop more advanced program management competencies, in much the same ways that establishing technically focused departments has (since the Industrial Age) enabled organizations to develop more advanced technical core competencies. It can provide a means of organizing program managers so that they can easily share their experiences, develop new insights, and (thereby) grow their professional competencies. It can enable organizations to develop "center of excellence" competencies in the management of outcome uncertainty, the resolution of outcome complexity, and the development of adaptive leadership. And it can promote the adoption of more consistent definitions of the roles, the responsibilities, and (most especially) the performance expectations of outcome sage program managers. Many stakeholders agreed that the potential benefits of establishing a program management department are significant—and well worth pursuing.

I have now had the opportunity to work with several organizations that have introduced program management departments to support third-generation programmatic oversight systems. Their collective experience confirms that these expected benefits are often realized; they report that their professional program managers have become highly valued contributors to their three-party programmatic oversight systems. As a group, they express high satisfaction about the value that their program management departments have brought.

Encouraged by their results, some stakeholders reported that their organizations have gone even further. Seeking to take advantage of the leadership synergies that could be achieved in a three-party program oversight system, they bureaucratically linked their organizations' program and project management departments as distinct and yet allied subfunctions within a "department of programmatic sciences." (That direction was taken by the organization from the case study in Chapter 11.) These stakeholders reported that by allying program and project management functions within a "programmatics department," they could ensure their collaboration as they strove to ensure the seamless management of programs and projects. In fact, it was observed by some stakeholders that establishing a department of programmatics was a viable alternative to establishing more traditionally described program or project management offices (PMOs). We do not yet have enough experience with third-generation (three-party) programmatic systems to compare the benefits of "departments of programmatic science" with those of the many types of organizational PMOs formed by various organizations. However, it will be fascinating to compare them in the future.

The experience available to date suggests that program management departments can contribute significantly to the success of three-party programmatic oversight systems. We might therefore expect that organizations pursuing third-generation programmatics approaches will pursue the establishment of program management departments with increasing frequency. However, stakeholders report that introducing program management departments as part of third-generation programmatics requires a good deal of organizational resolve. Establishing a separate program management department requires that an organization's bureaucratic hierarchy be modified—and such changes are often met with resistance. It often requires the re-assignment of current program managers from line function departments, and the need to address "headcount issues." It requires that executive stakeholders support the re-assignment of adaptive leadership responsibilities to managers who are outside of their bureaucratic empires. It is sometimes difficult to reach consensus about the value of such changes; coming to consensus requires that stakeholders come to believe that transforming an organization's bureaucratic structure will produce benefits that are themselves transformational.

As an advisor to organizations that seek to implement three-party systems, I have found it important that organizational executives firmly believe that they will realize significant organizational benefits. With high expectations comes a greater willingness to address the significant challenges that inevitably arise. I have found that it is best if these expectations remain focused on a singular promise: That by developing specific competencies in both program and project management (as we have defined them), organizations can more effectively and successfully manage their complex programmatic initiatives. Focusing on this promise ensures that organizations implementing third-generation programmatic approaches never lose sight of an important truth—that *success of the system is based on the promise that it will ensure the engagement of leaders who, as a result of their collective contributions, are effective in solving complex problems.* To ensure success of the system it is therefore important that we understand the nature of project and program (operational and adaptive) leadership.

Emerging research on program leadership competencies provides interesting insights about both.

CHAPTER **13**

Developing Programmatic Leadership Competencies

O ne needs only to visit the business sections of a local bookstore, or to peruse the latest list of bestselling books, to realize that the public has a seemingly insatiable appetite for new insights on the nature of leadership. It is tempting to speculate that the number of books available in the field is a sign that we know so very much about it, but it could be argued that the opposite is true. Our literary discourse about the nature of leadership might be equally well considered as evidence that we know far too little about it—that there is no singular perspective (or collection of perspectives) that is capable of satisfying all of our needs. Each of those leadership books might be considered to bear witness to our continuing search for perspectives that ring true and clear to our own particular needs.

While collecting the perspectives of stakeholders for this book, I have had many opportunities to discuss the nature of programmatic leadership with executives, programmaticists, and other organizational stakeholders. Over that period, I too have searched for key perspectives on leadership—and in particular, on "programmatic leadership." My search for a singular perspective that unlocks the secrets of programmatic leadership is also ongoing. It has, for the most part, been a pragmatic search, based on a fundamental observation that seems to be shared by many executives: Leadership is a bit like pornography; it is difficult to define to everyone's satisfaction, but most people feel that they know it when they see it.

THE NEEDS OF A LEADER

I have found that most organizational stakeholders are very comfortable in identifying programmaticists who they believe are exceptionally good

---

leaders. Within any one organization, it is likely that executives and pro-grammaticists will agree on who the best leaders are. However, when those same stakeholders are asked to explicitly define what specific attributes set the "best" leaders apart from the rest, they often struggle a bit. They usually begin by listing elements of leadership that we would all recognize—they speak about a leader's need for appropriate knowledge, skills, and experience. Because these elements would seem to be definable, it would seem that we should be able to identify good leaders using a checklist (of sorts) that enumerates key elements.

Over the course of the earlier chapters we began to assemble such a checklist. We have observed, for example, that a high level of performance in the project management role would require a strong *knowledge* of traditional project management principles, practices, tools, and techniques, as detailed in the Standards of project management practice. Understanding each of these elements ensures that modern project managers have assimilated the professional knowledge that has been refined over decades of practice by professional project managers who came before them. This understanding enables project managers to speak a common language that ensures that they are properly prepared to manage the operational uncertainty that their projects will face and to effectively lead their project teams as they work to resolve operational complexity.

We have also observed that a high level of performance in project management requires *skills* that are essential to the collaborative management of a project's operational plans—personal skills in effective communication, active listening, influencing without authority, and negotiation, for example. We have noted that being an effective project manager might require the ability to use a collaborative yet control-oriented leadership style to ensure achievement of operational goals. Each of these skills is critical to a project manager's ability to engage appropriately with the operationally focused stakeholders upon whom his or her project depends, and to deliver the desired operational results. They are critical to a manager's ability to fully understand and manage stakeholder and organizational complexities while negotiating solutions to operational issues.

We have similarly noted the knowledge and skills that would be important for a program manager. A program manager's ability to deal with outcome uncertainty and complexity might, for example, require *technical knowledge* related to the specific outcomes being targeted. It might require unique insights about how outcomes would or would not enable realization of a program's intended benefits or value. And it might require knowledge about how a program's value can best be predicted or assessed. The knowledge required of a given program manager might therefore be expected to vary somewhat, depending upon the nature of his or her program and the technical or strategic outcome uncertainties that the program faces.

We have also observed that a high level of performance in program management might require unique *technical skills*. The skills we noted for a project manager (in communication, listening, influencing, and negotiation) would of course be important. However, a program manager would need to combine them with skills in the analyses of technical or strategic uncertainties unique to the program. And he or she would need to engage appropriately with the technically focused stakeholders upon whom the project depends, so as to be effective in managing stakeholder or organizational uncertainties and complexities. Finally, an effective program manager must use his technical skills in a learn-and-adapt environment to stimulate innovation and creativity as part of his adaptive leadership role.

At first, my discussions with stakeholders seemed to provide a sound basis for defining the essential requirements for effective programmatic leadership based on knowledge and skills. As my discussions progressed, however, new insights emerged—insights that became more troubling over time. The checklist descriptions of the knowledge and skills required of program and project leaders did not usually provide an adequate basis for distinguishing the performance of "the best" of an organization's leaders from "the rest" of that organization's leaders. The knowledge and skills contained in each checklist were necessary, but not sufficient. As I explored this point further with executives and programmaticists, our discussions typically turned to the third of their commonly cited elements of leadership—*experience*.

Pressed to identify what made their best program and project managers stand out, stakeholders noted that these programmaticists had demonstrated unique insights that had seemingly grown over time. Their best leaders had developed a high level of understanding about how to get things done within the context of their organizations. They had differentiated themselves because they had the *experience* to know how best to use their knowledge and skills within their organizational environment and culture. I was reminded of the comments made by the interviewee in Chapter 8: "When I take my car to a specific repair shop, it is because I trust that its mechanic will understand my problem, and I trust his ability to do good work when fixing it. It is not because I believe that he has good tools; I have never asked to look at his toolbox. It is *how and when* he uses his tools that really matters."

In the minds of many of the stakeholders I interviewed, experience was the primary difference—the experience of the programmaticist in solving similar issues, and the stakeholders' own experience in having been satisfied with the results that a given programmaticist would deliver. Most stakeholders agreed that experience was important because it informed program and project managers as to what did or didn't work (or what was or was not an acceptable approach) when trying to resolve the various sometimes nuanced challenges of their organizational environments. They also noted that their organizations' broad needs for "experience" in its programmaticists were quite difficult to describe. They speculated *that* was why it was so hard to universally define the requirements for successful program and project leadership.

It was a logic that seemed to make sense, but it still seemed incomplete. When asked to describe why experience was valuable, stakeholders commonly focused on how experience enabled programmaticists to acquire more knowledge and skills (to put more tools in the toolbox). So was experience really an independent factor? Stakeholders often also described experience in measures of time, or with descriptors of the diversity or frequency of an individual's exposure to specific circumstances. However, none of these measures seemed to correlate directly enough with the kinds of experience that led to the broad recognition of a programmaticist's exemplary leadership. Each stakeholder I interviewed could easily identify examples of experienced programmaticists (those who had worked for many years on programmatic endeavors) who were not recognized as their organizations' best leaders, and also of programmaticists with far less experience who were more widely recognized for their exceptional leadership. It seemed that "experience" was necessary or important, but again not entirely sufficient.

Something was missing.

As I further explored the importance of experience with executives and programmaticists, two consistent observations could be made: (1) Stakeholders agreed that program and project managers who were recognized as performing exceptionally well had developed clearly defined "leadership personas"—they were recognized for their abilities to consistently and effectively fill a specific leadership need. Whether they functioned as Traditionalists or Operationalists or Inclusivists, their roles, responsibilities, capabilities, and competencies were well understood—both by themselves and by their organizations. And, (2) these exceptional program and project managers had demonstrated a significant *positive impact and influence* while serving in their respective roles.

Those in Traditionalist roles had demonstrated that they were effective in ensuring that their project outputs and outcomes would be delivered as promised (on time, on budget, and to expectations). They were highly effective in managing operational uncertainty and thereby reducing or preventing operational complexity.

Those in Operationalist roles had demonstrated that they could work independently to effectively and efficiently resolve operational issues that might threaten the delivery of project outputs and outcomes. They were highly effective in solving operational complexity.

Those in Inclusivist roles had demonstrated that they were effective in ensuring that their teams efficiently and successfully delivered their program's targeted outcomes, benefits, and value. They were highly effective in managing outcome uncertainty and in solving outcome complexity.

And programmaticists who were considered exceptional in any of these roles had also demonstrated that while they were managing operational or outcome complexity, they were highly capable of managing stakeholder or organizational uncertainties and complexities that might arise as a consequence.

Discussions with stakeholders seemed to suggest that "experience" could contribute to a programmaticist's perceived leadership competency in three ways: It could provide programmaticists with the opportunity to acquire new knowledge and skills important to their performance; it could provide opportunities for programmaticists and their organizations to come to a clearer understanding of the leadership role that a given programmaticist would be effective in filling (their leadership persona); and (in so doing) it could help programmaticists to understand the specific leadership behaviors and to acquire the specific leadership skills that would be most appropriate and effective for use in their roles.

These seemed to be important observations. Interviews with executives, programmaticists, and other stakeholders suggested that there were three critical components to effective programmatic leadership: knowledge, skills, and those specific leadership behaviors. The success of a third-generation programmatic system seems to depend upon a programmaticist's ability to use his or her knowledge and skills and *the most appropriate leadership behaviors* to produce the outcomes desired in their programmatic endeavors (see Figure 13.1).

Figure 13.1   Critical components of programmatic leadership.

We have previously discussed some of the knowledge and skills that might be required of a program or project manager under a three-party programmatic oversight system. And the project management literature seems replete with information about leadership approaches required from a Traditionalist project manager. But what specific leadership behaviors might be required of Operationalist and Traditionalist programmaticists as we have defined them? What individual behaviors might be necessary for their effective performance, and what constellation of behaviors might be sufficient for their overall success? These are important questions if we are to clearly define the operational savant and the outcome sage roles—and if we are to be effective in staffing those positions.

During early interviews with organizational stakeholders, there was great diversity of opinion about which leadership behaviors were "appropriate" for program or project managers who might assume an Operationalist or an Inclusivist role. Programmaticist behaviors that were considered to be acceptable by one executive might be considered to have "not gone far enough" by a second—and to have "gone too far" by a third. It was a problem that had fueled the angst of many Exasperados.

The differences between stakeholders' opinions were partly a consequence of their inconsistent assumptions about a programmaticist's roles and responsibilities. Stakeholders who held Traditionalist-dominated first-generation views of a project manager's role (and who believed that program and project management were qualitatively similar disciplines) tended to have a much more constrained view of the behaviors that would be appropriate for a project management professional. Stakeholders who had second- or third-generation programmatic perspectives, or who espoused Operationalist or Traditionalist visions of a programmaticist's role, tended to expect that a project or program manager would exhibit leadership behaviors that were more permissive—that would seek to influence stakeholders at higher levels and in greater numbers. However, differences of opinion existed even between stakeholders who generally shared Operationalist or

Traditionalist views. When discussing the specific leadership behaviors that a given programmaticist should exhibit—even a programmaticist who had been successful in their organizations—they still often differed in their views. As my interviews proceeded, it became apparent that many stakeholders had different interpretations of the programmaticist job descriptions used by their organizations.

Defining "Appropriate" Leadership Behaviors

Take, for example, a common job description statement—that a programmaticist should "proactively manage program or project issues." Is this description sufficiently explicit? What issues are being addressed?

Under a third-generation programmatic oversight system we might expand this description to state that a programmaticist should proactively manage uncertainty and resolve complexity that is either outcome-based (in the case of a program manager) or operationally based (in the case of a project manager). We might applaud such a description for its newfound focus on the management of uncertainty and complexity, and for its ability to reinforce the specific roles of either an outcome sage or an operational savant programmaticist. But what does "proactively" mean? Stakeholders commonly had different interpretations of that word. It was not unusual for them to conclude that it called for quite different leadership behaviors.

Consider, for example, the following scenario:

While walking down a hallway, a program manager encounters a senior executive who is a member of her program's governing committee. The executive stops her to ask about a technical outcome that the program has generated—an outcome that has exposed a technical issue that will need to be resolved. The executive then proceeds to tell the program manager what approach he believes the team should take as a means of resolving the issue. The program manager, however, is not her program team's most knowledgeable "expert" on the subject of the outcome, and the team's expert is not available at that moment.

What response should the program manager have? What behaviors might appropriately satisfy the program manager's mandate to "proactively manage outcome-based uncertainty and resolve outcome-based complexity"?

There are five distinct approaches that the program manager could take in responding to the executive's suggestion. Each involves the invocation of specific and distinct leadership behaviors.

1. She could listen to and (if necessary) clarify the executive's suggestion, then agree to communicate it to her team (and its subject matter expert). She might agree to inform the executive of their perspectives on his suggestion.

2. She could listen to the executive's suggestion, then offer to schedule a meeting between the executive, the subject matter expert, and key members of her team who might have important expertise or insightful perspectives relating to the suggestion.

3. She could listen to the executive's suggestion and, while noting that she is not the expert, inform the executive of the subject matter expert's likely views on the issue. She might question the executive about the expert's concerns and about how the executive would suggest that they be addressed. She would then discuss their conversation with the expert (and the program team) and ensure that the executive is informed of the team's collective perspectives.

4. She could listen to and interact with the executive as described in the previous scenario, but also weigh in with her own perspectives and opinions about how the issue could or should be resolved. She might propose a strategy for implementing changes, and negotiate with the executive if she felt it would advance the issue's resolution.

5. She could listen to and interact with the executive as described in (4) above, but also inform the executive of the likely positions of other team members, executives, influential stakeholders, and secondary governance committees. She might negotiate with the executive on behalf of any of these stakeholders if she felt it would advance the issue's resolution. In doing so she would be seeking to identify a solution that would be acceptable to all.

It is interesting to discuss with stakeholders which leadership behaviors would be considered "appropriate" or "ideal" for a program manager within their organizations. Each of these specific leadership behaviors arguably satisfies a program manager's mandate to be proactive in resolving outcome-based complexity. Yet each embodies a different vision of a program manager's roles and responsibilities.

In the first response, the program manager is proactively seeking to manage outcome complexity by ensuring efficient and rapid communication of complexity-solving proposals between the senior executive and a team member—communication that might not otherwise occur. In the second response the program manager goes further; she arranges a conversation between the executive and her team member(s). She proactively facilitates their direct interaction to enable their potential resolution of complexity.

Neither of these first two responses requires that the programmaticist have much personal knowledge about how the outcome-related issue can or should be resolved. Instead, they both depend upon the program manager taking action to ensure that the issue-solving capabilities of others are accessed—that an opportunity to develop adaptive responses is created (in an environment that could be recognized as a complex adaptive system).

A program manager who pursued the third response has gone further, however. In the third response, the program manager assumes some responsibility for communicating on behalf of the subject matter expert. She seeks to have her team benefit more immediately from the hallway meeting by immediately initiating a bidirectional dialog about the executive's ideas. This is a fundamentally different leadership behavior. It requires that a program manager assume some risk; she would need to trust in her ability to appropriately represent the expert's view and to engage in dialog with the executive about it. She would then need to speak with the expert to ensure that she had represented his or her perspectives appropriately.

To exhibit the third behavior, a program leader would need to have some personal understanding about the nature of the technical outcome, the issues that had arisen as a consequence of it, and the team's options for responding to it. The third leadership behavior thus requires that the program manager have greater technical knowledge than the first two behaviors, and that she be willing to assume personal responsibility for representing the sometimes complex views of her team members. In pursuing the third leadership behavior, the program leader seeks to turn the hallway meeting itself into a complex adaptive system (or at least an extension of one).

The fourth leadership behavior goes a bit further than the third. It requires that the program manager not only represent the subject matter expert's opinions, but that she also have opinions of her own. To pursue the fourth leadership response, the program manager would be required to have an even greater, more independent knowledge of the subject matter related to the outcome. It would require not only that she understand the opinions of her subject matter expert and of her executive, but also that she have the skills required to assess them and compare them to her own perspectives. It would require that the program manager have the skills, the ability, and the willingness to independently assess whether proposed solutions for outcome-related issues are viable. A program leader who exhibits the fourth leadership behavior becomes a more active contributor to complex adaptive systems as they seek to resolve complex outcome-related issues within the organization.

The fifth leadership behavior extends the fourth still further. It requires that the program leader be capable of understanding, representing, and analyzing the perspectives of many program team members, stakeholders, and organizational committees and subcommittees. It requires that she be capable of representing others in discussions that might otherwise only be possible in larger meetings—that she contributes as they otherwise would to promote the dynamic exchange of ideas that is critical to the success of complex adaptive systems. To pursue the fifth leadership response, the program leader would need to possess even broader knowledge of the disciplines, interests, and needs of her organization's various stakeholders, and she would need to possess greater skills in interpreting stakeholder opinions and in using those opinions to stimulate the resolution of issues. When the program manager exhibits the fifth level of leadership behavior, she has begun to "embody" adaptive leadership by anticipating and integrating the perspectives of her colleagues and then using them dynamically to identify adaptive solutions.

It is interesting to present these five behaviors to senior executives or programmaticists when exploring their views on the "ideal" leadership behaviors of a programmaticist. Many are at first surprised to observe that programmatic leadership behaviors can be described and organized in a way that enables their systematic examination. They often report that having the five behaviors presented in such a way gives them new understanding and insights about the various ways that a programmaticist could be expected to show leadership. It enables them to more clearly define and communicate which behaviors they consider to be appropriate and which they consider insufficient (because they have not done enough) or inappropriate (because they have gone too far). It enables them to more clearly identify the behaviors that they associate with excellence. Executives and programmaticists agree that examining such behaviors can help them to better define the roles that they expect programmaticists to play within their organization's programmatic oversight system.

Consider, for example, using the above-mentioned scenario to improve how an organization defines the roles and responsibilities of program and project managers under a third-generation programmatic (three-party) oversight system. The example, as described, is based on an executive's concern about a *technical* issue that has arisen as a consequence of *outcome uncertainty*. After examining the scenario, it would be reasonable for an organization to conclude that its *program* management professionals (as we have defined them) should be expected to exhibit high-level leadership behaviors and the knowledge and skills required to support them (perhaps level 4 or 5). However, an organization might also conclude that the same knowledge and skills should not be expected of a Traditionalist project manager; Traditionalist *project* management professionals might only be expected to exhibit lower-level leadership behaviors (level 1 or 2) in this situation.

Now consider a similar situation, in which the executive was addressing a complicated *planning* issue that had arisen as a consequence of *operational uncertainty*. One might expect, in this case, that a *project* management professional would need to exhibit high-level leadership behaviors, knowledge, and skill; lower-level behaviors would be acceptable from a *program* management professional.

By examining requirements for programmatic leadership using a framework based on knowledge, skills, and behaviors, organizations can more explicitly define the leadership expectations of both program and project managers. In a three-party programmatic oversight system, an outcome sage program manager might be required to exhibit high-level leadership when managing *outcome-related* uncertainty and complexity, while an operational savant project manager would exhibit high-level leadership when managing *operational* uncertainty and complexity. Very large programs that rely on highly uncertain outcomes would be best managed by a cohort of program and project managers who join together to collaboratively contribute their respective knowledge, skills, and high-level leadership behaviors.

When first working with organizations on the assessment and development of programmatic competencies, it is common to find that their executive stakeholders have diverse views about the ideal behaviors of a programmaticist. While some stakeholders might expect a programmaticist to exhibit level 3 or 4 behaviors, others might insist on level 5. Still others might never have thought to expect anything but level 2. These differences of opinion can be very disruptive to an organization's programmatic oversight system. A programmaticist exhibiting level 4 behaviors might be praised for doing an excellent job by one group of executives while being chastised for not doing enough or for going too far by other groups. (It is understandable that Exasperados abound in organizations that have not aligned their expectations.)

Aligning the views of internal stakeholders is an important first step in helping organizations to more precisely define their expectations of programmaticists, regardless of their programmatic oversight system. It is a critical step in any organization's development of more behaviorally focused competency models for its program and project management professionals.

As I have worked to help organizations define the programmatic leadership behaviors they consider to be ideal, I have found that organizations can have significantly different expectations—even if they work on quite similar programmatic endeavors. Organizations that seek first to empower their programmaticists (using operationally empowered or fully empowered leadership models) by delegating them more responsibility encourage high-level leadership behaviors of their program and project managers. Organizations that seek to ensure that their governing committees retain control over project or program changes (by using fully governed leadership models) often prefer that the majority of programmaticists exhibit lower-to-middle-level behaviors. They reserve high-level prerogative for their most senior executives. Programmaticists who are capable of exhibiting high-level leadership behaviors become exasperated when they are constrained to work in positions that limit them to lower-level behaviors.

Clarifying an organization's preferred leadership behaviors becomes, in many ways, an exercise in precisely defining that organization's leadership "culture." It enables the organization to divine and define its leadership expectations so that it can teach them to programmaticists (and other stakeholders) who would otherwise learn them over time, through "experience." Moreover, assessing an individual's characteristic or preferred leadership behaviors can be a valuable means of determining whether his or her views about leadership are a cultural fit for an organization. Organizations that require high-level leadership behaviors from their programmaticists do well to hire programmaticists who demonstrate their understanding of (and prior success using) those behaviors.

Defining an organization's preferred leadership behaviors can also be an important first step in defining how it might change its culture. By examining current perceptions of the most "characteristic" behaviors of a given organization's programmaticist leaders, and then comparing them to behaviors it might consider to be preferred or ideal, that organization can uncover the performance gaps between current and preferred behaviors. It can then define the specific competencies that need to be developed to ensure that it develops its desired behaviors.

The perspectives of organizational stakeholders can easily be examined using tools that enable organizations to study their programmatic leadership cultures. An example of one tool that allows the presentation of scenarios, the examination of preferred behaviors, and the diagnoses of performance and competency gaps is displayed in Figure 13.2.

Questions arise when initiating a survey of behaviors. Which behaviors are important to assess? What are the specific behavioral

The Executive in the Hall	Appropriate?	Most Characteristic	Currently Preferred	Future Ideal
Walking down a hallway, a program manager encounters an executive on her program's governing committee. He stops her to suggest an approach for resolving a technical issue that affects her program. The program manager, however, is not the teams "expert" on the subject of the issue. How should she first respond?				
Behavioral responses:				
1 Note details of the discussion, and communicate them to the expert. Advise the expert on the executive's perspectives and expectations for follow-up.				
2 Note details and offer to facilitate a follow-up meeting between the executive and the team expert(s).		✓		
3 Inform the executive of the experts probable view or concerns. Seek to clarify the executive's perspectives.	✓		✓	
4 Inform the executive of the expert's probable view or concerns, and also of her own views. Seek to clarify the executive's perspectives. Negotiate on behalf of the absent expert if it will advance the resolution of the issue.	✓			
5 Inform the executive of the probable views of the expert, herself, other stakeholders and committees. Seek to clarify the executive's perspectives. Negotiate on behalf of any absent stakeholders if it will advance the resolution of the issue. ge as a consequence of the discussions.	✓			✓

Figure 13.2 Examining the leadership behaviors of a professional program manager.

distinctions that reflect different levels of programmaticist behavior? The answers to such questions are important; the "executive in the hallway" example presents just one of many relevant situations that any given program manager might encounter. And because there are big differences between organizations' programmatic oversight systems, their leadership cultures, and the programs they pursue, one might speculate that there could be big differences in the kinds of reactions that programmaticists could consider. What should one focus on when designing such a survey?

We are fortunate that research has been conducted on competencies important to success in program management; it sheds light on these particular questions. It is important for programmaticists to study this research as they strive to extend their understanding of the programmatic sciences.

INSIGHTS FROM RESEARCH ON PROGRAM MANAGEMENT COMPETENCY

The key leadership behaviors required for successful program management were explored in a valuable research study conducted by Partington, Pellegrinelli, and Young, and published in a paper in 2005.[1] The conclusions from that study are fascinating.

The researchers sought to identify leadership behaviors that contribute to success in program management by exploring the perceptions that stakeholders from a variety of industries (including aerospace, software development, pharmaceuticals, construction, financial services, telecommunications, and public utilities) have about program leadership. Using a methodology known as "phenomenography," the researchers asked stakeholders to identify program managers who were recognized as successful in each of their organizations, and to define what it was that made them more successful than their colleagues. In so doing, the researchers sought (1) to identify the elements of work that were considered essential to the competence of a program manager, and (2) to identify how a program manager might demonstrate leadership in his or her approach to those elements of work. The information they collected and their methods of analysis led to important observations and conclusions. The data suggested

---

[1]Partington, D., Pellegrinelli, S., and Young, M.: Attributes and levels of programme management competence: An interpretive study, International Journal of Project Management 23: 87–95, 2005.

that program management competencies could be organized using a framework that focused on seventeen separate elements, organized into three different groups, each with four distinct "levels" of behavior.

The first group of elements was related to the programmaticist's views of the work that needed to be performed. The researchers noted that key elements that seemed to contribute to success were the programmaticist's:

- Focus on the details of his or her work,
- Degree of emotional attachment to the work,
- Willingness to take action related to the work, and
- Willingness to assume others' roles as might be necessary to advance the work.

(This last element is the one addressed in the "executive in the hallway" scenario discussed above.)

The second group of elements was related to the programmaticist's interactions with other organizational stakeholders. Here, the elements important to programmaticist success included his or her:

- Relationships with team members,
- Approach to conflict and disagreement,
- Ability to use questions,
- Willingness to establish expectations of others, and
- Willingness to provide education and support.

The third group of elements was related to a programmaticist's approach when interacting with the programmatic environment. In this category, the key elements that seemed important to a programmaticist's success included his or her:

- Willingness to be adaptive,
- Awareness of the organization's capabilities,
- Approach to communication,
- Approach toward risk,
- Approach toward governance,
- Attitudes toward time,

- Attitudes toward budgets, and
- Attitudes toward scope.

The researchers found that programmaticists exhibit a wide variety of leadership behaviors in each of these elements. On close examination, however, they observed that the behaviors associated with each element could be organized into one of four distinct groups that each represented a different "mindset" or "conception" that programmaticists applied when choosing their leadership behaviors. Most interestingly, these mindsets could be ordered hierarchically to reflect their progressively increasing association with programmaticist effectiveness and success.

The first-level behaviors exhibited for each of the seventeen elements were focused on managing a programmatic endeavor under prescribed conditions, according to defined assumptions, and with a focus on conditions specific to the programmatic endeavor. First-level behaviors tended to have an inward-facing perspective that assumed responsibility for the pursuit of endeavors according to their defined plan and approach. Programmaticists exhibiting first-level behaviors did not assume responsibility for the environment in which a program or project was being pursued. First-level behaviors could generally be recognized to conform to traditional conceptions of project management, its principles, and its practices.

Second-level behaviors for each of the elements focused more on the potential need to adapt. They reflected greater awareness of the potential impact of uncertainty and complexity on a programmatic endeavor, and greater vigilance about the possibility that programmatic assumptions might change in response to unexpected (or unwanted) results. These were behaviors exhibited by programmaticists who might break from Traditionalist protocol; they reflected a greater willingness to deviate from approved plans. Second-level behaviors revealed greater awareness of circumstances (both inside and outside of their programs) that could influence their endeavors and their teams. They were behaviors of programmaticists who were receptive to the need for adaptive change, but not necessarily of programmaticists who were responsible for initiating it.

Third-level behaviors for each of the elements focused more intently on defining how the delivery of programmatic benefits could be improved by embracing adaptive change in response to uncertainty and complexity. Third-level behaviors sought to focus more intently on actively managing the change inherent to a programmatic endeavor. They showed greater sensitivity to the diversity of interests and motivations of key stakeholders, to stressors that affected stakeholder perspectives, and to the organizational constraints under which their teams needed to operate. They reflected a greater willingness to establish new program visions and strategies to accommodate the change that is driven by uncertainty and complexity. And they were behaviors of programmaticists who were more likely to initiate change and to manage its implementation.

Fourth-level behaviors were highly strategic in their orientation. They focused on defining and pursuing a vision for the future. Fourth-level behaviors tended to manage programmatic endeavors not as standalone initiatives, but as contributors to the greater missions, visions, and strategies of the organization. They assessed programmatic outcomes using the broadest of perspectives to ensure that the actions taken were always aligned with the strategic and operational needs of the organization.

It can be observed from this hierarchical ordering of program leadership behavior that a programmaticist is perceived to be more effective and successful as his or her leadership behaviors became more holistically, strategically, environmentally, and systemically focused. High-level program leadership competence is attributed to programmaticists whose behaviors allow them to more autonomously embody and express the goals of their entire organization, and who are therefore prepared to manage their programmatic endeavors more independently on their entire organization's behalf.

These same behaviors would enable a programmaticist to adaptively manage outcome, operational, stakeholder, and/or organizational complexities. They would, for example, enable a programmaticist to be more capable of anticipating the views of stakeholders or secondary committees who might influence decision making. They also encourage sensitivity to the operational and strategic issues that arise when uncertain outcomes result in the need for adaptive change. In short, they are behaviors required of an outcome sage or an operational savant programmaticist.

The behavioral hierarchy also provides an initial blueprint for the development of new programmaticist competency models—models that are based not just on the *knowledge* and *skills* required of the program and project manager roles, but also on the *behaviors* required of successful programmaticists. In the "executive in the hall" case study, leadership behaviors that displayed "willingness to assume others' roles" were organized into a hierarchy of behaviors that might be exhibited by a *program* manager (because the issue was based on a technical outcome). Had it focused instead on an operational issue, the study could be used more specifically to define a hierarchy reflecting the behaviors of a *project* manager. Developing similar situational analyses might provide a valuable means of studying other leadership behaviors required of those who manage or lead programs and projects. The work of Partington, Pellegrinelli, and Young gives us a good place to start in this effort.

There are challenges, however, that will need to be addressed to enjoy the full benefits of this research.

LEADERSHIP CHALLENGES

The first of these challenges relates to the application of this research to the three-party programmatic systems that are central to the third-generation programmatic approaches we have described. We must study the leadership behaviors required of high-level program versus project management professionals, as we have defined them. The research on program management competence conducted by Partington, Pellegrinelli, and Young does not investigate this question directly. While it had presumed that there were distinctions to be made between the leadership behaviors of program and project management, it did not explicitly explore the potential need to distinguish the different leadership expectations that should be established for *three* distinct programmaticist roles—for Traditionalist versus Operationalist versus Inclusivist programmaticists.

Prior to the introduction of third-generation programmatic concepts, it was most commonly presumed that project and program management leadership behaviors would likely exist in a single hierarchical continuum in which higher-level behaviors were critical to program management competence. Conversely, lower-level behaviors would be associated with traditional project management competence. Such presumptions might lead to expectations that leadership behaviors of Traditionalist, Operationalist, and Inclusivist programmaticists should be displayed in a linear hierarchy that describes progressively greater leadership expectations.

There were reasons to believe that. The critical leadership competencies required of Traditionalist project managers might reasonably be expected to be more limited than those of Operationalists because Traditionalist project managers would have more limited responsibilities for initiating and managing operational change. Moreover, it might be presumed that Inclusivist program managers would need the highest-level leadership skills because of their need to manage technical issues *and* to understand the operational implications of the solutions that Operationalist programmaticists might propose.

However, third-generation programmatic principles encourage the contributions of Operationalists (project managers) and Inclusivists (program managers) to be more equal. Both roles are similarly important for the successful management of truly complex programmatic endeavors. Under third-generation programmatics, high-level leadership competency is required of both the Operationalist and the Inclusivist programmaticist. The resolution of complexity depends critically upon their respective contributions of operational and adaptive leadership.

Third-generation principles acknowledge that the separate focus of Operationalists on managing operational complexity and of Inclusivists on managing outcome complexity leads project and program managers to need different *knowledge* and *skills*. However, their need to collaboratively manage stakeholder and operational complexities is likely to require that they exhibit similar high-level leadership *behaviors*. Without high-level behaviors, it is unlikely that program and project managers could be effective in integrating the sometimes disparate views of organizational stakeholders and committees—it is unlikely that they could serve effectively in their operational savant and outcome sage roles.

The proposed requirement for high-level programmaticist behaviors is consistent with our observation that assignment of the "program manager" title in many organizations may be driven more by the expectation that a programmaticist will exhibit certain leadership behaviors than by the expectation that he or she will have specific knowledge or skills. In those organizations, programmaticists who carry the title of "program manager" may be a mixed group of professionals who are recognizable as either Operationalist or Inclusivist programmaticists. This should not be a surprising observation; the definitions of "program management" embraced by most program management Standards (and adopted by these organizations) are broad enough to include professionals who serve in either an Operationalist or an Inclusivist role. Under third-generation programmatics, we distinguish these roles based on the advantages of having large and highly complex programmatic endeavors jointly managed by *both* an Operationalist project manager *and* an Inclusivist program manager.

More research will be required to explore the leadership behaviors required for high-level performance in the Operationalist project management versus the Inclusivist program management roles. The tenets of complexity leadership theory, with its emphasis on the importance of operational and adaptive leadership, might lead one to expect that the ideal leadership behaviors of high-level project and program managers could be different (based on differences between the leadership behaviors that would best support command-and-control versus learn-and-adapt leadership styles). The specific *behavioral* requirements of leaders under third-generation programmatic systems warrant deeper study if we are to continue to expand our understanding of the programmatic sciences.

Clearly understanding the leadership behaviors that enable successful program and project management is only the first step, however. A second challenge commonly arises—the challenge of identifying and developing professionals to fill an organization's programmatic leadership roles.

Ongoing research will likely also lead to a better understanding of how to develop more advanced program and project leadership capabilities. However, I am confident that effective leadership can be developed today. We have observed that higher-level programmatic leadership capabilities often emerge once the roles and responsibilities of program and project managers (and of their primary and secondary governance committees) for managing complexity are clearly established—once organizations and their programmaticists attain a higher-level understanding of how their programmatic oversight systems should ideally work. Organizations that clearly define how they expect a programmaticist to behave when he or she meets an "executive in the hall" are much more capable of identifying and developing professionals who exhibit their targeted ideal behaviors. The research performed by Partington and his colleagues has already been beneficial in this regard.

Stakeholders whom I have worked with are often surprised to observe how quickly their programmaticists develop and employ an organization's desired leadership behaviors once that organization's expectations are clearly defined. They report that by closely examining those targeted behaviors, they can effectively assess whether or not a given programmaticist's leadership skills are appropriate and whether or not those skills can be effectively developed. They report that it becomes easier to tell whether that particular programmaticist's development is being limited (for example) by his or her knowledge, skills, or behaviors. Stakeholders often observe that defining and assessing their organizations' leadership behaviors enables them to more effectively focus their leadership education and development activities on those areas that are in the most need; it enables them to more clearly determine how and why a given programmaticist is not effective in filling his or her role.

The research described by Partington and colleagues also gives us a hint of what one might expect from assessments of knowledge, skills, and behaviors. It revealed that there can be fundamental differences between programmaticists who exhibit higher- versus lower-level leadership behaviors. While the researchers had observed that the higher-level leadership behaviors were attributed to success in the "program management" role (which in our parlance would include the Operationalist or Inclusivist roles), they saw that the lower-level behaviors were aligned with success in a more traditional project management role. Partington's "level 1" behaviors could be aligned with the competencies of our "Traditionalist" project manager.[2]

In their research, Partington, Pellegrinelli, and Young made another important observation: They found that stakeholders who exhibited lower-level behaviors sometimes had difficulty understanding and embracing higher-level leadership behaviors. Their findings suggest that not every Traditionalist programmaticist would be effective in assuming (or should be expected to assume) the broader responsibilities of the Operationalist or the Inclusivist programmaticist. Even the most successful of Traditionalist project managers might not be capable of transitioning from a role that focuses on the command-and-control limitation of uncertainty (to prevent issues) to a role that focuses on the resolution of operationally unavoidable or outcome-driven complexity.

Under third-generation programmatic oversight systems, that is acceptable. It is not necessary or even desirable that every programmaticist make such a transition. Third-generation systems require that organizations clearly understand and leverage the talents of *each* type of programmaticist. Managing a large and complex programmatic endeavor under third-generation programmatic systems will usually require the collaborative participation of Traditionalist, Operationalist, and Inclusivist programmaticists. Within such a system, projects that face less operational uncertainty or little outcome uncertainty can (and often should) be managed by Traditionalist programmaticists who are

---

[2]It should be noted that in our discussion of the "executive in the hall" case study above, we have expanded Partington's "Level 1" behaviors into two distinct behavioral levels, because we have found that this expansion is useful in our ongoing research. For that reason, our case study uses five levels of leadership behavior, in contrast to Partington's four.

overseen by a governance or program management function in a two- or three-party oversight relationship.

Defining "Ideal" Leadership Systems and Behaviors

During the course of my interviews and discussions with organizational stakeholders, many have asked: "What leadership behaviors are ideal?" The most truthful answer (once again) is: "It depends." What might be considered ideal depends upon the culture and needs of an organization, and also on the programs and projects it pursues. Organizations, their programs, and their projects each face different challenges; it is reasonable to expect that they would have different leadership needs.

But to just answer "it depends" can also be a copout. Too often, "it depends" becomes a convenient response for those who do not want to precisely define their organization's leadership expectations. It too often becomes a reason not to expect one's organization to identify the kind(s) of leadership it expects from programmaticists. After years of working with organizations and their stakeholders, I have reached this conclusion: Every organization does not need to have *the same* answer to the question of "What leadership behaviors are ideal?" but every organization should have *an* answer. And every organization should have its own answer. The challenge is to define what leadership behaviors are ideal for a given combination of an organization, its programs, and its projects. An organization's leadership expectations may be influenced by its culture, but that need not impede their clear definition. In fact, *organizations that learn how to clearly define their leadership expectations simultaneously establish a very powerful means of communicating their cultural expectations.*

Behavioral research assessments (such as "the executive in the hall" assessment above) provide valuable tools for assessing an organization's current programmatic leadership behaviors and for establishing a new "vision" for its ideal future behaviors. We have found that using them enables organizations to take an important step in defining expected leadership behaviors. However, the advancement of programmatic leadership requires more than tools and neatly planned processes; it is not a project which, if properly executed, will always deliver its preconceived outputs.

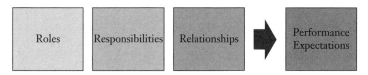

Figure 13.3 Critical components of a programmaticist's performance expectations.

The advancement of programmatic leadership requires that individual programmaticists acquire new knowledge, develop new skills, and learn new behaviors. Often, it also requires that the organization's stakeholders (who supervise or enable programmaticists) learn how their relationships with (and demeanor toward) a programmaticist can have a profound effect on that programmaticist's leadership effectiveness. And it requires that new partnerships be established between program managers, project managers, and the executive stakeholders with whom they work. It is not just about defining the roles and responsibilities of a programmaticist; it is also about achieving an organization-wide understanding of the *relationships* that are required for the effective management of programmatic endeavors (Figure 13.3).

The advancement of programmatic leadership usually requires the adaptive pursuit of somewhat-uncertain and often complex leadership goals. It requires a behavioral change *program*. Such leadership development programs (like all programs) are most effective when they focus on a clear (and presumably ideal) vision of their success. The paths for achieving that success may be uncertain. They are likely to be different from one organization to the next. (After all, each of them starts in a slightly different place.) Yet many organizations have found that the journey is worthwhile and the benefits to be realized are substantial. The secret, it seems, is that the programs be effectively managed—and (again) always focused on their vision of success.

In the next (and final) chapter, we will review those elements of a "vision" that I have found to be especially important for organizations that seek to introduce third-generation programmatic approaches.

CHAPTER 14

Becoming a Third-Generation Programmatics Organization

APPLYING THE PRINCIPLES OF
THIRD-GENERATION PROGRAMMATICS

It is difficult to identify a single third-generation programmatic over-sight model that would satisfy the needs of every complex programmatic endeavor. The unique demands of complex projects and programs for technical and operational oversight, for example, often lead to requests for their interaction with a variety of organization-specific secondary review and oversight committees. Program-specific regulatory, compli-ance, and quality assurance requirements frequently lead to requests for interactions with specialty governance committees. Resource allocation and prioritization issues create the need for program and project teams to consult with business governance committees. And partnerships, alli-ances, and co-development agreements frequently trigger requirements for interactions with external governance and relationship review com-mittees. As a result, the "review and oversight maps" for individual pro-grams (the "mess" depicted in Figure 7.10) can be quite different for individual programs being managed under third-generation program-matic systems.

That should not be surprising; we have observed (especially in Chapter 7) that the same is true for first- and second-generation pro-grammatic oversight systems. For some organizations, however, it can be befuddling. Stakeholders find themselves asking: "How should our orga-nization pursue third-generation programmatics?" "How can our current programmatic oversight system be transformed into a third-generation system?" The ideal solution for each organization, program, and project might be quite different.

It is best, I believe, to start with a conceptual re-framing of the roles of those who are primarily responsible for managing programs and projects. One such re-framing is depicted in Figure 11.6. In that figure programmatic oversight is presented as the shared responsibility of three functional parties that support a third-generation programmatic oversight system—the governing committee, program management, and project management. These three parties are envisioned to assume primary responsibilities for providing (respectively) the enabling, adaptive, and operational leadership required by organizations that pursue complex programmatic endeavors. In filling their roles, the three parties are expected to take a leadership role in managing environmental, outcome, and operational complexities (respectively). Governing committees, program managers (or leaders), and project managers (or leaders) each assume distinct responsibilities and accountabilities.

The governing committee is expected to assume primary responsibility for understanding and integrating the knowledge, insights, perspectives, and positions of the organization's stakeholders and secondary committees as they relate to (1) the pursuit of organizational strategy, and (2) the enablement of programmatic teams. To accomplish that, governing committee members need to establish and maintain close relationships with the secondary governance and review committees that are responsible for pursuing individual elements of the organization's strategy. The governing committee is expected to assume a leadership role in defining the organization's strategic goals and in ensuring that stakeholders and secondary committees agree to support the pursuit of those goals through sanctioned programmatic endeavors.

The project manager (or project management function) is expected to assume primary responsibility for understanding and integrating the knowledge, insights, perspectives, and positions of stakeholders and secondary committees as they relate to (1) the pursuit of operational goals, and (2) the conduct of operational activities to support the organization's programmatic endeavors. To accomplish that, the project manager also needs to establish and maintain close relationships with the secondary governance and review committees that are also responsible for managing or overseeing operational activities within the organization. The project manager is expected to ensure that work is completed efficiently—according to a sound organizationally supportable operational plan.

The program manager (or program management function) is expected to assume primary responsibility for understanding and integrating the knowledge, insights, perspectives, and positions of stakeholders and secondary committees as they relate to (1) the pursuit of uncertain outcomes that are expected to provide benefits (or contribute to the provision of benefits), and (2) the adaptation of program strategies and plans. To accomplish that, the program manager needs to establish and maintain close relationships with secondary governance and review committees that are responsible for generating and assessing outcomes that support the organization's pursuit of its goals. The program manager is expected to ensure that program benefits are pursued adaptively and that stakeholders and secondary committees support the adaptation of program strategies and plans as might become necessary as a consequence of emergent program outcomes.

Working together, these three functions (each exhibiting the personal leadership behaviors, knowledge, and skills that make them uniquely qualified for their roles) provide a means for ensuring that the perspectives of the entire organization are effectively represented in critical decision-making venues. They jointly satisfy the leadership requirements of a high-level team because they dynamically interact and function as a complex adaptive system (as depicted in Figure 11.2). They become collectively and collaboratively responsible for identifying solutions to complexity-related issues. And they assume *individual* responsibilities for ensuring that environmental, operational, and outcome-based complexities are effectively managed and resolved, while *collectively* ensuring that stakeholder and organizational complexities are worked out—according to the framework that was depicted in Figure 11.1.

The result is a conceptual model for the evolution of organizations to a third-generation programmatic oversight system (depicted in Figure 14.1). The model does not presume or exclude the involvement of any of the secondary review committees that might be required by a given organization or program. Instead, it focuses on more clearly defining the *relationships* that need to exist between those committees and a programmatic endeavor's governing committee(s), program manager(s), and project manager(s). It is a model that focuses on how best to ensure that the knowledge, skills, and experience of

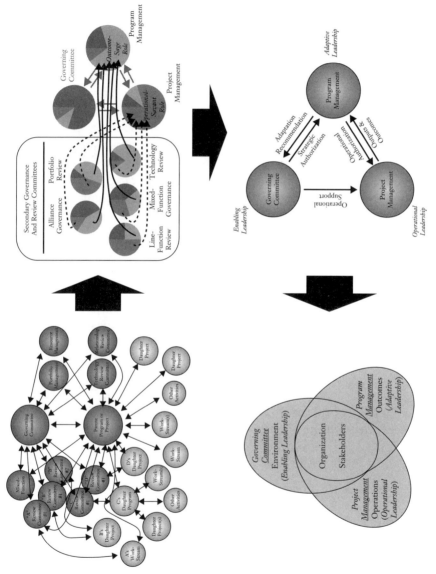

Figure 14.1 Emergence of a third-generation oversight system for the pursuit of complex programmatic endeavors.

organizationally dispersed stakeholders—each working within their own complex adaptive systems (for example, their individual secondary committees or line functions)—are effectively aggregated by professionals with appropriately developed skills.

Within the third-generation programmatics model, a system is created whereby governance committees, program managers, and project managers assume primary responsibility for each of the leadership roles required of an effective complex adaptive system. This high-level complex adaptive system becomes accountable for aggregating and integrating the views of a bigger organization, so that issues can be efficiently and effectively addressed.

As understanding of and experience with third-generation systems have grown, an increasing number of organizations have asked whether they might benefit from such a system. I would suggest that it depends—mostly on the answers to questions that too many organizations still neglect to ask and answer. It would be beneficial if we took a moment to review them.

TWELVE QUESTIONS TO ANSWER

When assessing the potential value of a third-generation programmatic oversight system to any given organization, the first questions that should be asked relate to an organization's current oversight system. It is important for organizations using first- or second-generation two-party programmatic oversight systems to ask:

1. Is our current (two-party) programmatic oversight system effective in aggregating and integrating the information that is critical for decision making?

2. Is our current system recognized as being both efficient and effective?

We have observed in Part 1 of this book that the answers to these questions are too often "No" in organizations that have grown to be very large, in organizations that pursue a large number of programs and projects, and in organizations that pursue uncertain and complex programmatic endeavors. If the answer to either of these questions is "No," there is reason to examine *why*, in order to improve the organization's programmatic oversight system.

Sometimes it is not the oversight system's structure that is broken. Instead, what needs to be improved is stakeholder performance within that structure. For example, an inefficient two-party system can sometimes be "fixed" by establishing new (or re-asserting old) agreements about the relationships that should exist between an organization's governing committees, its programmaticists, and its secondary governance and review committees. At other times, it can be repaired by ensuring that project managers are better trained and recognized for their abilities to function in an operational savant role.

Sometimes, however, it is worthwhile to consider whether an organization would be better served by a third-generation (three-party) programmatic oversight system. To assess whether an organization might benefit from such a system, it is best to use questions that provoke examination of the types of uncertainty and complexity that need to be faced by the organization's programs and projects. We have discussed some of those questions earlier:

3. What kinds of uncertainties and complexities are associated with the organization's programmatic endeavors?

4. How significant is the potential impact of those uncertainties and complexities?

5. Can responses to them be planned in advance?

6. How frequently might they be expected to arise?

7. Can we predict when uncertain and complex conditions might arise?

8. Is specific knowledge (technical or behavioral) required of (or desired in) the programmaticists who are responsible for managing those uncertainties and complexities?

Answering these questions enables an organization to determine what complexity-management skills will be required for managing programmatic issues; these questions enable an organization to assess what degree of readiness it needs to maintain for solving complex issues.

Organizations with programmatic endeavors that principally face operational uncertainty or that face outcome uncertainty of little significance might be able to manage their initiatives principally as projects; they might be best served by two-party programmatic oversight systems.

Organizations that sponsor initiatives that face infrequent outcome uncertainty, or that face outcome uncertainty that can be mitigated with predictable responses, might also consider managing their programmatic endeavors as projects; they might be best served by a two-party system that uses a phase-gate approach. Alternatively (as outcome uncertainty increases) these organizations might also consider using a three-party system.

But circumstances are often different for organizations that sponsor initiatives with significant, frequent, or unpredictable outcome uncertainty. Organizations that sponsor these kinds of initiatives are often better off managing them as programs that are overseen by programmaticists with specialized knowledge or experience relevant to the endeavor's outcome uncertainty and complexity. For such organizations it is worthwhile to seriously consider the introduction of a third-generation three-party programmatic oversight system.

Organizations that conclude (based on the above questions) that they should consider implementing a third-generation system next need to ensure that they can staff the system appropriately; they need to determine how best to fill their programmaticist positions (and in particular, their program manager positions) with individuals who would be effective in their respective roles. They need to ask and answer additional questions:

9. What specific knowledge, skills, and behaviors should be required of the programmaticists who will fill our organization's program and project manager roles?

10. How can we ensure that programmaticists have (or that they develop) the appropriate knowledge and skills, and that they are capable of exhibiting the required leadership behaviors?

11. How can we establish a culture that encourages programmaticists and their stakeholders to exhibit the leadership behaviors required for high-level performance of our third-generation programmatic oversight system?

12. What relationships need to be established between our programmaticists, stakeholders, and the primary and secondary committees with whom the programmaticists work?

Answering each of these questions enables an organization to assess how best to prepare its *people* for the introduction of a third-generation programmatic system.

By asking what specific knowledge, skills, and behaviors are required of program and project managers within an organization's third-generation system, the organization can begin to assess which programmaticists have the competencies necessary to fill each programmaticist role. It can begin to assign its programmaticists to positions for which they are best suited.

Question 9 prompts an organization to clearly identify those programmaticists who are best suited to fill its Traditionalist versus its operational savant (Operationalist) project manager roles, and its outcome sage (Inclusivist) program manager roles. It challenges an organization to make these assignments deliberately—based on objective assessments of knowledge, skills, and behaviors, and not just on historical assignments or time-based measures of "experience."

Question 10 prompts an organization to identify any gaps that might exist between the competencies required of its programmaticists and the competencies that they are currently equipped to provide. It prepares an organization to take steps to close any competency gaps that might exist—either by providing opportunities for programmaticists to develop new knowledge, skills, and behavioral competencies, or by hiring (or assigning) new programmaticists who have the required skills.

Question 11 stimulates an organization to carefully examine its leadership "culture," to determine whether members of the organization are currently exhibiting and encouraging the behaviors required of its third-generation programmatic system. It encourages an organization to remove any obstacles to the development of appropriate leadership behaviors—to align its leadership expectations with the requirements of its new system.

Question 12 challenges organizations to more clearly define the relationships that are expected to exist between programmaticists and the variety of stakeholders and committees with whom they interact. For example, it encourages an organization to clarify whether the relationship between a programmaticist and a given secondary review or governing committee is intended to be principally for the exchange of insight or for oversight; is it advisory or supervisory? This question seeks to ensure that an organization clearly establishes the authority and autonomy of its programmaticists and its committees, so that its programmatic oversight system functions more smoothly.

Each question in this final group highlights the need to ensure that the people who are most responsible for the performance of a third-generation programmatic oversight system are capable and prepared to contribute appropriately to its success. They are all critical questions.

There is one additional question that I have found to be important. I would encourage every organization to ask it. This question is different from the rest because it is not specifically related to the introduction of a third-generation programmatic system. It is equally relevant to all programmatic oversight systems, and is related to question 12 above: *Have we done everything possible to minimize organizational uncertainty and complexity in our programmatic oversight system?*

This question challenges organizations to consider whether it might be possible to reduce the amount of organizational complexity within a given programmatic system. The discussions of Chapter 7 (and the mess in Figure 7.10) highlight just how frustrating organizational complexity can be. Organizational complexity is less endeavor-specific than other forms of complexity, however. It is often a consequence of the actions taken by an organization as it tried to manage programmatic endeavors using a two-party system. The introduction of a three-party system sometimes presents an organization with an opportunity to undo some of those earlier actions. In my interactions with organizations and their stakeholders, I have commonly observed that reducing organizational complexity significantly improves the efficiency of programmatic oversight systems, and so this last question is well worth asking.

Stakeholders from various organizations have reported that the above questions have been invaluable to them. Many have observed that the questions helped their organizations to carefully examine their needs, their readiness, and their willingness to introduce a third-generation programmatic oversight system.

Some stakeholders have observed that the questions were also valuable when used to audit the function and performance of their existing programmatic oversight systems. These stakeholders noted that they could expose reasons for their system's underperformance by asking whether each question had been adequately addressed. Some reported, for example, that asking the questions had enabled their organizations to establish clearer expectations about the relationships that were intended to exist between their programmaticists and their secondary committees. Others indicated that it had prompted them to re-examine the criteria they had been using for assigning programmaticists to their programmatic endeavors.

DECIDING TO USE A THIRD-GENERATION PROGRAMMATIC OVERSIGHT SYSTEM

Experience to date suggests that third-generation programmatic oversight systems can be highly effective when used to manage programs that are complex and/or fraught with outcome uncertainty.

The strength of such systems lies in their ability to leverage the different leadership talents of each of their principle parties. Third-generation systems enable the assignment of program managers, project managers, and governing committee members who have competencies that are uniquely suited to the specific needs of the programmatic endeavors that will be pursued. Organizations choose to use third-generation systems to ensure that their diverse leadership needs can be efficiently and adaptively satisfied.

Third-generation programmatic oversight systems also enable many organizations to embrace a new concept of program oversight—one that is less focused on the linear transfer of information or the sequential conferral of authority according to traditional bureaucratic hierarchies. Third-generation programmatic oversight models support a more holistic approach that is instead based on the cross-functional sharing of leadership authority within a dynamic, interactive, and integrated system. As a consequence, we have found, third-generation systems often provide the best approach for managing complex initiatives. Organizations choose to use third-generation systems to ensure that they are prepared to pursue the knowledge-based programmatic endeavors that are increasingly undertaken by modern organizations.

The final question that many organizational stakeholders face when considering the implementation of a third-generation system is: *"Should I expect that it will work for my organization?"*

Based on our earlier discussions of stakeholder experience and program management standards, literature, and research, it seems reasonable to expect that combining the enabling, adaptive, and operational leadership skills of individual "leadership specialists" would result in a highly effective programmatic oversight system. But the decision to supplant a more traditional system can be nerve-wracking. Stakeholders often observe that there are good reasons to be nervous. They raise objections that are based on two distinct concerns.

Some people worry that third-generation programmatic approaches seem to rely on a small group of accountable professionals. They express concern that the three principle participants in any given program's third-generation oversight system (governing committees, the project managers, and program managers) might not be effective in understanding, aggregating, and integrating insights from the many other stakeholders who can be affected by programmatic decisions. Often, they express concern that adoption of the system might result in the marginalization of stakeholders whose individual contributions would be valuable.

It is a legitimate concern.

Individual governing committees, program managers, and project managers might have difficulty effectively filling the enabling, adaptive, and operational leadership needs of a programmatic endeavor. To limit others' contributions might be a mistake.

However, the proposal of a third-generation programmatic oversight system that is based on the contributions of three principle parties should not be construed to suggest that *only* those three parties can (or should) be involved in program oversight or decision making. Third-generation programmatic systems are not meant to exclude the involvement of stakeholders who might contribute valuably to the effective oversight of programs; they are meant to ensure that all stakeholder positions are adequately represented. In their aggregation of enabling, operational, and adaptive perspectives, third-generation systems should be expected to be inclusive, and not exclusive. As we continue to investigate three-party approaches for managing programmatic endeavors, we should expect that we will learn more about the best ways to strike a balance between leadership and stakeholder participation.

Other people have quite different concerns. They worry that third-generation programmatics' focus on developing a team of "leadership specialists" who separately provide enabling, adaptive, and operational leadership might distract individual leaders' from their need to develop proficiencies in all three types of leadership. These stakeholders are more focused on the prospect of developing valuable centaur-like super-leaders who can more effectively assume personal decision-making responsibility for "all things programmatic." (It is not uncommon for them to believe that they are such leaders!)

This is also a legitimate concern.

It is important that organizations pursuing third-generation programmatics approaches never lose sight of the potential contributions and value of such leaders. Super-leaders are consistently recognized for their organizational contributions and for the success they seem to always deliver. In fact, such leaders might be considered an example (in essence, a personification) of what can be achieved when all three types of complex adaptive leadership are brought together under a circumstance that allows completely seamless, fluid, and collaborative integration.

It seems reasonable to suggest that many of our organizations' most inspirational and insightful super-leaders (those who seem to flourish in *any* situation that demands leadership) may actually be effective because of their abilities to function effectively in the enabling, adaptive, *and* operational leadership roles—and their abilities to move effortlessly between them. We should recognize such leaders as uniquely talented individuals who emulate and embody the power of complex adaptive systems. It is intriguing to think that we should study the performance and behaviors of such leaders as an idealized example of a third-generation programmatic oversight system.

LIFE, VIEWED PROGRAMMATICALLY

In some sense, I think it is important to recognize that we are each capable of emulating all of the elements of leadership that are represented in complex adaptive systems. We have each come to understand all three types of programmatic leadership, because (to some degree) we embody each in our personal lives.

Consider, for example, a story about Casey, an individual who wants to improve her life by advancing her education (a strategic goal that demands initiation of a "personal development program"). Casey needs to save or borrow money to pay for classes (thereby enabling and governing her program). She needs to plan a curriculum, to register for classes, and to work hard to complete her course requirements (she initiates and manages projects). Her purpose is to earn credits toward her college degree (to generate the outputs required by her program). In so doing, Casey earns grades (achieves outcomes) that might determine whether she will be capable of achieving her goals and realizing her desired benefits. Based on her performance and enjoyment of each of her classes (class outcomes) and the perceived value of each of them in providing her opportunities (potential benefits), Casey might decide to change her course of study or her major (in an adaptive response to her outcomes). She would then need to make more plans (initiate more projects) to fulfill her requirements. She would register for more classes, and again work hard (thereby generating more outputs and outcomes). All the while, Casey might need to limit her social activities so that she would have the money that she needs for classes and the time that she needs to study (she would need to continue enabling and governing her actions). When she was successful in getting her degree, Casey might be qualified to pursue a new career (thereby achieving her targeted goal).

In her pursuit of an educational program, Casey became her own (one-party) programmatic system. She was her own governing committee, project manager, and program manager. She dynamically transitioned between the roles of an enabling, operational, and adaptive leader to optimize her pursuit of benefits. Casey personified a three-party programmatic oversight system in a one-party body.

Each of us emulates complex adaptive systems. Our lives are our programs—driven by goals, enabled by opportunities, realized through work, and made resilient through adaptation. In our lives (as in our professional careers) we may be better in some roles than others: Some of us work hard but find it difficult to adapt; others have ideas, but don't get things done. If we are lucky, we have people in our lives whose strengths complement our weaknesses, so that we might each function better in the company of others.

It is tempting to speculate that the study of three-party programmatic oversight systems could benefit us in interesting ways—in both our professional and our personal lives.

FINAL THOUGHTS

There is no doubt that we still have much more to learn about the potential of third-generation programmatic systems. Some people will question whether three leadership functions can adequately represent an organization's diverse stakeholders. Others will question whether we can replicate our super-leaders using those same three leadership conceptions. The purpose of the system is not to replace either the larger organization or the super-leaders among us. Instead, its purpose is to build a framework that bridges the two. The third-generation programmatic oversight system seeks to ensure that each part of an organization becomes more accessible to the others. Given the struggles that our organizations have faced when trying to use two-party programmatic systems, it seems that such a framework would be valuable.

For the most part, I can attest, our Exasperados agree.

AFTERWORD

The perspectives communicated in *Managing Complex Projects and Programs* could not have been generated without the active participation of many colleagues and friends. The insights so generously shared by many of these people provided a foundation for the concepts described herein, and for development of the third-generation programmatic approach. It would be presumptive, however, to think that *Managing Complex Projects and Programs* has captured all views that are important and relevant, or that it has considered all of the circumstances that have been faced by organizations.

As I continue to pursue research on the value of third-generation programmatic approaches (with the continued help of my colleagues), I would be delighted to hear the perspectives of readers who could contribute to our understanding. Please let me know where you believe we got it right, and also where you believe we may have gotten it wrong. I am especially interested in hearing from readers who would like to share their experiences related to the implementation and function of three-party third-generation programmatic oversight systems.

For further information on how best to share your experiences and understanding, I invite you to visit: www.programmaticsciences.com

GLOSSARY OF NEWLY INTRODUCED TERMS

Business governance committee

A committee of stakeholders convened to govern how projects or programs utilize an organization's assets. Common business governance committees include portfolio review committees and resource review committees. Business governance committees usually assume responsibility for compiling and maintaining accurate information about resource needs of organizational projects and programs, for conducting analyses of those needs according to preferred organizational practices, and for ensuring that resources are used in a manner that is consistent with an organization's defined priorities. The decision-making versus advisory responsibilities of such committees may vary from organization to organization. (Chapter 7)

Directional complexity

See stakeholder complexity. (Chapter 4)

Directional uncertainty

See stakeholder uncertainty. (Chapter 4)

Enabling conditions

Organizational conditions that support the pursuit of organizational projects or programs. Enabling conditions established by organizations might be expected to include, for example, the conditions that provide support in the form of resources (human and financial), infrastructure (technological and physical), and oversight (leadership, management, and governance) of an organization's projects and programs. (Chapter 6)

Environmental complexity

The complexity associated with managing environmental uncertainty. (Chapter 4)

Environmental uncertainty

The uncertainty that is external to a project or program, but that may influence its direction. Environmental uncertainty is a lack of surety that environmental conditions will remain stable, and thereby continue to support the pursuit of a project or program as planned. (Chapter 4)

Exasperados

A group of experienced and successful project management professionals who have grown exasperated with trying to function within the increasingly complex programmatic oversight systems used by their organizations to manage complex programs and projects. An examination of the causes of Exasperado frustration and of the common experiences of Exasperados led to the proposal of third-generation programmatic approaches for the management and oversight of complex projects and programs. (Chapter 4)

First-generation programmatics (first-generation programmatic approach)

An approach for managing organizational projects that is characterized by strict governing committee control over project strategies, plans, timelines, budgets, and specifications. Under first-generation programmatic approaches managing committees authorize projects and approve their strategies and plans, and project teams (usually under the direction of project management professionals) assume accountability for pursuing those plans precisely as defined to assure that their intended outputs are efficiently delivered—on time, on budget, and to specifications. (Chapter 2)

Five-complexities framework

A framework used to categorize the types of uncertainty and complexity faced by programs and projects, and to assign responsibilities for complexity management. Under this framework, the five types of programmatic uncertainty and complexity are defined as: operational, outcome-based, stakeholder, organizational, and environmental uncertainties and complexities. (Chapter 4)

Fully empowered programmatic oversight model

An organizational management model in which a program's strategy and plans are managed by an "outcome sage" – program manager who is given broad authority to manage a program's pursuit of its intended benefits and value. Fully empowered programmatic oversight models seek to enable program managers to more agilely and adaptively manage their program's strategies and plans by allowing them greater freedom to implement changes without the formal approval of governing committees. (Chapter 12)

Fully governed project (or programmatic) oversight model

An organizational management model in which the strategies and plans of projects or programs are closely managed by organizational governance committees. Within a fully governed project oversight model, approval of one or more organizational governance committees is required before establishing or changing a project's or program's strategy or plans. Fully governed project oversight models maximize an organization's control over its projects and programs by assuring governing committee review and approval of a project's or program's planned approach. (Chapter 6)

Inclusivist perspective

A view that a given programmaticist should assume personal responsibility for delivering outcome-dependent benefits from his or her program(s) and project(s). Stakeholders who have an Inclusivist perspective believe that a programmaticist should be personally responsible for managing or ensuring the management of outcome-based, operational, stakeholder, and organizational uncertainties or complexities. Stakeholders who have an Inclusivist perspective believe that governance committees should principally serve an enabling function—providing an appropriate organizational environment, adequate resources, and the benefits of their knowledge, experience, and insight. (Chapter 5)

Operational complexity

The complexity that is associated with managing project planning uncertainty. (Chapter 4)

Operational uncertainty

The uncertainty that is associated with defining, scheduling, and completing those activities required to generate the outputs and outcomes of a project or program—the project or program plan. Operational uncertainty is a lack of certainty that a project plan, in its current form, can be completed precisely as prescribed to deliver the intended outputs on time, on budget, and to specifications. (Chapter 4)

Operationalist perspective

A view that a given programmaticist should have a broad mandate for defining a project's operational plans and for independently managing operational uncertainty and complexity that might affect those plans. Under the Operationalist perspective a programmaticist is recognized to be an operational planning expert. He or she is expected to ensure that projects deliver their outputs as expected (on time, on budget, and to specifications), while autonomously managing any operational uncertainty and complexity that those endeavors might face. (Chapter 5)

Operationally empowered programmatic oversight model

An organizational management model in which a project's operational plan is managed by an "operational savant" project manager who is given authority to initiate and manage change in a project's operational plans. Operationally empowered project oversight models seek to enable project managers to more agilely and adaptively manage their project plans by allowing them freedom to implement operational changes without the formal approval of governing committees. (Chapter 12)

Organizational complexity

The complexity associated with managing organizational uncertainty. (Chapter 4)

Organizational uncertainty

The uncertainty that is associated with trying to align the views and secure the endorsements of organizational committees with distinct roles, responsibilities, perspectives, and priorities. Programmaticists must manage organizational uncertainty whenever the approvals or endorsements of different committees must be obtained before a project's or program's strategies and plans can be implemented or changed. Organizational uncertainty is a lack of certainty that any given proposed strategy or plan will be supported by each of the endeavor's governing or review committees. (Chapter 4)

Outcome complexity

The complexity associated with managing outcome uncertainty. (Chapter 4)

Outcome uncertainty

The uncertainty that is associated with a plan's dependence on activities that do not have known or predictable results. Outcome uncertainty is a lack of certainty that a project plan will produce the results (outcomes) that are intended or desired. (Chapter 4)

Program

An endeavor that seeks to deliver benefits via activities that by their nature have uncertain outcomes. The uncertainty associated with programs dictates that they need to be managed adaptively, so that their strategies and plans can be modified in response to emergent outcomes. As a result, programs may be highly complex. The outcomes required by programs are pursued via projects, subprograms, and other program-related activities. (Chapter 10)

Program management

A profession in the programmatic sciences that ensures the optimal delivery of program benefits by adaptively managing program strategies and plans. Program management involves the application of specialized knowledge, skills, tools, and techniques to ensure that programs are responsive to the outcomes they generate as they pursue their intended benefits Program management is practiced by program managers who work collaboratively with project managers, subprogram managers, and other members of program teams to ensure the completion of required program activities and the delivery of important program outcomes. (Chapter 10)

Program manager

A professional who is responsible for managing a program's pursuit of its intended benefits. Program managers are responsible for ensuring that a program's strategy and plans are adapted appropriately in response to program outcomes, to ensure the most effective pursuit of targeted program benefits. Program managers are adaptive leaders who work closely with project managers, subprogram managers, and other members of their program teams to ensure completion of required program activities. (Chapter 10)

Programmatic

Of or relating to programs and/or projects, or the managerial systems and principles used by organizations to oversee their programs and/or projects. (Chapter 1)

Programmatic complexity

A characteristic of projects and programs that reflects the difficulty of understanding and defining the most appropriate strategy or plan for pursuing project or program goals. Programmatic complexity grows larger when the uncertainty associated with a project's or program's strategy or plan increases, and when the number of possible responses to that uncertainty increases. Managing programmatic complexity can be difficult because it must be done dynamically—as elements of a project's or program's strategy or plan are completed, the impact of their uncertainty is realized, issues emerge, and viable options for responding to that uncertainty are clarified. (Chapter 4)

Programmatic science

The study of managerial systems, principles, practices, and processes used by organizations to pursue their goals via programs and/or projects. The purpose of programmatic science is to develop and advance an understanding of those strategies that contribute to organizational success when managing programs and projects, and the leadership competencies that are required by those responsible for executing these strategies. Programmatic science should be viewed as a social science that seeks to study and understand the dynamics of managing programs and projects within an organization, much the same as "political science" is a social science that seeks to study and understand the dynamics of managing governments and governmental institutions. (Chapter 1)

Programmaticist

A professional leader or manager of an organization's projects or programs. A programmaticist is responsible for assuring that projects or programs are effectively pursued and for managing the interactions of a project or program team with its sponsoring organization. (Chapter 4)

Programmaticist's credo

Manage the uncertain; solve the complex; deliver the value. (Chapter 4)

Programmatics (or, programmatic approach)

A specific combination of applied systems, principles, practices, and processes, used by an organization for the purpose of managing its programs and projects. (Chapter 1)

Project

A temporary endeavor that seeks to deliver unique value and benefits via activities that are thought to have predictable outputs and/or outcomes. Projects are managed in a manner that seeks to ensure efficient delivery of work products with precisely prescribed specifications, on time and on budget. (Chapter 10)

Project management

A profession in the programmatic sciences that focuses on the design and completion of work plans to ensure the efficient delivery of specified work products on time, on budget, and to specifications. Project management is practiced by project managers who apply professional knowledge, skills, tools, and techniques to ensure the effective management of operational uncertainty and the resolution of operational complexity. (Chapter 10)

Project manager

A professional who is responsible for managing a project's pursuit of its intended outputs and/or outcomes. Project managers are operational leaders who are responsible for assuring that a project meets its operational goals for delivering work products with prescribed specifications—on time and on budget. (Chapter 10)

Second-generation programmatics (second-generation programmatic approaches)

Approaches sometimes used to support the oversight of programmatic endeavors whose timelines, budget, and/or specifications need to be managed adaptively because pursuing the project is expected to result in the generation of outcomes or the acquisition knowledge that will (and should) influence the endeavor's strategy or plans. Under second-generation programmatic approaches, programmaticists are given authority for managing the adaptation of their project's timelines, budget, and/or specifications (usually within previously established constraints) so as to enable more effective pursuit of the benefits desired from a project or program. Examples of second-generation programmatic approaches include those approaches used in the disciplines of Agile Project Management, Complex Project Management, and Extreme Project Management. (Chapter 2)

Secondary governance or review committee

A committee that is asked (as part of the organization's project oversight process) to review project results, analyses, needs, and proposals before they are presented to the project's primary sponsoring governing committee. Secondary governance or review committees usually have a narrower scope of responsibilities than a primary governing committee. They may, for example, be responsible for work being performed within an individual line function, work being conducted in a specific technological field, support of an individual client group, or support of other business processes of the organization (such as budget, resource, or portfolio management). (Chapter 7)

Stakeholder complexity

The complexity associated with managing stakeholder uncertainty. (Chapter 4)

Stakeholder uncertainty

The uncertainty that is associated with a reliance on stakeholders to support the strategy or plan used by a project or program to achieve its goals. Stakeholder uncertainty might also be thought of as *directional uncertainty* because it relates to a reliance on stakeholders to support a project's or program's *direction*.

Stakeholder uncertainty is a lack of certainty that stakeholders will support the strategy or plan of a programmatic endeavor as desired, or that they will agree to support changes in the strategy or plan that may become necessary. (Chapter 4)

Third-generation programmatics (third-generation programmatic approaches)

An approach for managing organizational programs that relies upon the collaborative contributions of two unique types of programmaticists: a project manager (or leader) responsible for providing operational leadership, and hence for delivering project outputs and their outcomes, and a program manager (or leader) responsible for stimulating and embodying adaptive leadership, and hence for optimizing delivery of program-level outcomes. Third-generation programmatics employs a three-party framework for managing programs through leadership that is collectively provided by governing committees, project management professionals, and program management professionals. (Chapter 11)

Traditionalist perspective

A view of programmaticist roles and responsibilities based on traditional first-generation project management systems. Under Traditionalist perspectives, programmaticists are expected to deliver value by efficiently and effectively managing the completion of work according to approved plans—on time, on budget, and to specification. Those who espouse a Traditionalist perspective believe that a given programmaticist's primary role should be defined so as to maximize organizational control over operational uncertainty and variance, to improve the likelihood that projects or programs will deliver their expected results precisely as predicted. The Traditionalist perspective advocates that governing committees (or a program team responsible for project governance) should retain responsibility for authorizing any significant changes to the plan or strategy of a project or program. (Chapter 5)

SUGGESTED READINGS

STANDARDS AND GUIDES IN PROGRAM AND PROJECT MANAGEMENT

Association for Project Management. *APM Body of Knowledge*, 6th ed. Buckinghamshire: Association for Project Management, 2012.

Ohara, Shigenobu. *P2M: A guidebook of project & program management*, 2005 ed. Tokyo: Project Management Association of Japan, 2005.

Project Management Institute. *A Guide to the Project Management Body of Knowledge (PMBOK Guide)*, 5th ed. Newtown Square, PA: Project Management Institute, Inc., 2013.

Project Management Institute. *The Standard for Program Management*, 3d ed. Newtown Square, PA: Project Management Institute, 2013.

The Stationery Office. TSO. *Managing Successful Programmes*, 2011 ed. Norwich, UK: The Stationery Office, 2011.

FIRST- AND SECOND-GENERATION PROGRAMMATICS

Cobb, Charles. *Making Sense of Agile: A Project Management Perspective*. Hoboken, NJ: John Wiley & Sons, Inc., 2011.

DeCarlo, Doug, James P. Lewis, and Robert K. Wysocki. *EXtreme Project Management: Using Leadership, Principles, and Tools to Deliver Value in the Face of Volatility*. San Francisco, CA: Jossey-Bass, 2004.

Goodpasture, John C. *Project Management the Agile Way: Making It Work in the Enterprise*. Ft. Lauderdale, FL: J. Ross Publishing, 2010.

Kerzner, Harold. *Project Management: A Systems Approach to Planning, Scheduling, and Controlling*, 11th ed. Hoboken, NJ: John Wiley & Sons, Inc., 2013.

Norman, Eric S., Shelly A. Brotherton, and Robert T. Fried. *Work Breakdown Structures: The Foundation for Project Management Excellence*. Hoboken, NJ: John Wiley & Sons, Inc., 2008.

Shenhar, Aaron, and Dov Dvir. *Reinventing Project Management: The Diamond Approach to Successful Growth and Innovation*. Boston, MA: Harvard Business School Press, 2007.

Wysocki, Robert K. *Effective Project Management: Traditional, Agile, Extreme*, 7th ed. Hoboken, NJ: John Wiley & Sons, Inc., 2014.

DISTINCTIONS BETWEEN PROJECTS AND PROGRAMS, PROJECT MANAGEMENT AND PROGRAM MANAGEMENT

Cicmil, Svetlana, Terry Williams, Janice Thomas, and Damian Hodgson. "Rethinking Project Management: Researching the Actuality of Projects," *International Journal of Project Management* 24, no. 8 (2006): 675–686.

Lycett, Mark, Andreas Rassau, and John Danson. "Program Management: A Critical Review," *International Journal of Project Management* 22, no. 4 (2004): 289–299.

Maylor, Harvey, Tim Brady, Terry Cooke-Davies, and Damian Hodgson. "From Projectification to Programmification," *International Journal of Project Management* 24, no. 8 (2006): 663–674.

Pellegrinelli, Sergio, David Partington, Chris Hemingway, Zaher Mohdzain, and Mahmood Shah. "The Importance of Context in Programme Management: An Empirical Review of Programme Practices," *International Journal of Project Management* 25, no. 1 (2007): 41–55.

Pellegrinelli, Sergio. "What's in a Name: Project or Programme?," *International Journal of Project Management* 29, no. 2 (2011): 232–240.

Thiry, Michel, and Mannon Deguire. "Program Management as an Emergent Order Phenomenon," *Proceedings of the PMI Research Conference* (2004).

Thiry, Michel. *Competitive Program Management*. Farnham, UK: Gower, 2010.

Thiry, Michel. "Combining Value and Project Management into an Effective Programme Management Model," *International Journal of Project Management* 20, no. 3 (2002): 221–227.

COMPLEXITY MANAGEMENT

Beer, Stafford. *Designing Freedom: With Sketches by the Author*. London: John Wiley & Sons, Inc., 1974.

Cicmil, Svetlana, Terry Cooke-Davies, Lynn Crawford, and Kurt Richardson. Exploring the Complexity of Projects. Newtown Square, PA: Project Management Institute, 2009.

Contractor, Noshir S., Leslie A. DeChurch, Jay Carson, Dorothy R. Carter, and Brian Keegan. "The Topology of Collective Leadership," *The Leadership Quarterly* 23, no. 6 (2012): 994–1011.

Curlee, Wanda, and Robert L. Gordon. *Complexity Theory and Project Management*. Hoboken, NJ: John Wiley & Sons, Inc., 2011.

DeRue, D. Scott. "Adaptive Leadership Theory: Leading and Following as a Complex Adaptive Process," *Research in Organizational Behavior* 31 (2011): 125–150.

Friedrich, Tamara L., William B. Vessey, Matthew J. Schuelke, Gregory A. Ruark, and Michael D. Mumford. "A Framework for Understanding Collective Leadership: The Selective Utilization of Leader and Team Expertise within Networks," *The Leadership Quarterly* 20, no. 6 (2009): 933–958.

Jackson, Michael C. *Systems Thinking: Creative Holism for Managers*. Chichester, West Sussex: John Wiley & Sons, Inc., 2003.

Lichtenstein, Benyamin B., Mary Uhl-Bien, Russ Marion, Anson Seers, James D. Orton, and Craig Schreiber. "Complexity Leadership Theory: An Interactive Perspective on Leading in Complex Adaptive Systems," *Emergence: Complexity and Organization* 8, no. 4 (2006): 2–12.

Maylor, Harvey, Richard Vidgen, and Stephen Carver. "Managerial Complexity in Project-Based Operations: A Grounded Model and Its Implications for Practice," *Project Management Journal* 39, no. 1 (2008): S15–S26.

Remington, Kaye, and Julien Pollack. *Tools for Complex Projects*. Aldershot, England: Gower, 2007.

Uhl-Bien, Mary, Russ Marion, and Bill McKelvey. "Complexity Leadership Theory: Shifting Leadership from the Industrial Age to the Knowledge Era," *The Leadership Quarterly* 18, no. 4 (2007): 298–318.

Uhl-Bien, Mary, and Russ Marion. *Complexity Leadership. Part 1: Conceptual Foundations*. Charlotte, NC: IAP, Information Age Publishing, 2007.

Uhl-Bien, Mary, and Russ Marion. "Complexity Leadership in Bureaucratic Forms of Organizing: A Meso Model," *The Leadership Quarterly* 20, no. 4 (2009): 631–650.

PROGRAM LEADERSHIP COMPETENCY DEVELOPMENT

Association for Project Management. *APM Competence Framework*. High Wycombe, Buckinghamshire, UK: Association for Project Management, 2008.

Partington, David, Sergio Pellegrinelli, and Malcolm Young. "Attributes and Levels of Programme Management Competence: An Interpretive Study," *International Journal of Project Management* 23, no. 2 (2005): 87–95.

Pellegrinelli, Sergio. *Thinking and Acting as a Great Programme Manager*. Houndmills, Basingstoke, Hampshire, UK: Palgrave Macmillan, 2008.

Project Management Institute. *Organizational Project Management Maturity Model (OPM3): [Knowledge Foundation]*, 3d ed. Newtown Square, PA: Project Management Institute, 2013.

INDEX

Ackoff, Russell, 136
Archeology, organizational, 134

Background documents, 83–87,
    105, 116, 219
Burning platform, 225–226

Centaur:
  building a, 148–153,
    218–219, 236
  of excellence, 152
  programmaticist(s) as 147–148
Clinical study outputs versus
    outcomes, 20, 202
Coffee house project, 3–4
Committee(s):
  cross-functional, 14–19, 93,
    105, 108, 116–117
  governing
    agility of, 89–92
    business 117–121, 287
    capabilities, 92–94
    capacity, 83, 91, 102, 228
    decisions, 85, 107–108,
      189–192
    delegation of responsibilities,
      139–140, 234–235, 241
    efficiency, 86–92
    integration role, 272, 281
    limitations, 81–83
    meetings, 87
    members, 83, 86, 90, 114–115
    oversight of programs,
      204–209

    oversight of projects, 14,
      77–83, 202–204
    primary, 98, 105, 127
    roles and responsibilities
      30, 64, 77–82, 88, 94–95,
      115–116, 163–164,
      196–209, 223, 227, 272
    secondary, 98, 100–105,
      118, 293
    specialty, 95, 123,
      130–134, 139
  review
    benefits of, 98, 101–102
    business, 117–121
    governance by, 107
    mixed function, 116–117
    operational, 102–103
    portfolio, 117
    resource, 117
    secondary, 98, 100–105,
      293
    specialty, 123, 131
    strategic, 103
    technical, 103
    unintended consequences,
      105–109, 111, 119–121,
      133–134
Complex adaptive system(s),
    159–169, 198, 211, 220,
    255–256, 275, 283
Complexity:
  directional. *See* Stakeholder
  environmental
    definition, 50, 287

Complexity (*continued*)
  management of, 50–57,
    151–152, 196–199, 204,
    223, 272–273
  mystery, misery, and mastery, 57
  operational
    definition, 44, 289
    management of, 44–45,
      141–148, 151–152,
      184, 196, 198, 204, 209,
      231–232, 251, 257, 271
  organizational
    definition, 52, 290
    management of, 52–53,
      141–144, 147, 279
  outcome
    definition, 46, 290
    management of, 46–47, 141,
      144–149, 151–152, 168,
      179, 192–193, 196, 227,
      229, 251, 263–268
  programmatic, 41, 142–148,
    292, 296–297
  Rubik's Cube, 57–59
  stakeholder, 48–49
    definition of, 48, 293
    management of, 48–49, 196,
      198, 204, 219
Complexity leadership theory,
    159–164, 167–168, 172,
    183, 266
Credo(s), 17, 30, 39–41, 141, 292
Crown vetch, 94–95

Enabling conditions, 78, 82, 287
Enterprise-resource and project
    management (ERPM)
    systems, 111
Exasperados:
  complexity management,
    71, 162

definition of, 35, 288
perspectives of, 35–40, 53

First-generation programmatics.
    See Programmatics, first
    generation
First-generation programmatic
    systems. *See*
    Programmatics, first
    generation
Five-complexities framework:
  definition of, 42–43, 288
  reactions to, 53–55
  use(s) 55

Gantt charts, 17, 45
Guide to the Project Management
    Body of Knowledge
    (PMBOK), 183

Handey, Jack, 34

Industrial Age, 13, 16–17, 64,
    74, 100–101, 124, 200,
    212, 231
Inclusivist approach (or
    perspective), 68–70, 74,
    144–148, 231–232, 289
Inclusivist(s), 68–75, 145–148,
    162, 231–232, 251–252,
    264–268

Leadership:
  administrative, 161–164
  adaptive, 161–169, 171–181,
    189, 191, 196–198, 201,
    203–212, 217–220, 227,
    234, 249, 256, 274
  behaviors, 73–74, 223,
    252–269, 278
  challenges, 264–268

competency research,
260–264, 297
enabling, 161–166, 196–198,
201, 203–212, 219–220,
234, 274
operational, 163–167, 173,
196–198, 201, 203–212,
217–220, 234, 274
persona(s), 250–251
programmatic, 152, 173, 193,
247, 249, 252, 256–258,
266–269, 282
project and program, 4–6,
173–181, 250, 297
responsibilities, 19
shared, 152, 220
specialists, 280–281
style(s), 22, 74, 188, 212,
218, 248
command-and-control 22,
25, 71, 173, 179, 217,
237, 266
learn-and-adapt 22, 25, 173,
179, 217, 237, 266
system, 9, 167, 196, 201–202,
268–269
Line function(s):
advantages of, 13–17
executive(s) (leaders) opinions,
14, 73, 79–80, 100–137,
144, 241–242
subgroups, 100–101

Managing Successful
Programmes, 176–177

Operational Integrator. *See*
Operational savant,
integrator role
Operational savant, 141–143,
147–148, 151–152, 184,
186, 193, 195, 218–220,
231, 238, 252–253, 257,
274, 276, 278
integrator role, 142–143,
166–167, 219–221, 265,
272–273, 281
Operationalist approach (or
perspective), 66–67,
70–75, 140–145, 231–232,
252, 290
Operationalist(s), 66–67, 70–75,
140–145, 231–233,
250–252, 264–267, 278
Organization(s):
downsizing, 137–139
growth, 99–100, 110, 114, 137
breakdown structure(s),
101, 212
Outcome sage, 144–148, 151–152,
167–168, 171, 183, 186,
191, 193, 195, 218–221,
228–231, 235, 238–239,
244, 252, 253, 257, 263,
274, 278
integrator role, 167, 169,
219–221, 256, 265,
275, 281
Oversight model(s) or system(s):
fully empowered, 232,
258, 289
fully governed, 77–95, 144, 159,
166, 191, 226, 231–232,
258, 288–289
adaptations of, 97–135
multi-party, 107, 117,
160, 230
operationally empowered, 232,
258, 289–290
three-party. *See also*
Programmatics, third
generation

Oversight model(s) or system(s)
  (*continued*)
  benefits of, 150–151, 158,
    167, 195, 198–199, 213,
    219, 222–225, 229, 246
  challenges, 229–244, 264–268
  choosing, 226–229, 276–282
  defining, 148–153, 197–202
  managing projects and (sub)
    programs, 203–213
  two-party. *See also*
    Programmatics,
    first generation, and
    Programmatics, second
    generation
  adaptations of, 97–135, 140,
    148, 229–235
  challenges, 97–135, 150–151
  choosing, 226–229, 275–276
  limitations of, 81–83, 164, 167
  traditional, 77–95, 144,
    200–206, 212

PERT chart, 17, 45
Phase gate approaches, 25–26
PMO (project or program
    management office), 111,
    213, 245
Product manager, 189
Program(s):
  benefits of distinguishing from
    projects, 213–217
  definition(s), 128–129,
    174–180, 185–192, 214,
    290–291, 296
  leadership, xii–xv, xix, 3–8, 173,
    193, 221, 247–260
  outputs and outcomes, 7, 18–22,
    25–40, 59, 89–91, 103, 129,
    185–192, 202, 207, 210

  managing, 43–47, 53–55, 66,
    72, 145
  sponsorship of subprograms,
    209–212
Program manager(s). *See also*
    outcome sage
  autonomy and authority, 142,
    144, 203, 230–235, 278
  assigning, 235–240
  definition, 182, 291
  reporting relationships,
    240–244
  responsibilities, 146–149,
    171–174, 182–186,
    195–213
  titles, 38, 146, 185–186,
    233, 265
Program management:
  behaviors, 143, 251–260
  benefits of distinguishing from
    project management,
    217–223
  competency research, 260–264
  definition, 180–181, 291, 296
  departments, 244–246
  reporting relationships,
    240–244
  standards, 45, 49–50, 53, 65, 69,
    174–177, 180–182, 192,
    248, 275, 280, 295
Program management office.
    See PMO
Program oversight model. *See*
    Oversight model
Programmatic science:
  definition 9–10, 53, 181,
    184, 291
  departments of, 174, 241,
    244–246
  maturity in, 229–230

Programmaticist(s). *See also*
    Program Manager and
    Project manager
  autonomy and authority,
    230–235
  credo, 40–41, 141, 198, 292
  definition of, 38, 292
  organizational athletes, 36
  roles and responsibilities
    Inclusivist(s), 68–69, 70,
      145–150, 231–233, 250–
      252, 264–268, 278
    Operationalist(s), 66–67,
      70, 142–144, 231–233,
      250–252, 264–267, 278
    re-examining, 140–148
    significance of differences,
      72–75
    Traditionalist(s), 63–66, 70,
      163, 231–233, 250–253,
      264, 267–268, 278
  titles, 38, 146, 185–186, 233, 265
Programmatic approach. *See*
    Programmatics
Programmatics:
  definition, 10, 292
  first-generation
    application of, 30–32, 39,
      197, 295
    approach, 17–19, 45, 75–80,
      153, 203, 218, 252
    definition, 18–19, 288
  second-generation
    application of, 29–33, 47–49,
      197, 295
    approach(es), 26–29, 37, 146,
      153, 158
    definition, 22–23, 293
    Exasperado reactions,
      35–37, 40

third-generation
  application of, 271–275
  approach, 153, 197–213, 246
  assessing value of, 275–279
  benefits, 213–224, 229
  choosing, 226–229, 276–282
  definition of, 197–200,
    231, 294
  evolution to, 273–275
  introducing, 195–197
  implementing, 225–226,
    229–244
  roles and responsibilities,
    200–209, 230–235,
    242–243, 256
  twelve key questions,
    275–279
Project(s):
  benefits of distinguishing from
    programs, 213–217
  creation, 16
  daughter, 123–129, 205, 209,
    211
    unintended consequences,
      126–130
  definitions, 15, 184, 214,
    292, 296
  infrastructure, 111, 123–130
    benefits of, 123–126
    unintended consequences of,
      126–130
  leadership, xii–xv, xix, 3–8,
    146–152, 184, 227,
    233–234, 246–260
  number, impact of, 111–115
  outputs and outcomes, 7, 18–22,
    25–40, 59, 89–91, 103, 129,
    185–192, 202, 207, 210
  managing, 43–47, 53–55,
    66, 72

Project(s) (*continued*)
  parent, 85, 123–124, 127–128,
    210–211
  phases, 17, 26, 132,
    139–140, 205–208, 277
  prioritization, 22, 78, 82, 103,
    108, 112–118, 271
  team
    agility, 75, 89
    composition, 78
    formation, 15–20
    high-performance, 68
Project manager(s). *See also*
    operational savant
  assigning, 235–240
  autonomy and authority, 142,
    144, 203, 230–235, 278
  definition, 184, 293
  responsibilities, 144, 149,
    184–186, 195–213, 272
  role as a conductor, 125
  title(s), 15, 38, 146, 185–186,
    233, 265
Project management:
  agile, 26–27, 29, 31, 33, 37
  beginnings, 13–16
  benefits of distinguishing from
    program management,
    217–223
  complex, 27, 29, 31, 37
  credo, 17, 30, 39–41, 141
  definition, 184–192, 292, 296
  departments, 244–246
  exasperation of, 6–9
  exhilaration of, 4–5
  extreme, 28–29, 37
  identity crisis, 31, 35–36, 70, 73,
    146, 183, 186, 209
  introduction of, 15
  processes, 17–19

  standards, 45, 49–50, 53, 65, 69,
    174–177, 180–183, 192,
    248, 280, 295
  vending machine analogy, 10
Project Management Institute 58,
    128, 175, 180, 183
Project management office. *See*
    PMO
Project oversight model. *See*
    Oversight model

Resource(s):
  allocation, 44, 50, 67, 79, 82,
    100, 111–114, 126, 133,
    138, 140, 203
  competition for, 111–114
  estimates, 113
  review committees, 117–120,
    163, 203, 205, 207, 271

Secondary governance
    committee(s). *See*
    Committee(s), governing,
    secondary
Secondary review committee(s).
    See Committee(s), review,
    secondary
Second-generation
    programmatics. *See*
    Programmatics, second
    generation
Second -generation
    programmatic systems. *See*
    Programmatics, second
    generation
Stakeholder engagement and
    management, 47–49, 58
Subprograms, 128, 179–182,
    208–212, 217
Super-leaders, 281

Traditionalist approach (or perspective), 63–66, 69–75, 88, 101, 231–232, 252–253, 294

Traditionalist(s), 70–75, 231–233, 250–252, 264, 267–268, 278

Uncertainty:
environmental
definition of, 49–50, 288
significance of, 50
managing, 43–52, 77–78, 138–146, 151, 157, 168, 179, 184, 192–193, 196–199, 204, 209, 218, 227–231, 237, 244, 248, 251, 253, 257
operational
definition of, 43, 289

significance of, 43–44, 141, 184, 196
organizational
definition of, 51, 290
significance of, 51–52
outcome
definition of, 45, 290
significance of, 46, 168, 178–179, 193, 196, 216
stakeholder
definition of, 47–48, 293–294
significance of, 48
University of Pennsylvania, xv, xix

VosSavant, Marilyn, 33

Work breakdown structure(s), 125–126